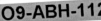

HITLER'S SECRET LIFE

Also by Glenn B. Infield:

Leni Riefenstahl:
The Fallen Film Goddess

Eva and Adolf

Big Week

The Poltava Affair

Disaster at Bari

Unarmed and Unafraid

HITLER'S SECRET LIFE

The Mysteries of the Eagle's Nest

GLENN B. INFIELD

STEIN AND DAY/*Publishers*/New York

Copyright © 1979 by Glenn B. Infield
All rights reserved.
Designed by Ed Kaplin
Printed in the United States of America
Stein and Day/*Publishers*/Scarborough House
Briarcliff Manor, N.Y. 10510

Library of Congress Cataloging in Publication Data

Infield, Glenn B
  Hitler's secret life.

  Bibliography: p. 301
  Includes index.
  1. Hitler, Adolf, 1889-1945.   2. Heads of state
—Germany—Biography.   I. Title.
DD247.H5I543   943.086′092′4   [B]   79-65109
ISBN 0-8128-2674-4

To Gary

Contents

Preface   xi

Acknowledgments   xiii

| 1 | The Secret Hideaway   1

| 2 | The Mysterious Wealth   13

| 3 | Hitler Territory   26

| 4 | The Führer's Strange Habits   47

| 5 | Hitler and the Actress   60

| 6 | Operation Seduction   76

| 7 | The Eagle's Nest   91

| 8 | Hitler's Famous Visitors   104

| 9 | Sex Under the Swastika   119

| 10 | The Mysterious Doctor   137

| 11 | Eva: The Secret Mistress   155

| 12 | A Day at Hitler's Berghof   174

| 13 | Nazi Gays and Addicts   193

| 14 | Hitler's "Jewish Princess"   207

| 15 | *How Hitler Duped J. Edgar Hoover*   223

| 16 | *The Führer and the Cowboys*   230

| 17 | *Eagle's Nest or Berlin?*   242

| 18 | *The Bunker Mystery*   256

| 19 | *Hitler's Final Secret*   272

Notes   289

Selected Bibliography   301

Index   304

List of Illustrations

Dietrich Eckhart	2
General Erich Ludendorff	9
Taking Hitler's belongings home from prison	16
Reich President von Hindenburg and Chancellor Hitler	27
Hitler's first house on the Obersalzberg	29
Hitler and his driver, Julius Schreck	31
Hitler studying	31
Hitler, Speer, and Bormann inspecting farmers	33
The Berghof	33
The Berghof conference hall window	35
A section of the Berghof conference hall	37
The Führer's study in the Berghof	39
Map of the Berghof bunker system	41
Hitler and his dog, Blondi	41
Hitler's bunker beneath the Berghof	43
The Platterhof	44
Map of the Obersalzberg complex	45
Hitler and staff at Wolfsschanze	48
The Führer's Mercedes stuck in the mud	53
Hans Baur, Hitler's personal pilot	59
Leni Riefenstahl and Hitler plan "Triumph of the Will"	62
Riefenstahl at film premiere	62
The Führer with Olympic officials	72
Nude photos Hitler obtained for private viewing	72
Riefenstahl filming *Olympia*	75
Goebbels and wife with Count Ciano	85
Hitler greets his half-sister and Magda Goebbels	87
Winifred Wagner's home	88
Winifred Wagner	89

The Eagle's Nest and tunnel below   93
The Eagle's Nest atop the Kehlstein   97
Hermann Göring and Charles Lindbergh   107
Admiral Darlan of the Vichy regime arrives at the Berghof 117
Reinhard Heydrich   127
Gerda Bormann   129
Yosuke Matsuoka, Inge Ley, and Robert Ley   134
Julius Streicher, Robert Ley, and Heinrich Himmler   135
Hitler at the Brown House   141
The Berghof "gang"   144
Dr. Karl Brandt   145
Hitler and Dr. Brandt   153
Eva Braun, sister Ilse, and friends   156
Eva and Adolf   162
Eva, Adolf, and Blondi   166
Hitler, Eva, and daughter of Eva's friend   169
Eva Braun   176
Hitler's bedroom door   179
Hitler's library   179
The Berghof winter-garden room   181
Hitler's birthday cake and gifts   185
The Führer's birthday party   189
Hitler leaving a church   198
Ernest Udet   198
The Führer considers art for his hometown museum   204
Hitler admiring nude statuary   204
Hitler's favorite bust   205
Hitler reviewing honor guard   214
Luis Trenker   231
The Karl May cowboy-and-Indian museum near Dresden 239
Hitler and Nicolaus von Below   248
The Goebbels family   265

Preface

Undoubtedly, Adolf Hitler is more studied, discussed, and written about than any other man of this century. We've always been more interested in someone who causes the world trouble than in someone who promotes peace. Hitler's infamy is immutable but people will always seek the causes of his actions. He fascinates historians, psychologists, and laymen who cannot fully understand how evil incarnate could have been so revered. In recent years there has been a rush to upgrade Hitler's reputation, an effort to convince the world that Hitler wasn't so bad after all because he loved dogs and children. At times he is pictured as a staunch fighter against inflation and unemployment. The Holocaust, according to some revisionists, was the result of the actions of his associates, not of Hitler himself. He didn't even know about Dachau or Auschwitz until late in the war, they say. They don't explain, of course, how he could have lived so much of the time in Munich, a mere fifteen miles from Dachau, and not have known about the camp.

In 1970 former members of Hitler's inner circle at Berlin, Munich, the Berghof, and the military headquarters, were quick to denounce the Führer. They admitted that they had been completely duped by him, that they'd had no idea Hitler was the type of man postwar documentation has proved him. Today, however, many of these same intimates qualify their criticism. The line is now, "Yes, he did some things that were wrong, but he did much more good for the world than harm." Many other Germans, less intimately associated with the Führer, have tried to forget him; consequently their children are not told what actually happened during the Third Reich.

A number of German schoolchildren were recently asked to write essays to the topic, "What I have heard about Adolf Hitler." The results reveal a wide gap between reality and their understanding of the man. Here are some excerpts:

"Hitler was strict with his people and everybody had respect for him. . . ."

"The neighbors still wish sometimes that he was back again. . . ."

"He was great in the war, too. His soldiers were courageous and even laughed when they went to war. . . ."

"Hitler did not tolerate youth wearing long hair. . . ."

"Hitler still lives and is doing much to restore Germany from the devastation of the war. . . ."

Even college students have trouble correctly characterizing Adolf Hitler and his works. The former accouterments of the SS elite guard—shiny high boots, leather jackets, whips, chains, and motorcycles—are now sexual symbols for many campus-age youth. Ask them, however, about the SS organization or its members and you draw a blank. They know what Hitler looked like and laugh at his Bohemian mustache, but most have little or no knowledge of the man or of what he did . . . except that he outfitted the SS with the symbols they now adore.

This book is about Hitler not when he was posturing in the public eye but when he was "at home." During the Third Reich Hitler had several residences: the Brown House, in Munich; an apartment in the Reich Chancellery, in Berlin; the various military headquarters; and, last and most important, his beloved mountain complex, the Berghof and the Eagle's Nest. In these places, and especially at the Berghof, Hitler was out of the public eye and revealed his true personality. His strange habits, his treatment of women, his attitude toward drugs and homosexuals, his cowboys-and-Indians antics . . . these were all exposed when he was secreted within his personal domain. It is this secret life that explains Adolf Hitler. Action is reality, and this is a book of Hitler's personal and enigmatic actions.

Acknowledgments

This book has had many contributors, for whose advice and aid I am very grateful. For facts about Hitler's life at the Berghof and the Eagle's Nest it was, of course, necessary to speak with those who were at these places with him. Among those I interviewed were Traudl Junge, Gerda Christian, Albert Speer, Adolf Galland, Hanna Reitsch, Ilse Braun, Nicolaus von Below, the late Otto Skorzeny, and many others of lesser status. Rudolf Jaeger directed me to many individuals in the Berchtesgaden area who were on the staff at the Berghof during the years of the Third Reich.

The papers of the late Michael A. Musmanno were invaluable to me, since they included over 200 interviews of Hitler's associates immediately after the end of the war. This material was made available to me through the kindness of Justice Musmanno's nephew, William F. Cercone, judge of the Superior Court of Pennsylvania.

Marianne Loenartz, Herr Witzenrath, and Dr. Haupt, of the Bundesarchiv in Koblenz, were very helpful. Dr. Faltlhauser, of Transit Film in Berlin; Manfred Kube and Elisabeth Hercht, of Süddeutscher Verlag in Munich; Renate Strasser, of the Institut für Zeitgeschichte in Munich; Daniel P. Simon, of the Berlin Document Center; and Dr. Roland Klemig, of the Bildarchiv Preussischer Kulturbesitz in Berlin answered my questions and supplied documentation about Hitler's personal life. In England much material and help was given by Dave Roberts, of the RAF Museum; Gita Johnson, of the Wiener Library; J. S. Lucas, of the Imperial War Museum; and David Irving.

At the National Archives in Washington, D.C., Charles A. Shaughnessy, Dr. Robert Wolfe, and Donald E. Spencer directed me to information that otherwise I would not have located. Leonard N. Beck, of the Library of Congress, provided detailed information about Hitler's private library. At the Hoover Institution, Adorjan I. de Galffy and my research assistant, Jonathan Zorach, discovered a great deal of material relevant to the personal life of Hitler. Allen H. McCreight, of the Federal Bureau of Investigation, guided me to documents I was seeking.

Others whose help was invaluable are Robert L. Parkinson, of Circus World Museum; Lyman W. Riley, of the University of Pennsylvania's Charles Patterson Van Pelt Library; Christine Schelshorn, of the State Historical Society of Wisconsin; and Vaughn Young, of the National Commission on Law Enforcement and Social Justice.

The book would have been impossible without the patience and help of Benton Arnovitz, my editor, who guided me over the rough spots a writer always encounters while researching and writing such a manuscript.

There are many others in Germany, Austria, and Spain who helped by telling me their experiences during the Third Reich but wish to remain nameless because of extenuating circumstances. To them, too, my thanks.

Last, but certainly not least, I want to express my appreciation to my wife, Peggy, who aids and abets me in all my projects.

HITLER'S SECRET LIFE

1

The Secret Hideaway

Two men leaned over the chessboard in Pension Moritz, the first boardinghouse opened on the Obersalzberg, the mountainous area in south Bavaria known as "the paradise of Bavaria." The older, Dietrich Eckart, had a large round head, a high forehead, and small, piercing eyes that were staring at his opponent. At 54 years of age in 1922, Eckart was 21 years the senior of the medium-built man with the Charlie Chaplin mustache and long face who was seated opposite him. Adolf Hitler was frowning as he stared at the chessboard, looking so serious that Eckart laughed. Immediately Hitler jumped to his feet.

"I didn't come to the mountains to sit around a chessboard all day," Hitler muttered. "Let's go for a walk."

Eckart sighed but didn't object. He knew there was no use protesting, because Hitler always got his own way, a fact that puzzled the older man at the same time that he admitted it to himself. There was a persuasive quality about this 33-year-old struggling politician, a persuasiveness that was amazing. In fact it was this quality that had earlier attracted the wealthy, famous poet Eckart to Hitler's entourage. Many Germans couldn't understand why a well-known writer such as Eckart, whose words *"Deutschland Erwache!"* ("Germany Awake!"), from his poem *Jeurjo,* later became the battle cry of the movement associated with the radical Hitler—the NSDAP (National Socialist German Workers' Party), or Nazi, movement. Or why he had provided the funds that enabled Hitler's followers to purchase the newspaper *Völkischer Beobachter,* which developed into the Nazi party's official organ. But Eckart knew. He was aware of the strong anti-Semitic ideas that Hitler held even during these

Dietrich Eckart, Hitler's friend and mentor during his early political career and the man who introduced Hitler to the Obersalzberg. *(National Archives)*

early years of his political career. Those ideas exactly coincided with Eckart's own.

In his earlier years Eckart had been a heavy drinker and a morphine addict who had spent time in an asylum for the mentally diseased. He was much more at ease sitting at a chessboard than hiking in the brisk air and rough terrain of the Obersalzberg. So it was with reluctance that he joined Hitler outside Pension Moritz a few minutes later. Eckart's wife, Dulcinea, who was 30 years younger than he, went with the pair. She easily kept stride with Hitler, but Eckart trailed behind, puffing and stopping every few minutes to rest. The abuse his body had endured earlier from the alcohol and morphine had sapped his strength, and he was to die of a heart attack in these same mountains within a year.

One of the rest stops was near a small cottage that had been built in 1916 for the councillor of commerce of Bavaria, Herr Winter, from Buxtehude. Constructed by the firm Josef and Stefan Amort of Berchtesgaden, it was a beautiful but unpretentious home located on one of the finest building lots on the Obersalzberg. From Haus Wachenfeld—the name given the cottage by its owner—there was an excellent view of the city of

Berchtesgaden several hundred feet below. A short distance above the cottage was the Hotel Zum Türken, a popular inn. While Eckart regained his strength, Hitler inspected Haus Wachenfeld, examining every detail of the cottage. Evidently he liked what he saw, because after his release from Landsberg prison, where he was jailed after his unsuccessful Beer Hall Putsch of November 8, 1923, Hitler moved into Haus Wachenfeld. The powerful hold of the mountains didn't end until his death in 1945, when his Third Reich collapsed.

He spent as much time as possible at Haus Wachenfeld, which later, after extensive remodeling, became known around the world as the Berghof. In these mountains of southern Bavaria, a virtual recluse except for the members of his inner circle and those who received a special invitation from the Führer himself, Hitler made most of his important political and military decisions, planned his world conquest, met world leaders and celebrities, entertained his women, took his drugs, and did the multitude of things he dared do only in the privacy of the Berghof. It has taken more than three decades to learn many secrets of the Berghof—the strange but fascinating actions of Hitler behind the high fences that kept the public away.

Until 1933, when the Obersalzberg became "Hitler territory," this section of Bavaria was an open resort area devoted to fun, health, and sports. The name Obersalzberg (Upper Salt Mountain) derived from the large vein of hazelrock that runs through this area of the mountains at the 3300-foot level and the salt residue remaining from the ice age. For centuries past, residents of Berchtesgaden and surrounding villages had worked in the salt mines of the Obersalzberg. Gradually they built small homes there at the foot of the Hoher Goll and Kehlstein mountains, where there are more slopes than flat spots. Settlers cut down trees to increase the grazing space and gradually started farms with a few cows and sheep. Succeeding generations scattered settlements across the entire Obersalzberg area.

Romance, including romantic love, played an important role in the developing history of the Obersalzberg. It inspired a best-selling novel by Richard Voss, one of Germany's most successful writers of the 19th century. The novel, *Zwei Menschen (Two People)*, is a tragic love story whose mystique was echoed at least faintly in the love affair of Hitler and Eva Braun many years later. The heroine of this novel, Judith Platter, was based on Mauritia Mayer, a mysterious and beautiful woman who was the real-life owner of the Platterhof pension on the Obersalzberg. Mayer is credited with turning the area into a resort mecca. With 13,500 marks in 1877 she purchased the Hofreiter estate and surrounding farms on the Obersalzberg. She immediately converted the Hofreiter estate into the Platterhof and one of the other buildings on the farms into Pension Moritz, the boardinghouse that later attracted Hitler. The Pension Moritz soon became known far and wide and attracted the wealthy, the famous and the royal. The Bavarian royal family and the Austrian imperial family often stayed at Pension Moritz. An especially frequent royal guest was the Bavarian Prince-Regent Luitpold, who was very fond of Mauritia Mayer. Famous authors and artists gathered at the boardinghouse. There Franz von Lenbach painted Mayer's portrait, Johannes Brahms composed many songs, and Clara Schumann often entertained. Ludwig Ganghofer wrote his novel *Das Gottesleben* (The Divine Life) while at the Pension Moritz, but it was the novelist Richard Voss who had the greatest impact on both Mayer and the Obersalzberg, by writing the tragic love story of "Judith Platter."

Voss and the beautiful owner of the Pension Moritz were very close friends. Critics are convinced that the heroine's lover in the novel, Rochus, was Voss himself.

Judith and Rochus were childhood friends, she an orphan from her early teens who had to earn her own living by managing a farm called the Platterhof, he an only son whom his mother has convinced to become a priest. On a sunny afternoon the two take a boat ride, are caught in a violent thunderstorm, and are thrown upon an island when their boat capsizes. Staying in a ramshackle cabin on the deserted island that night, they fall in love. Rochus, ignoring the wishes of his mother that he become a priest, proposes to Judith and, as evidence of his love, puts on her finger a ring he was given by his mother. However when they are finally rescued and his mother sees the ring, she is brokenhearted and dies. Rochus feels responsible for her death, breaks off his romance with Judith, and becomes a priest. Through the years they see each other now and then, and both realize their love has not dimmed. In the end, seeing no way out of her dilemma, Judith climbs the rocks of her beloved Obersalzberg and leaps to her death. Thus concludes the novel *Zwei Menschen,* a tragedy that was well known to Pension Moritz guest Adolf Hitler in 1922, 23 years before he and Eva Braun committed suicide together.

Zwei Menschen was very popular in Germany, and when it became known that Judith Platter was patterned after Mauritia Mayer, the owner of Pension Moritz and the Platterhof, the Obersalzberg area gained a great deal of publicity. Wealthy and influential Germans visited the Obersalzberg, and many decided they would build vacation homes in the area. Carl Von Linde, the developer of a process to manufacture liquid air, bought an estate on the Obersalzberg and later built the Pension Antenberg, which he eventually donated to the government as a convalescent home for navy personnel. He also built a mountain road with his own funds and gave another home he owned on the Obersalzberg to his parish to be used as a hotel for the aged. Others followed Linde: singer Terina; painter George Waltenberger; piano manufacturer Carl Bechstein—whose money and wife, Helene, became important factors in the career of Hitler within a few years; and Councillor of Commerce Winter, who built Haus Wachenfeld, the house that changed the fate of the Obersalzberg. In 1911, while Hitler was trying to eke out a living in Vienna by painting pictures and posters, Hotel Zum Türken was built; it too would play an important role in the life of the future Führer.

A post office was established, and skiing facilities, including a hazardous jump, were opened in the Obersalzberg area.

A Doctor Seitz had a sanitarium constructed for the use of sickly children. The facility was later taken over by the infamous Martin Bormann.

While this construction was going on, Hitler made only infrequent visits to the Obersalzberg, mostly with Eckart. Eckart had joined Hitler's NSDAP political movement early, and it was his money that financed the post–World War I trips to the mountains. But Hitler's political activity limited his visits to the Obersalzberg. On January 12, 1922, he was sentenced to three months' imprisonment for causing a disturbance at a meeting. He actually served only 33 days in Stadelheim prison, Munich,

but on his release he had to fight a Bavarian government
movement to deport him back to his native Austria. On December 13, 1922, shortly after a stay at Pension Moritz with
Eckart, Hitler organized and held 10 mass Nazi demonstrations
in Munich and, in the same city a month later, the first NSDAP
party rally.

By the middle of 1923 the party had grown in membership
and power to a point where unifying action was demanded if
he was to maintain rigid control. The SA *(Sturmabteilung,* or
Storm Detachment), Hitler's private army, which had originally
been formed to protect party members at mass meetings and to
oppose rival political parties, was now a large group of street
brawlers demanding action. No longer were they satisifed to
stand back and protect Hitler while he made his impassioned
speeches—speeches that, in their collective estimation, were getting the party nowhere. They wanted to take over the government by force, not with words. In fact the Bavarian government
had found a mass muster of the SA in Oberwiesenfeld on May
1, 1923, so disruptive and threatening that its president, Gustav
Ritter von Kahr, had summoned the state troops to disperse
them.

Hitler spent several days in June at Pension Moritz, trying to
decide his next move. His political party was not making any
dramatic advaances, and his own status was rapidly sinking to a
new low in the confused politics that were the aftermath of
World War I in Germany. He was well aware of the restlessness
of his storm troopers and understood very clearly their desire to
use violence to overthrow the present leaders instead of waiting
until the NSDAP could assume power by legal means. Walking
in the heavily wooded area of the first level of the Obersalzberg, which extended from the post office to the foot of the
Kehlstein, Hitler recalled the promise he had made a few
months earlier to Doctor Franz Schweyer, the Bavarian minister of the interior, who had wanted to deport him to Austria.
Sitting in Schweyer's office off the Odeonsplatz in Munich,
discussing his political aims and his goal of "smashing Marxism," he had become distressed when Schweyer said, "If you
continue your propaganda in its present form, it will inevitably
lead to a violent explosion some day, whatever your intentions.

You can't just go on talking for years, some day you will have to act."

Hitler was distressed: Schweyer was speaking the truth, was aware that sooner or later words would stop and action begin. Hitler threw up his hands in protest and vowed, "Herr Minister, I give you my word of honor, never as long as I live will I make a putsch!"

Now, in June 1923, as he hiked alone on the Obersalzberg, he recalled the promise he had no intention of keeping. Later, in his book, *Mein Kampf,* he would outline in detail his plans for world conquest, plans that were ignored by world leaders; but his actions even during 1923 were indicative of his intentions. His lies, big and small, were transparent to the world at large but were shunted aside as the wild statements of a radical politician who would soon be forgotten. This dismissal was a mistake that cost millions of lives.

"You can tell the people anything," Hitler once told the members of his inner circle. And he did!

Later Franz Halder, chief of staff of the German Army from 1938 until 1942, said, "Nothing would work with him from the point of view of legal reasons or what we call honor and decency."

The ardent self-righteousness with which he lied was remarkable. Whenever possible he included an oath or at least a word of honor with the lie, just as he did in Schweyer's office in 1922. The truth was that before he left the Obersalzberg to return to Munich in June 1923, he had made up his mind that a putsch was necessary. And he selected Munich as the site, having concluded that if he could gain control of Bavaria and obtain the support of the German Army officers in that area, he could bring Berlin into the NSDAP fold without trouble. A second reason for choosing Munich was decisive: If the coup failed, he could escape to the Obersalzberg and hide. Knowing the mountains of the area as well as he did, he concluded that his chance of recapture was slight. He ignored the welfare of those who would be involved in the putsch with him. In his opinion their well-being was their problem. As he headed back to Munich from the Pension Moritz by the Rosenheim road that June day, Hitler saw many small paths leading off into the mountains and was confident he could disappear from sight within hours. It was a personal secret, this intent, as an integral part of the planned putsch, to hide in the mountains— should it be necessary to leave Munich in a hurry.

In August 1923 Hitler had a stroke of luck. The Weimar Republic, Germany's central government, ended its passive resistance against the reparations payments demanded by the Allies after Germany's defeat in World War I. This angered the Bavarian leaders; they saw the move as cowardice, a step that would forever hinder the recovery of Germany. Hitler saw his opportunity. He decided to take over the government of Bavaria and make a clean break with Berlin, effecting the plan he had formulated in general terms while on the Obersalzberg in June.

The original plan was devised in detail by Hitler and Alfred Rosenberg, after Hitler, the leading NSDAP ideologist and editor of the *Völkischer Beobachter (People's Observer)*. Knowing that in the first days of November a celebration to honor the war dead would be held in Munich and that the highest officials of the Bavarian state government would be there, Hitler and Rosenberg selected this time to make their move. Kahr, the president, General Otto von Lossow, commander of the armed forces in Bavaria, and Colonel Hans von Seisser, chief of the Bavarian State Police, were the three men vital to Hitler's plan. With their cooperation, willing or unwilling, the putsch would be successful. Hitler knew that Kahr, Lossow, and Seisser would be standing in a side street not far from Feldherrn Hall, waiting for the marching troops to pass, and that the three would then join in the procession. Hitler's plan was to move a few hundred of his SA into this street just before the parade, surround the Bavarian leaders, and inform them that the German revolt had started.

On the day of the celebration, however, it was discovered that a large, armed police escort was with the Bavarian leaders in the side street. The putsch was called off at the last minute.

On November 8, 1923, Hitler decided to try again. Kahr was scheduled to make a political address at the Bürgerbräu Keller, a large beer hall in Munich, and Lossow, Seisser, Schweyer, and other government, military, and social leaders of Bavaria would be there. Hitler infiltrated the beer hall with several

Gen. Erich Ludendorff, the revered hero of World War I, who helped Hitler during the 1923 putsch. *(National Archives)*

hundred of his storm troopers and waited for the opportune moment to take control of the meeting and the Bavarian leaders. He also had an ace-in-the-hole: He had sent one of his associates out to the suburbs of Munich to bring Gen. Erich Ludendorff to the Bürgerbräu Keller. Ludendorff was a revered hero of World War I, a man respected by virtually everyone in Germany. Ludendorff was embittered by Germany's defeat and consequently was devoted to right-wing nationalist efforts to restore Germany's independence and former power. Hitler felt that if the putsch went as planned, Ludendorff would support it, and his support would give status to the Hitler administration. It was a "loner" decision that Hitler had made while on the Obersalzberg, one that he didn't impart to his associates until the last moment.

Once the SA had set up machine guns at the exits, Hitler motioned for the lights at the doors to be extinguished. He then leaped onto a chair and fired a shot into the ceiling to attract attention. When the startled beer drinkers and visiting notables became silent, Hitler made his dramatic announcement.

"The national revolution has begun!"

This "revolution," like many of the decisions Hitler subsequently made alone during the Third Reich, was not planned in detail; it had no depth. Hitler didn't know what he wanted to do beyond the first few minutes. Neither was he certain what role he would attempt to persuade Ludendorff to play once the general had arrived at the Bürgerbräu Keller. Consequently, after reaching the speakers' platform and "capturing" Kahr, Lossow, and Seisser, Hitler not only looked the way Charlie Chaplin would in the movie "Great Dictator" but also acted that way. The putsch turned into a farce, a comedy of errors that would have made a great Broadway play except for the tragic ending of the event, when a number of men lost their lives because of Hitler's foolhardiness, and the worldwide tragedy foreshadowed by Hitler's actions during the putsch. For the first time the public was given manifest warning of the unpredictable personality of Adolf Hitler, the "outlaw" characteristic of this little-known politician. Instead of taking the warning seriously, however, the world laughed at the funny-looking man who tried to take over Germany by using a beer hall as his headquarters and beer as the tranquilizer.

After taking Kahr, Lossow, and Seisser prisoner, Hitler wasn't quite sure what he should do with them. Threatening the trio with a gun, he forced them to accompany him to a small side room. Meanwhile, as the crowd became restless and menacing, Hitler's associate Hermann Göring, thought of a way to soothe them.

"Don't worry," Göring yelled, "we have the friendliest intentions and, anyway, you can be happy, you have your beer."

Meanwhile in the side room Hitler was having problems. He threatened to shoot Kahr, Lossow, and Seisser unless they joined him in the revolution, or to shoot himself instead. The trio, of course, voted for the latter; but Hitler flew into a rage, and they became silent. At an impasse, Hitler followed the advice Göring had given the patrons of the hall.

"Get me a stein!" he ordered. One of the SA troopers hurried back into the main room to get him a beer.

About this time Ludendorff appeared on the scene. Since Hitler had not consulted him about the putsch, he was both confused and angry. He berated Hitler for starting such an action without first contacting him. But the crowd, unable to hear Ludendorff's words, thought the famous military hero was supporting the NSDAP cause and began cheering. Hitler regained his confidence despite Ludendorff's rebuff, and Kahr, Lossow, and Seisser decided their best move was to pretend, at least, that they too supported Hitler.

When a brawl was reported between the SA and the German Army soldiers at a nearby barracks, Hitler rushed to the scene to break it up, leaving the three Bavarian leaders in the custody of Ludendorff at the Bürgerbräu Keller. After a few minutes Lossow nonchalantly informed Ludendorff that he was going to return to his office, and Kahr and Seisser joined him. When an SA officer protested, Ludendorff ignored him and gave the trio permission to leave the beer hall. When Hitler returned to the Bürgerbräu Keller and discovered his hostages gone, he knew the putsch had failed. The three Bavarian leaders quickly renounced Hitler, explaining they had been coerced at gunpoint to cooperate. Berlin ordered the German Army to quell the revolt. The army preferred to avoid involvement in the putsch and turned the matter over to the police.

During the night Hitler, Ludendorff, and the others holed up in the beer hall debated on their next move. Hitler concluded that Ludendorff's prestige was useless now. To save the situation he needed someone who had more power and influence with key Bavarian and German government officials. Hitler decided to send a messenger to Crown Prince Rupprecht of Bavaria, the pretender to the throne, who lived in a large castle in Berchtesgaden, not far from Hitler's beloved Obersalzberg and Pension Moritz. The messenger was to ask Prince Rupprecht to intercede with Kahr and Lossow and obtain a pardon for Hitler and Ludendorff so that bloodshed and criminal charges could be avoided. When the messenger couldn't find a car and was forced to take the train to Berchtesgaden, he arrived much too late to do Hitler any good, and the plan failed.

But the Obersalzberg area still figured in the putsch plans. Rudolf Hess, another close associate of Hitler, forced Minister of the Interior Schweyer into a car and headed towards the mountains. Two SA guards accompanied them. At a clearing near Berchtesgaden Hess stopped the car and ordered the guards to take the minister into the woods, insinuating that they were to shoot him. But it was just another act in the putsch farce, an attempt to bluff the minister into interceding for Hitler. This bluff too failed, and Hess ordered the minister back into the car and drove off.

In a last show of bravado Hitler assembled his cohorts and, with swastika banners flying, began a demonstration march towards the Marienplatz in the center of Munich at 11:00 the next morning. The front row of the group consisted of Hitler, Ludendorff, Göring, and the Jew-baiter Julius Streicher. There were 3000 Nazis behind them, and at the Odeonplatz they met 100 policemen barring their way. Hitler ordered the police to surrender. Instead they began firing. When the battle ended a few minutes later, 16 Nazis and 3 policemen were dead. Göring was seriously wounded. Ludendorff escaped injury despite his refusal to take cover. Streicher, lying flat on the pavement, managed to crawl to safety while bullets flew over his head. Hitler, meanwhile, reverted to his original plan. He ran to a car waiting near by, leaped in, and headed for the Obersalzberg.

Within a few days Hitler was under arrest. He had been unable to reach the mountains, where he had intended to hide. During the incident at the Odeonplatz his left arm had been dislocated. Turning away from the route to the Obersalzberg, Hitler ordered the driver to take a side road, near Marnau, that led to a villa at Uffing owned by Ernst Hanfstängl, another Nazi associate. At Uffing Helene Hanfstängl, his friend's wife, hid him in an upstairs room, where two doctors managed to get his arm back into the shoulder socket. It was a short stay, however. While Hitler was still trying to arrange transportation to the Obersalzberg, the police arrived and arrested him.

In 1924 Hitler was found guilty of conspiracy to commit high treason and was sentenced to five years in fortresslike Landsberg prison, not far from Munich. He served only nine months, a pampered prisoner who was permitted to entertain friends and accept gifts from outsiders. Hess, who had kidnapped Schweyer and then abandoned the minister and the car when he heard about the Odeonplatz incident, was also sentenced to Landsberg; and it was there that Hitler started dictating *Mein Kampf* to him.

It was also at Landsberg prison that Hitler made plans to establish his personal headquarters on the Obersalzberg as soon as he was free.

2

The Mysterious Wealth

On December 20, 1924, Adolf Müller, a publisher from Munich, and Heinrich Hoffmann, a photographer friend of Hitler and the man destined to become official photographer to the Führer and the NSDAP, drove west from Munich to Landsberg am Lech. Instead of a chauffeur, the publisher himself was behind the wheel of Müller's huge Daimler-Benz. This surprised Hoffmann, who thought they were merely going to the prison to visit Hitler. When they had covered half the 60-mile distance to Landsberg, Müller turned to Hoffmann and explained the purpose of the trip.

"Very few people know the exact time and date of Hitler's release," he said, smiling, "but I do. We're going to fetch him."

The gates of the prison swung open shortly before noon, and Hitler walked directly to the Daimler-Benz waiting outside the walls. He stepped inside and motioned for Müller to drive off. It was obvious he was glad to be free after nine months; obvious, too, that he wanted to get away from the prison as fast as possible. The only package he carried was his partially completed manuscript of *Mein Kampf*. He had nothing else to take. At the time of his release he'd had 282 marks, but at the last minute he gave it all to the prison inmates he left behind. This donation left Hitler with no money, and the remnant of his NSDAP was nearly bankrupt.

In fact Göring was trying to convince Benito Mussolini, the Italian dictator, to lend the NSDAP two million lire, but his attempts had been unsuccessful. How, then, did Hitler obtain the large sums of money he needed—and, by 1929, had—to support his SA, to buy the expensive automobiles he used, and to staff a luxury apartment in Munich and purchase House Wachenfeld on the Obersalzberg?

The years 1924–1928 were particularly lean ones for Hitler, years during which he contracted considerable indebtedness. Many of those individuals who had previously supported him now turned their backs on him because of his prison sentence and the disreputable reputation of the NSDAP. Hitler was on parole, fearful of deportation as an undesirable alien and prohibited from making political speeches in Bavaria. Hoffmann provided a room in his home in the Schellingstrasse for Hitler to work in when he felt like it. But Hitler couldn't concentrate, nor could he find the solitude he desired. Finally he returned to the Obersalzberg, to the Pension Moritz, where he once again found the inspiration he needed. Actually he lived in a small cottage above the main building; and it was in this cottage, which he named Kampfhaus, that he completed *Mein Kampf.* The cottage and the surrounding mountains also gave him the opportunity to get out into the fresh air and hike, something he had not been able to do while in prison. He could dress as he wished, do as he wished.

꙾ "Having to change into long trousers was always a misery to me. Even with a temperature of ten below zero I used to go about in leather shorts. The feeling of freedom they give is wonderful," Hitler said later.

On May 1, 1925, Hitler was notified by the Munich Finance Office that he had not filed an income tax return for 1924 and that he also owed a quarterly declaration for the first quarter of 1925. Hitler's reply was short and to the point:

"I had no income in 1924 or in the first quarter of 1925. I have covered my living expenses by raising a bank loan."

Yet it was known at the Munich Finance Office that in February 1925, despite the fact that Hitler had not turned in a quarterly return, he had purchased a Mercedes-Benz automobile costing at least 20,000 marks. Once again he was contacted; once again he insisted that he had paid for the car with a bank loan. Investigators also learned that Hitler had visited Zurich, Switzerland, where he had stayed at the Hotel St. Gotthard. Where had the funds for this trip come from? Why had he not reported the income on his tax form? The Munich Finance Office never was able to prove that Hitler had any income during this period. It wasn't until October 31, 1925, that he finally acknowledged, on his third-quarter income tax form, that he had accumulated some money.

On this date he reported a gross income of 11,231 marks, but from this he deducted 2245 marks as interest payments on his bank loan and 6540 marks for professional expenses. To prove the interest payments Hitler explained that he had no resources after his release from prison and was in debt for his trial expenses so he was forced to take a bank loan. Regarding the professional expenses, including travel, that Hitler claimed, it was obvious that while he lived as a near-recluse at the small cottage on the Obersalzberg, he was not exactly "roughing it." He listed deductions for the salaries of a private secretary, an assistant, and a chauffeur who drove his new Mercedes-Benz. Hitler devised a unique approach to the deductions he claimed for political activity:

Without my political activity my name would be unknown and I would be lacking materials for the publication of a political work. Accordingly, in my case as a political writer, the expenses of my political activity, which is the necessary condition of my professional writing as well as its assurance of financial success, cannot be regarded as subject to taxation.

The first volume of *Mein Kampf* was published in July 1925, and by the end of the year 9473 copies had been sold at 12 marks each. In closing his letter to the Munich Finance Office, he further explained his viewpoint toward the deductions:

I am quite willing at any time to make a sworn statement with regard to my personal expenses and expenditures. The Finance Office can then see that out of the income for my book for this period, only a very small fraction was expended for myself; nowhere do I possess property or other capital assets that I can call my own. I restrict of necessity my personal wants so far that I am a complete abstainer from alcohol and tobacco, take my meals in the most modest restaurants and aside from my minimal apartment rent make no expenditures that are not chargeable to my expenses as a political writer. I [list] all this so that the Finance Office will see in my representations not an attempt to avoid a tax obligation but rather a sober proved statement of actual circumstances. Also the automobile is for me but a means to an end. It alone makes it possible for me to accomplish my daily work.

It was a "creative" presentation, but it failed. During the final audit of his 1925 income only half the total amount of deduction was allowed. Hitler's contention that his main occupation was that of a political writer, not a politician, was bluntly rejected by the Munich Finance Office. The final audit decision stated: "This taxpayer travels mainly in order to spread his political ideas among the people and to attend to party affairs. Also his employees are for the most part engaged in work of this kind. The stated expenditures are not in and of themselves professional expenses within the meaning of the income tax law. Since, however, this activity at the same time provides material for his work as a political writer and increases the sales of his book, one half of the claimed expenditures for travel and salaries is allowed as a deduction from income."

Rudolf Hess, right, with Julius Schaub and Walter Hewel next to him, take Hitler's and Hess's belongings home from Landsberg prison in 1924. *(National Archives)*

Hitler's attempt to convince the Munich Finance Office that his main activity since his release from Landsberg prison was writing *Mein Kampf* was just another of the falsehoods that flowed so easily from him. His goal had not changed, and all his energies were devoted to that goal—to become the leader of Germany. When he stepped from prison in December 1924, the NSDAP had officially been disbanded, but on February 26, 1925, Hitler refounded the party. He also started the printing presses of the party newspaper, the *Völkischer Beobachter,* once again. The following day, February 27, he returned to the Bürgerbräu Keller for the first time since the debacle of his putsch. The beer hall was jammed with more than 4000 party members and sympathizers, while another thousand stood outside. If there was any doubt that Hitler was back in the political arena full time, the speech he made that night erased it. Once again, just as he had done many times prior to his prison stay, Hitler called on those who remained loyal to the party to unite behind the swastika flag and crush their two enemies: Marxism and the Jews. The posters advertising this first postprison public appearance of Hitler gave the party members and sympathizers an indication of what to expect:

NATIONAL SOCIALIST GERMAN WORKERS' PARTY
National Socialists! Old Party Members!

Men and Women!

On Friday 27 February at 8 P.M. the first great public Mass Meeting for the Reconstruction of the National Socialist German Workers' Party will take place at the Bürgerbräu Keller, Rosenheimerstrasse in Munich. Our party comrade Adolf Hitler will speak on Germany's future and our Movement. Admission 1 mark to cover cost of hall and publicity. All additional moneys will be used to start the Movement's Fighting Fund. Jews not admitted. Summoner: Amann. Advance sale of tickets from Thursday 26 February at 15 Thierschstrasse (bookshop).

The audience loved every word of his speech and clamored ——

for more. There is no doubt that this February 27 speech gave the NSDAP its second life and Hitler the opportunity to try once again for the national leadership. But it wasn't to be an easy path.

The first obstacle was the Bavarian government. When it became apparent that Hitler once again had a large, enthusiastic following in the palm of his hand, the Bavarian cabinet made its move. On March 9, 1925, the cabinet forbade Hitler to speak in public again in Bavaria. Since he was on parole from Landsberg, Hitler knew that if he ignored the order, he would be sent back to prison. He was also banned from speaking in Prussia, Baden, Saxony, Hamburg, and Oldenburg. These bans lasted until May 1927 and aggravated his second problem—money.

Lack of finances was as serious an obstacle to the NSDAP as was the opposition of the Bavarian government. Hitler depended upon his public appearances to raise the funds necessary to re-establish his party; to pay for the upkeep of the ever-growing SA; and to publish the *Völkischer Beobachter,* his only media outlet. Now that he was prohibited from speaking in most centers of influence in Germany in public, he had to seek other financing.

Industrialists who wanted Hitler in power were one source of funds, because they thought they would benefit personally. Fritz Thyssen, whose father, August Thyssen, had become enormously wealthy during the reign of the last kaiser, was made furious by the French occupation of the Ruhr in 1923, and he contributed generously to the NSDAP. Carl Bechstein, the famous piano manufacturer, supported Hitler, not only because he thought it would be good for business but because his wife Helene was enamored of the "shy" politician. Hugo Bruckmann, a Munich publisher, was in the same situation. His wife, Elsa, was a Hungarian noblewoman who tried to make Hitler forget Helene Bechstein by doing more for him and the NSDAP than the Bechsteins were doing. These supporters and others provided funds to help the party through the lean years.

Hitler's personal earnings were still poor; *Mein Kampf* had achieved a satisfactory sale when first published, but by 1928 sales were down. In that year only 3000 copies, counting both volumes, were sold.

Hitler was in arrears in his income tax payments in 1927. He still owed a final installment on his 1926 tax and had not paid any of the quarterly remittances for 1927. Finally, in October of that year, he notified the Munich Finance Office that he was unable to settle the full amount and requested permission to make monthly payments. The request was granted. In 1928 he was able once again to meet his tax obligations quarterly, although, through neglect, he paid late. But it was the abrupt change in Hitler's financial status in 1929 that has remained an unsolved puzzle. Historians have searched the archives for the answer. Tax records have been studied. The royalty ledgers of Eher Verlag, the publisher of *Mein Kampf,* were discovered at the end of World War II, but the detailed sales figures of Hitler's book, figures that had always been secret, failed to explain his sudden affluence in 1929.

Officially Hitler's income in 1929 was slightly less than his income in 1925-1926, the years immediately after his release from prison. Yet the interest payments on the loans, which he had always deducted during previous years, completely disappeared from his income tax form in 1929, indicating that he had liquidated his considerable indebtedness. From what sources did he obtain the funds to pay off the bank loans? Where did he obtain the money to lease, furnish, and staff a luxury apartment on Prinzregentenplatz in Munich? And where did he get the wealth to move from the Pension Moritz to the coveted Haus Wachenfeld on the Obersalzberg?

There has never been an adequate explanation of the sudden influx of funds that came Hitler's way in 1929. A recent investigation into the matter, however, revealed that a member of a U.S. Army foreign area studies program submitted a thesis to his commander on May 30, 1944. According to Harvey M. Berg, the man whose conclusions these are, his report was "placed under tight wraps" by the Security Intelligence Corps (SIC), a little-known World War II organization that was a component of the Counter Intelligence Corps of the U.S. Army. It is a shocking allegation, and even at the risk of having its inclusion here being thought a contrivance, the theory deserves a hearing. In any case, it will surely intrigue those who take a conspiratorial view of history.

To understand the interpretation advanced by Berg it is nec-

essary to go back in history to the year 755 A.D. when the
popes of the Roman Catholic Church gained control of several
provinces and cities, including Rome, in central Italy. This area
became known as the Papal States. For many centuries, with
slight interruptions, the popes held temporal sovereignty over
16,000 square miles and more than three million people. In
1860, however, the Papal States became subject to Victor Emmanuel II, King of Italy, because after the Reformation the
political power of the pope gradually declined. When Victor
Emmanuel seized Rome by force in 1871 and the citizens voted
to accept the monarchy and establish the city as the capital of
Italy, Pope Pius IX shut himself up in the Vatican and regarded
himself as a prisoner.

From that moment on there was a deep schism between the
papacy and the national government. Italian citizens were torn
between their duty as Catholics and their loyalty to the Italian
government. Benito Mussolini understood this divided loyalty
and was convinced that no regime in Italy could survive indefinitely without the papacy's approval. He was determined to
secure it. On January 19, 1923, at the same time that Hitler was
making final preparations to hold 10 mass rallies of his NSDAP
in Munich, Mussolini met with Cardinal Pietro Gasparri, the
Vatican secretary of state. They met secretly, both men approaching the meeting place, a senator's apartment in Via del
Gesu, by separate entrances and stairways. The two men discussed the dissension between the Vatican and the government,
and Mussolini vowed that he would, if necessary, go so far as to
change the electoral laws in order to obtain a chamber of
deputies that would vote in favor of giving the pope temporal
dominion over a sector of Rome.

It took six years for Mussolini to fulfill his promise to the
Vatican. During that period, however, while Hitler served a
prison term and struggled to reestablish his NSDAP, Mussolini,
already a world figure and the virtual dictator of Italy, made
many concessions to the Vatican. He gave orders to restore the
crucifix to state schoolrooms and hospitals and reintroduced
compulsory religious education. Mass was a part of every public function. Mussolini also took public money and gave it to
the clergy in the form of increased salaries. At the same time he
exempted novices of the church from military service. During

this period Pope Pius XI became a supporter of Mussolini. So did Eugenio Pacelli, who, the Berg theory alleges, had supported Hitler and the NSDAP in Germany while he was papal nuncio in Berlin. Both church officials, it was reported, had felt Hitler and Mussolini were safeguards against the communists.

Finally, at noon on Monday, February 11, 1929, a long line of automobiles passed through the rainy streets of Rome and halted at the Lateran Palace, residence of the bishops of Rome for more than six centuries. In the Hall of Missions Cardinal Gasparri and Mussolini signed the agreement that has been known since that day as the Lateran Treaty. The following day the Italian tricolor and the yellow-and-white papal flag flew side by side for the first time since 1870. All over Italy that night people celebrated by thronging the churches for services of thanksgiving. They prayed for Pius XI, who had "given God back to Italy and Italy to God," and for Mussolini, whom, the Pope said, "Providence ordained that we should meet."

Perhaps Hitler too should also have been down on his knees praying that night in February 1929, because, according to the Berg report, he and the NSDAP benefited at least as much as the Vatican and Mussolini from the Lateran Treaty.

On June 7, 1929, *The New York Times,* in its front-page article reporting the ratification of the Lateran Treaty, signed nearly four months earlier, explained the details of the agreement:

The high contracting parties at the moment of exchange of the ratifications of the Lateran Treaty again affirm their desire loyally to observe in letter and spirit not only the treaty of conciliation in its irrevocable reciprocal recognition of sovereignties and in its definite elimination of the Roman question but also are concerned at its lofty aims tending to regulate the condition of religion and the Church in Italy.

Some other clauses of the treaty were:

"The treaty reaffirms the principle contained in the first article of the Constitution of the Italian kingdom, by which the Catholic Apostolic Roman religion is the only state religion in Italy.

"The treaty recognizes the full property and exclusive dominion and sovereign jurisdiction of the Holy See over the Vatican as at present constituted.

"For this purpose the City of the Vatican is created and in its territory no interference by the Italian government will be possible for there will be no authority but the authority of the Holy See.

"The Vatican territory will always be considered neutral and inviolable.

"The Italian government accepts the canon law in cases of marriage, separation, and other matters over which the Church has jurisdiction.

"The Holy See, as a definite settlement of all its financial relations with Italy in consequence of the fall of temporal power, accepts 750,000,000 lire cash and 1,000,000,000 lire in Italian State consols at the rate of five per cent." (Italics added.)

It is this last-quoted part of the agreement that provoked the investigation by Berg. On the basis of facts known in 1944, at the time of his report, and facts made available since the end of the Third Reich, his conclusions may merit some consideration. Berg claimed that he had "irrefutable circumstantial evidence that $92,500,000 in cash and negotiable gold bonds settled on the Holy See by the reason of the Treaty of the Lateran concluded with the Kingdom of Italy in 1929 was gradually funneled into the Nazi Party coffers under the aegis of one Eugenio Pacelli, the papal nuncio there [in Germany], afterwards chosen Pope Pius XII."

In 1944, when Berg submitted the report to his commanding officer, not nearly as much was known about Hitler, the SA, Pope Pius XII, or the internal workings of Third Reich as is known today. It is easy to see why such a report might have been placed under wraps by the Security Intelligence Corps, as Berg charges. The "laundering" of money has, for centuries, been a practice of politicians trying to get huge financial resources into circulation without the authorities being aware of it. Yet to accuse the Vatican, or someone in the Vatican, of funneling millions of dollars to Hitler with or without the knowledge of the Pope was a sensitive matter that could have alienated Allied Catholic supporters.

One piece of "evidence" submitted by Berg to document his

conclusion is the cost to maintain the ever-growing SA, Hitler's private army. He calculated that one mark and 25 pfennigs, or 30 cents, a day at the then rate of exchange was required for the rations, quarters, and administration of each SA member.

"This meant nine dollars a month or $91,800,000 for the period of years in question, within 1% of the [Lateran Treaty] settlement amount. During the terrible depression years of the early 1930s these funds provided the support for the Storm Troopers (SA) who in turn were directly responsible for Hitler's rise to power," Berg has written.

Why would these funds be given to Hitler and the NSDAP? Berg's theory also answers this puzzling question.

"In return for these loans," states Berg, "all of which were afterwards repaid, Hitler made certain promises to Eugenio Pacelli, the Papal Nuncio."

Included in the secret agreement, according to Berg, were Hitler's vow of a legal dissolution of the German Freemasons when he took power, a concordat between the Holy See and Germany within six months after a NSDAP takeover, the downfall of the European Jews because of their presumed "deicide," and the defeat of communism because of its anti-Christ policy. As for the Freemasons, Hitler certainly would have had no qualms about a dissolution, legal or illegal, of that fraternal society. As early as 1923 Hitler had stated that so-called world pacifism was a Jewish invention and that the Freemasons were tools of the Jews.

The concordat between the Vatican and the Reich was signed on July 20, 1933, *six months and 20 days* after Hitler took power. It was the first Concordat with a German state since the Reformation. By this time Eugenio Pacelli had completed his 11 years of service in Germany, first in Bavaria and then in Berlin, and had become Vatican secretary of state. Franz von Papen, Hitler's vice-chancellor during the early years of the Third Reich, handled the matter of the Concordat with Pacelli, whom he knew well.

"When [Pacelli] left Germany his departure was much regretted," Papen said, "even in non-Catholic circles which had come to appreciate his extraordinary personal qualities."

After several discussions in Rome and Germany during the

six months and 20 days, a final agreement was drafted on July 8, 1933, and signed on July 20 by Pacelli and Papen. Article 1 guaranteed "freedom of the profession and the public exercise of the Catholic religion" as well as the right of the church to regulate and administer freely its own affairs independently, within the law, and to issue, within the framework of its own competence, laws and ordinances binding on its members. Additional clauses guaranteed diplomatic representation, legal status of the clergy, and the church's right to appoint Catholic teachers of religion and to operate Catholic parochial schools. There was even a secret clause that dealt with the clergy in case of universal military training. The world was amazed that Hitler—at a time when he was severely limiting the rights of the individual and organizations by his Enabling Act of March 24, 1933, and by party orders enforced by his SA—would grant such concessions to the Vatican. Was it because he was financially indebted to the Holy See, as Berg believes? Even more amazing was the fact that the Holy See made such an agreement with Hitler when it was obvious he was a morally bankrupt dictator intent on devastating the Jews. During the first six months of his regime he initiated the discrimination that would eventually lead to the gas chambers. He ordered the boycott of Jewish shops, lawyers, and doctors, demanded that Jewish pupils and teachers be expelled from universities, and forced many prominent Jews to flee the country.

As Papen said later, when critics of the Concordat questioned him, "The Vatican had an intimate knowledge of conditions in Germany in 1933. Suggestions that my visit to Rome and the subsequent signing of the Concordat were planned as a trap are rubbish."

His statement was true.

The actions of Eugenio Pacelli—a prominent Catholic figure in latter-day Weimar Germany, the signer of the concordat, and pope during the years when Hitler destroyed six million Jews—have been the subject of controversy over the years. Why did he favor the concordat when his 11 years in Germany made him aware of Hitler's non-Christian attitudes? Why did he keep quiet during the war, when he was aware of the death camps and the brutal mistreatment and execution of millions, including a large percentage of the European Jews? Perhaps no one really knows. Yet if, as Berg believes, Pacelli funneled millions of dollars to Hitler and the NSDAP after the signing of the Lateran Treaty in 1929, he may have feared to speak out, knowing that Hitler, in retaliation, might very well reveal a secret that, if known to the world, would have meant disaster for the Vatican.

Even if the Berg thesis is not accepted, one must still explain Hitler's sudden affluence. For a reason never explained his living habits changed drastically in 1929. Prior to that year he had stayed in a sparsely furnished two-room apartment or at the Pension Moritz, spent little money on clothes, and lived quietly and abstemiously. In 1929, however, his attitude toward luxury changed. He moved into the large, plush apartment on Prinzregentenplatz, one of Munich's most fashionable areas, bought a new and expensive wardrobe, acquired a fleet of modern automobiles, and hired 12 people to take care of his living quarters and his personal belongings.

Robert Ludlum based his novel *The Scarlatti Inheritance* on two photographs he saw in an old English magazine. One photograph, he said, showed a man wheeling a barrow full of marks to the store to buy a loaf of bread; the second showed thousands of men with boots and shovels at a rally in Munich.

"I got to wondering who paid for those boots and shovels in a country where it took millions of marks to buy bread," Ludlum answered, when asked where he got the idea for his book. "Nobody ever explained to me where the money for the Nazis did come from on the scale it was made available."

His work of fiction blames international financiers. Berg's theory blames Eugenio Pacelli. The question of Hitler's financial miracle in 1929 may never be answered satisfactorily, but the mysterious wealth he acquired then produced a marked effect on his life, personal and public. It enabled him to begin the construction in the Bavarian Alps of the complex that was to become known the world over as "Hitler territory."

3

Hitler Territory

The area known as "Hitler territory," in the mountains of Bavaria near Berchtesgaden, has always been an enigma to the public. The mystery is understandable, since the area was Hitler's private retreat, well guarded, hidden from view, inaccessible except by personal invitation.

When, in 1928, Hitler bought Haus Wachenfeld, the home built in 1916 by Herr Winter, it was an average, two-story mountain chalet at the foot of the Kehlstein. There was a front porch, from which Berchtesgaden could be seen. But because the house had small windows, the view from inside was limited. Painted beer mugs and stuffed deer heads decorated the inside walls, hanging above the heavy, rough-hewn, Bavarian furniture, which had been made locally. Visitors to the Obersalzberg noticed the place not because of its beauty or outstanding architecture, but because it was brightly painted. It was a cheerful-looking house with a large porch and a yard, more suitable for a family with several young children than for a moody politician hatching a plot to gain control of Germany.

Hitler brought his stepsister, Angela Raubal and her daughter Geli to Haus Wachenfeld to keep house for him, a move that would mean tragedy in 1931. Outwardly, everything stayed the same in the Obersalzberg for a while after Hitler purchased the house. His neighbors didn't pay much attention to him, nor did Hitler pay much attention to them. He was too busy trying to advance his political career. Other than adding a small terrace to the house, he made no changes inside or out before 1933.

The years between 1929 and 1933 were harsh ones for Hitler,

leaving him little time to concentrate on plans for large real-estate holdings on the Obersalzberg; he would spend more time on that later. In an attempt to gain further prestige for himself and the NSDAP, Hitler joined forces with Alfred Hugenberg, Germany's leading film and press lord and head of the right-wing German National People's Party. However the connection turned out to be a disappointing one for Hitler. On June 7, 1929, when the plebiscite was held for the Young Plan, a new method for the defeated Germans to pay off the reparations due the victors, the Hitler-Hugenberg alliance suffered a resounding defeat. Needing 21 million votes to overthrow the proposal, they received only 6 million. Hitler immediately abandoned his associate to try a new approach to power. He didn't want to be paired with a loser.

His next chance to gain publicity for himself and the NSDAP came with the death of Horst Wessel in February 1930. Wessel was a 21-year-old member of the NSDAP who had written a poem dedicated to those members of the party who had died in

Reich President Paul von Hindenburg and newly elected Chancellor Hitler at a 1933 ceremony honoring the war dead. *(National Archives)*

street battles with the communists. When Wessel himself was killed in a street brawl in Berlin, Hitler used the slaying as a propaganda ploy. In an effort to immortalize Wessel, party officials made speeches honoring him, and each NSDAP function was closed by the singing of his poem. When, on Wessel's death, the party had staged an extravagant funeral for him, the funeral procession had ended in a running battle between the NSDAP and the communists. Hitler's use of Wessel was a brutal and ghoulish way to gain publicity but a successful one: The young Nazi's death and the resulting controversy made Hitler's name a household word in Germany.

With this new impetus Hitler campaigned long and hard during the summer of 1930, preparing for the fall national election. He had little time to visit the Obersalzberg and Haus Wachenfeld. The long, difficult campaign tour paid off. In the September national parliamentary election the NSDAP won 6,371,000 votes, over 18 percent of the total, making Hitler's party the second largest in the country. It was an amazing comeback from the ragtag remnants that had been the NSDAP when Hitler stepped from Landsberg prison in 1924.

Despite some setbacks that made Hitler more bitter than ever, setbacks that he often blamed on "Jewish influence," he was not to be stopped. In Bremen an NSDAP member was elected president of the city council in 1931; the NSDAP vote doubled in the Hesse election that same year; on March 13, 1932, Hitler received 13.7 million votes for president of the republic—not enough to win, but a very creditable showing; two months later the NSDAP won 230 seats out of 608 in the Reichstag elections; and finally, after secret dealings between Franz von Papen, Hitler, and banker Kurt von Schröder in January 1933, Hitler was named chancellor by President Paul von Hindenburg on January 30. These steps in his path to the dictatorship are well known, but a step he took next is seldom mentioned. Hitler immediately moved to establish a secret, elaborate complex on the Obersalzberg from which he could rule Germany and, someday, the world.

Heinrich Hoffmann, the official photographer for the NSDAP and Hitler, and Joseph Goebbels, the propaganda expert of the Third Reich, gave Haus Wachenfeld a new name

Haus Wachenfeld on the Obersalzberg, the first house Hitler bought. He later had it remodeled and enlarged and renamed it the Berghof. *(Bundesarchiv)*

after Hitler became chancellor. Referring to the "small lodge of Volkskanzler Hitler," they named it the Berghof. "Berghof" can imply a neat farm building with the characteristics of a mountain house, thereby giving an impression of modesty. But the word literally means "mountain court." The Berghof was anything but a modest home, and the enclave eventually became one of the most elaborate and unusual secret retreats ever constructed.

As soon as Hitler became chancellor, thousands of his followers began flocking to the Obersalzberg to get a glimpse of the new Führer. Approximately 5000 visitors a day came to see Hitler, and at first he enjoyed this attention. He would walk to a young lime tree at the side of the road to the Berghof and return the salutes and salutations of the crowd, pose for photographs, and occasionally hold a conversation with a pretty girl. He even ordered Martin Bormann, at the time Hitler's private secretary, to remodel Pension Moritz to accommodate visitors who had traveled a long distance to see him and wanted to stay overnight.

Gradually, however, the Hitler retreat changed from the little alpine house where the Führer greeted visitors. Rudolf Hess, close friend of Hitler and now deputy Führer, was commissioned to bring order to the Obersalzberg when the crowds became so large that Hitler had no semblance of privacy. Hess, realizing that Hitler needed more land if he was to have the desired solitude, began negotiations with farmers and wealthy residents who owned nearby homes. Hess, instantly recognizable because of his deep-set eyes and square-cut face, was liked by citizens living on the Obersalzberg. He treated them fairly. He even paid some of the farmers exceptionally high sums for their land rather than risk controversy. Before long, though, Hess was preoccupied with political assignments given him by Hitler and had no time to continue his development of the Obersalzberg complex for the Führer. Martin Bormann replaced him in this activity.

Bormann, a thick-set, stocky NSDAP member and Hitler's closest collaborator in later years, was entirely different from Hess. A brutal, cruel man, he had taken part in the murder of Walther Kadow, a young schoolteacher whom he considered

Hitler and Julius
Schreck, his chauffeur,
at Haus Wachenfeld in
1933. *(Bundesarchiv)*

Hitler studying in the living room of Haus Wachenfeld. *(Bundesarchiv)*

an enemy of the NSDAP, and had served a prison sentence. Bormann was obsessed with the power and money his position as an intimate of the Führer provided him, and he used them both for his own personal gain as well as for the benefit of Hitler. It was discovered at the end of the war that the entire area of Hitler's enclave on the Obersalzberg was owned by Bormann, not Hitler.

Hess had tried to be fair with owners of homes on the Obersalzberg, but on the contrary Bormann was ruthless. If the owner of a desired property tried to haggle over Bormann's initial offer, Bormann didn't raise the ante. He threatened. Soon he had deeded over to him a large area surrounding Hitler's house. Approximately 10 square kilometers were ultimately "obtained" from private owners, the forest administration, and hotel operators.

One farmer, Heinz Jager, had lived and tilled his acreage on the Obersalzberg all his life and was reluctant to sell. Bormann told him bluntly, "Take my offer or I'll throw you off the property."

Jager, who knew nothing about the NSDAP official and wasn't aware of the influence Bormann had with the new Führer, just grinned. Twenty-six years old in 1934, when Bormann demanded his farm, standing 6 feet 2 inches and weighing 230 pounds, he was certain the pudgy, shorter Bormann couldn't "throw him off the property." He didn't realize that Bormann had no intention of handling the matter alone. A few days after Jager had refused to accept the offer, an automobile stopped in front of his farmhouse, and six SA officers stepped out. Without a word they forced Jager from his home, pushed him into the back of the Mercedes, and took him to the Berghof.

"For the first and only time in my life," Jager said later, "I had a personal interview with the Führer. Hitler was sitting on the small terrace in front of his house when we drove up. Bormann was sitting beside him. The SA men pushed me from the car and led me directly to them. I was angry, but by this time I realized I was also in trouble. Everywhere I looked there were uniformed SA men, armed and mean looking."

Jager said Hitler greeted him politely, invited him to sit, and

Hitler, Albert Speer, and Martin Bormann enjoy a day in the country viewing the work of farmers. Bormann had been brutal in dispossessing Obersalzberg farmers to assemble the Berghof enclave. *(National Archives)*

The Berghof, where Hitler led much of his personal life. *(Hierzegger)*

then asked why he wouldn't sell his farm. When Jager explained that he had lived on the farm all his life, that he wanted to continue to live there and till the land, Hitler nodded and was silent.

"Then he looked me right in the eye and said, 'For the sake of Germany I ask you to sell your farm.'"

Jager, more stubborn than wise, refused.

"I never saw a man change so quickly in my life," he recalled. "His eyes seemed to be boring right through me, and his little mustache twitched a couple of times. He turned to Bormann, ignoring me completely, and shook his head. I heard him say, 'Go ahead.'"

Jager listened as Bormann called the senior SA officer over and told him to take "the stupid farmer to Dachau where he can learn some sense."

At the time Jager was unaware that Dachau was a concentration camp 12 miles northwest of Munich, one of three such camps that Hitler had ordered established shortly after he became chancellor in 1933. Jager was not even permitted to return to his farm to bid his relatives good-bye. He was taken directly from the Berghof to the concentration camp, where he remained until his release in 1938. Surprisingly, he returned to the Obersalzberg to work with the construction crews building the Eagle's Nest.

Others were not so fortunate. The owner of the Hotel Zum Türken, the popular inn located just above the Berghof, also wouldn't sell voluntarily. He too was sent to Dachau, where he died of a lung ailment. Three young sisters who had inherited a farm a short distance west of the Berghof hesitated too long before agreeing to Bormann's offer. They were sent to a brothel set up in Munich for the SA.

One way or another Bormann soon had all the acreage he needed to start his huge reconstruction program. He hired Professor Roderich Fick, an architect from Munich, to lay out the complex, and once Hitler had approved the plans, construction began. A remodeling of the Berghof was first. An additional floor was added, and wide steps at the front of the building, seen in hundreds of photographs distributed by Hoffmann during the years of the Third Reich, were constructed. A Gothic type hall, with pillars of marble obtained from the nearby mountains, formed the lobby of the large conference room on the first floor, where Hitler met with his visitors. Here the famous picture window was installed. This window, which took up one entire wall, could be opened when Hitler wanted an unobstructed view of the mountains. But there was one problem.

"The garage was directly underneath the large window," Albert Speer, Hitler's favorite architect and, later, minister of munitions and armaments, explained after the war. "When the window was opened the fumes from the exhausts of the automobiles threatened to asphyxiate anyone in the conference room."

ironic? gas chamber

Also on the first floor were a vestibule, a dining room, a large kitchen, a terrace, and two rooms for the adjutants. On the second floor were Hitler's living room, his bedroom, his study, three rooms for staff members, four rooms for the permanent bodyguard, five rooms for Hitler's guests, and an apartment for

The huge window in the conference hall at the Berghof. The window could be raised, but exhaust fumes from the garage below would then seep into the conference hall. *(Bundesarchiv)*

the caretaker. The third floor had the same number of rooms as the second, but it was used only by staff, bodyguards, and guests, not by Hitler personally. Underneath the Berghof's first floor were the garage, the supply rooms, the heating system, and a bowling alley.

Hitler insisted that only the very best materials be used in the Berghof. Expensive woods, marble, artificial and natural stone were brought to the Obersalzberg for use by the contractor. All the windows were lined with lead. Most of the furniture was in Biedermeier or baroque style, and many of the pieces were decorated with inlaid mosaic. Hitler had a special film projector and screen and watched a movie nearly every night until the war was launched.

Elisabeth von Stahlenberg was one of the few relative outsiders to view Hitler's mountain house. She was invited in 1937 because her husband was an associate of Goebbels' in the Ministry of Propaganda. She later described the conference room to her friends.

"The salon is like something out of a fairy story. It is like a room for a giant. An enormous window, a vast clock with a terrifying bronze eagle crouching over it, a table which has to be twenty feet in length, a sideboard at least ten feet high (it turned out to conceal gramophone records), huge paintings, tapestries—one of which hid the movie screen which I was astonished to find as part of the evening's entertainment. The room seems roughly divided in half, the window half and the fireplace (very, very big) half. We began in the window half, the tapestries were lifted (the projector was also hidden behind one) and with some slight rearrangement of seating by Hitler, we were treated to what seemed like five hours of *La Jana,*" she explained.

After the film, a musical, Stahlenberg said Hitler asked them to move to the half of the room dominated by the fireplace. The Führer again determined the seating arrangement. The conversation, mostly a monologue by Hitler, lasted until the early hours of the next morning and ended only when Hitler excused himself and went to bed.

The dining room, also on the first floor, was another unusual room. Pauline Kohler, a maid at the Berghof, retained her memory of the room as she had first viewed it, on arriving from Munich.

"This particular room was sixty feet long by forty feet wide. A massive oak table ran down the center. There were no lights visible. A soft glow came from cunningly concealed lighting. Four etchings by Dürer hung on the walls. A vast Persian carpet covered the floor."

Later, when she helped set the table, she discovered that Hitler did not live modestly, as her countrymen were told.

"When the dinner was an informal one the service was of magnificent Dresden china but when important guests were

A section of the large conference hall in the Berghof. *(Bundesarchiv)*

visual description

present they ate off solid silver—most of it plate from the Jewish merchants of Nürnberg, stolen from them by Himmler's agents," Kohler wrote. Himmler was SS chief and leader of the Gestapo, the secret police.

Each of the guests' bedrooms at the Berghof had a private bathroom. Each bath, except the bathroom used by Hitler, was constructed of stone and marble quarried from different parts of Germany. The Führer's bath was built with marble from Italy, a gift from Mussolini. The walls of the bedrooms were of gray plaster decorated with paintings from German mythology. On the ceilings naked fauns and nymphs represented scenes from Greek legends. In each bedroom there was a copy of *Mein Kampf* beside pornographic books from Paris. Over each bed was a portrait of Hitler. One guest has said, "The French books looked as though they were used much more than the copy of *Mein Kampf.*"

The Berghof's kitchen was magnificent, equipped with every modern appliance available. All cooking was done by electricity, and at one time the former chef of the Adlon Hotel in Berlin was in charge of the kitchen. Hitler, however, had his own personal cook, whose every move was watched by a Gestapo agent. The Führer was always afraid he might be poisoned.

Hitler used an enormous desk in his study on the second floor. He could automatically flood the room with tear gas if an intruder slipped into the study. An alarm bell would sound as the tear gas was released, alerting Hitler's personal bodyguard. Not that there was much danger of an intruder's reaching his study. Every door in the Berghof was equipped with an electric-eye detector that would sound an alarm if an unexpected visitor tried to use it; and the electric eye at the doorway of Hitler's study also detected any metal object that a guest might have on his person. In addition, with few exceptions, every visitor to the Berghof was searched before being permitted to meet Hitler.

One of Hitler's favorite rooms in the Berghof, until his empire began to crumble late in the war, was the map room. He spent a great deal of time in this room, since he had a mania for maps. Drawers along the walls of the room were filled with maps of every part of the world. Over the fireplace in this room was a very large bronze map of Germany and Central Europe. He always kept the frontiers of his Third Reich up to date on his maps, and during the war he daily outlined the battle lines.

Another installation in the house that aided Hitler in keeping abreast of political and military affairs was the communications room. Three men were on duty there night and day. A direct telephone line ran from the Berghof to Berlin and Munich. All Hitler's official messages were electronically scrambled, but his private calls, such as those he made to his female friends, were made in the clear because there was no device at the other end to translate scrambled messages.

Next to the communications room on the second floor was Hitler's private post office, where he received an average of 600 letters a day. Most of the letters came from his supporters in Germany; about 15 percent arrived from abroad. No parcel was allowed into the Berghof for fear it might contain a bomb. All parcels were opened in the barracks, and presents sent to Hitler were given to his bodyguard contingent. One Christmas Hitler received more than 12,000 parcels.

Hitler's study in the Berghof. He could automatically flood the room with tear gas if an intruder slipped in. An electric scanner at the doorway also detected any metal object that a guest might have on his person. *(Bundesarchiv)*

A well-kept secret of the Berghof was the powerful radios, both receivers and transmitters, installed in a locked, guarded room. One high-powered transmitter kept Hitler in contact with his military commanders all over Europe without a second's delay.

Artur Kasche, a skilled radio operator who was on duty at the Berghof for three years, believes that it was the failure to exploit information gained with these radios just before the Allied invasion of Europe that caused Germany's defeat.

"We had been briefed many weeks earlier that the French Resistance organizations would be alerted to the Allied invasion when the BBC broadcast two lines of a Paul Verlaine poem," he explained. "At noon on June 1, I picked up the broadcast of the first line of the poem: *'Les sanglots longs des violons de l'automne.'* I immediately notified General Jodl."

Alfred Jodl, who was at the Berghof during this period, was chief of the operations staff of the German armed forces.

"I don't know what Jodl told the Führer. Then at 9:15 P.M. on June 5 I received the second line of the poem: *'Blessent mon coeur d'une langueur monotone.'* That meant the invasion would begin within 48 hours. Again I notified Jodl, but I learned later that Jodl decided to await further news before telling Hitler. When first reports of Allied ships were radioed to the Berghof, I relayed the message to Jodl. Hitler was in bed by this time and the general was afraid to awaken him for fear the news was a false alarm. By the time Hitler learned of the radio messages I picked up, it was too late to repel the invasion forces on the beaches, as Rommel wanted to do."

From Hitler's private suite in the Berghof an elevator dropped down through 300 feet of solid rock to the underground bunker, an extensive tunnel system unique to the Berghof and Hitler's other installations on the Obersalzberg. The main part of the tunnel system was provided for Hitler, Eva Braun, and guests who stayed at the Berghof. The system consisted of caverns and subtunnels branching off both sides of a main corridor. The subtunnels contained the ventilation, electric power, water, communication cables, and heating facilities. The caverns, or side rooms and suites, were immediately claimed by the various Berghof inhabitants and designed to please their special tastes.

Hitler had an
underground kennel
built for his dog Blondi
in the Berghof bunker.
(National Archives)

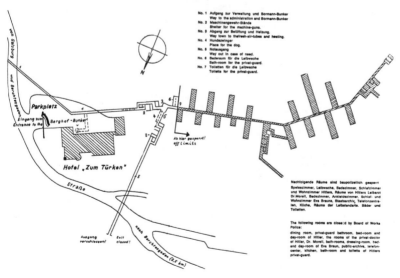

No. 1 Aufgang zur Verwaltung und Bormann-Bunker
       Way to the administration and Bormann-Bunker
No. 2 Maschinengewehr-Stände
       Shelter for the machine-guns.
No. 3 Abgang zur Belüftung und Heizung.
       Way down to thefresh-air-tubes and heating.
No. 4 Hundezwinger
       Place for the dog.
No. 5 Notausgang
       Way out in case of need.
No. 6 Baderaum für die Leibwache
       Bath-room for the privat-guard.
No. 7 Toiletten für die Leibwache
       Toiletts for the privat-guard.

Nachfolgende Räume sind baupolizeilich gesperrt
Speisezimmer, Leibwache, Badezimmer, Schlafzimmer
und Wohnzimmer Hitlers, Räume von Hitlers Leibarzt
Dr.Morell, Badezimmer, Ankleidezimmer, Schlaf- und
Wohnzimmer Eva Brauns, Staatsarchiv, Telefonzentra-
len, Küche, Räume der Leibstandarte. Bäder und
Toiletten.

The following rooms are closed by Board of Works
Police:
dining room, privat-guard bathroom, bed-room and
day-room of Hitler, the rooms of the privat-doctor
of Hitler, Dr. Morell, bath-rooms, dressing-room, bed-
and day-room of Eva Braun, public-archive, telefon-
center, kitchen, bath-room and toiletts of Hitlers
privat-guard.

Map of the Berghof bunker.

Eva Braun, for example, wanted her own bathroom; Bormann demanded room below ground for his entire headquarters and also a special dining room; the cooks demanded complete kitchens and a refrigeration system. Hitler had his private dining room, dressing room, bedroom, archive space, study, bathroom, space for his bodyguard, and a room for his personal physician, Dr. Theodor Morell. Even after the demands of the elect were met, petty jealousies surfaced. Bormann claimed that Göring had more space underground than he did, so he confiscated several rooms from the defense command. These he filled with personal booty from the conquered countries—heavy brass locks, silver candlesticks, pewter plates, jewelry, paintings, and such. Göring insisted that the tunnel from his house connect with Hitler's tunnel. Bormann, however, perhaps trying to conceal from the Führer the extent of some of his looting and other activities, had 10 meters of dirt left between his tunnel and Hitler's. For his part Hitler ordered underground kennels built for his and Eva Braun's dogs. In the end he had 17 rooms, Göring 10, and Bormann 5, not counting the rooms Bormann had taken from the defense command.

The rooms were not cold, damp, prisonlike cells, as were most air-raid shelters. They had polished, inlaid floors covered by heavy rugs. Each wall had wainscoting, and the doors and door frames shone with lacquer. All office furniture was of hardwood, and the underground offices were as well-equipped as those above ground. There were even safes built into the rocks for valuables.

One of the largest construction projects other than the work done on the Berghof resulted from Hitler's order to modify the Pension Moritz (called the Platterhof after a change in ownership) so that citizens who traveled to the Obersalzberg to see him would have a place to stay overnight. Bormann, with unlimited NSDAP funds at his disposal, decided to tear down the old Platterhoff and build a completely new hotel. To justify the cost Bormann's office announced that a "national hotel would be erected. And here every German who participated in a pilgrimage to the beloved Führer would have the opportunity to spend one day and one night close to the Führer for only one Reichsmark."

Instead the new Platterhoff ended up as a deluxe hotel much too expensive for the ordinary German citizen.

Bormann spent millions of marks on the new hotel, much of the expenditure a result of his own incompetence and idiosyncrasies. He used his considerable cunning to dupe Hitler about the grandiose plans he had for the new Platterhof. More than once he ordered an already constructed section torn down and built again to meet his revised specifications. This happened so often, in fact, that Hitler muttered, "If I did not know that so much money has been spent already I would . . . blow everything up."

Once, when Hitler was inspecting the building site, he asked Bormann where the bar would be located. Bormann, knowing that Hitler did not drink alcohol, had not included a bar in the plans for the Platterhof, but he didn't tell Hitler that. As soon as he realized that Hitler favored having a bar available for the guests, he ordered that a basement be constructed underneath the courtyard to accommodate the bar. This meant digging

Hitler's bunker beneath the Berghof complex. *(Hierzegger)*

attitude of Hitler

through solid rock at great expense. Later, when he was shown a model of the bar, a model that had cost 10,000 marks to build, he threw it angrily against the wall of his office, smashing the miniature, because it displeased him. Another, incorporating his "suggestions," had to be built.

When completed the new Platterhoff consisted of this added basement and two floors above ground. It included a reception hall adorned with expensive paintings, heavy rugs, and other lavish furnishings. There was a barbershop and a beauty parlor, a reading room, a mirrored hall, a library, a beer room, a breakfast room whose ceiling alone cost 25,000 marks, bomb-proof bowling alleys, and 150 guest rooms. Brass and chrome, both in short supply in Germany at the time, were used for door handles and toilets; copper served for the roof and the gutters; and the decorative lanterns were made of gold. After the gold lanterns were installed, Bormann decided he didn't like them, so he had lanterns made of silver put up. Once they were in place he decided he didn't like silver, so they were taken down and the gold ones put back up.

Spoiled rotten

The Platterhof, the hotel Hitler had Bormann build on the Obersalzberg. Ostensibly built for ordinary Germans who wanted to spend a night in the vicinity of their Führer, it was so expensive only high-ranking Nazis could afford its accommodations. *(Hierzegger)*

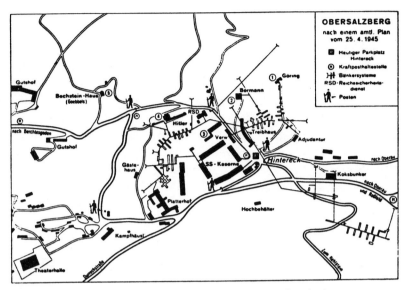

Map of the Obersalzberg complex as it stood very late in the war.

Bormann decided a new road was needed to serve the Berghof, the new Platterhoff, a new post office, barracks for the SS, garages, hotels for the employees, and the many other buildings associated with the complex. The Klaushöhe road was built; and the Rossfeld-Eckersattle highway was begun, although it was still not completed at the end of the war.

A fence two meters high was erected around the entire enclave, which reached from the Obersalzberg to the foot of the Kehlstein mountain. An inner fence divided the area into two sections: an inner circle, called "Hoheitsgebiet" (sovereign territory), where the Berghof and Hitler's close associates' houses were located, and an outer circle, where employees, construction workers, and those not intimately associated with Hitler lived. The inner circle was guarded by the *Schutzstaffel* (SS), or Elite Guard, Hitler's black-shirted personal bodyguard. The outer ring was the responsibility of the State Security Service. At the entrance to the outer circle all persons had to show valid passes to the guards, whom Bormann had instructed: "A minis-

ter's uniform is no authorization to pass through these gates."
Relatives of those who were employed on the Obersalzberg
were issued a one-hour or, at most, a one-day pass to visit
within the outer circle.

The SS, guards of the inner circle, were housed in stone
buildings at the entrances, buildings that cost as much as 130,-
000 marks each. No one passed through these well-guarded
gates without verification from within the Berghof of a personal
invitation from Hitler. And these invitations, as we shall see,
were issued by Hitler only for reasons he considered very
important.

"Hitler Territory" was seen by relatively few persons, and the
strange events that took place there were known to even fewer.

4

The Führer's Strange Habits

"You will never learn my real intentions. Not even my closest colleagues, who are convinced they know them, will ever find them out."

With these words Hitler greeted Franz Halder when he made him chief of staff of the German Army on August 22, 1938, and Hitler never spoke truer words. For many the ultimate in evil, disloyalty, hypocrisy, banality, desperation, and obscenity, Hitler was able to conceal these characteristics from even his closest associates when he so desired. No one completely understood him. He was a "man of a thousand faces" who presented to each person he confronted the aspect he deemed most advantageous at the given time.

Even his domestic staff at the Berghof, who saw him in off-guard moments more than most others, could never be certain how he would treat them. Sometimes he ignored them completely, just as though they didn't exist. At other times he became furious on finding his coffee cup not full enough or too full, the bedspread not perfectly smoothed, a speck of dirt in the corner of his room. But there were occasions when he treated the domestics warmly.

"Once when I entered Hitler's room to serve his meal at his desk," says Pauline Kohler, "he told me I was pretty and gave me a thousand-mark note as a reward for faithful service. I was amazed."

The servants became accustomed to this erratic behavior, but outsiders who had very little contact with Hitler and met him only on formal occasions were shocked, pleased, or frightened, depending upon the mood Hitler was in at the time. By keeping them off balance in this manner he often achieved his aims before his guest realized what had happened.

His personal habits and behavior were both predictable and unpredictable. Hitler constantly complained about stomach trouble, and his food, prepared on his instructions, was nearly always the same. A Viennese dietician, Frau Marlene von Exner, was hired by Dr. Theodor Morell, Hitler's personal physician. The doctor paid Exner a bribe of two thousand marks just to get her to the Berghof, and she received a tax-free salary of 800 marks a month to cook for Hitler. One of the best culinary experts in Austria, she soon discovered there was no need of her talents at the Berghof, that Hitler was certainly not a gourmet. A typical Führer-requested menu consisted of orange juice with linseed gruel, rice pudding with herb sauce, and crisp bread with butter and nut paste.

At Hitler's military field headquarters in East Prussia the Führer ate alone in his bunker, since he ate at odd hours and tired of the conversation that was required when he ate with

Hitler and members of his staff take a walk at Wolfsschanze, his military headquarters in East Prussia. (National Archives)

others. He had a camp cook who was very good, a Berliner who used his imagination to prepare special Bavarian meals for Hitler. His surname was Günther, but only a few knew him by this name. Even Hitler called him by his nickname, Krümel ("Crumbs"). Over the kitchen door was displayed a large sign: "Who does not honor Crumbs is not worthy of the cake." "Crumbs" was accustomed to cooking for soldiers, and he had a difficult time getting used to the demands of a vegetarian such as Hitler. In fact he was prejudiced against vegetarians, but since Hitler was the most feared man in Germany Crumbs took pains to work out a special menu for the Führer. Basically it pleased Hitler. However Crumbs never got over the opinion that people could not live without meat, and for that reason he put into every kettle of soup he made for Hitler a little meat broth or a small piece of pork fat. Most of the time the Führer noticed the deception, became angry, and complained that it was the cause of his stomach trouble. Finally he had Crumbs cook only gruel, mashed potatoes, and other dishes that he could be certain were cooked without animal ingredients. This, of course, made Hitler's menu more boring, more predictable.

Hitler insisted that his work rooms be kept comfortably cool. While he enjoyed the fireplace at the Berghof and the Eagle's Nest and kept the living rooms of his apartment in Munich and the Reich Chancellery at normal temperatures, his conference rooms, map rooms, and studies were always much too cold for the average person.

Traudl Junge, Hitler's private secretary, told about her first experience with the temperature of the Führer's study.

"I left Hitler's work room with ice cold feet and a hot head. I ask the servants why it was always so cold in Hitler's work room. In a fleeting glance at the thermometer I saw that it was 11 degrees Celsius [52°F]. A head of state certainly should be able to provide heat to his study. After all the whole installation was centrally heated and it was warm everywhere else. They told me that Hitler only felt well at that temperature and never let it get any warmer in his work rooms. Now it was clear to me why the general staff officers and the generals themselves always came out of the conferences, which often lasted for hours, with red noses and blue frozen hands. They would immediately pour themselves a warming Schnapps in the serving room or the mess. In fact, General Jodl said he had chronic rheumatism because of his conferences with Hitler."

On June 22, 1941, when he sent German troops into action against the Russians, Hitler decided to move to his new military field headquarters, in the Görlitz forest near the town of Rastenburg, East Prussia. He arrived two days later with the field detachment of the Wehrmacht Operational Staff and his own private secretaries, adjutants, and other staff members. Named Wolfsschanze (Wolf's Redoubt or Wolf's Lair), the headquarters consisted of eight bunkers hidden in the woods plus various wooden buildings. It was a depressing site, made more frustrating when Russian air raids forced Hitler and his staff to stay inside the windowless bunkers for hours at a time. As Jodl said later, "The Führer's headquarters was a cross between a monastery and a concentration camp."

It was at Wolfsschanze that some of the most momentous decisions concerning the invasion of Russia had to be made, yet Hitler would insist that his generals and their staffs halt all work periodically to join him for what he apparently considered a much more important event. They had to gather together to watch Hitler's Alsation, Blondi, perform her tricks! The dog was undoubtedly one of the greatest pleasures of the Führer's strange life. Not only did he have kennels built for her in the underground tunnels of the Obersalzberg; but at the Reich Chancellery and at his Munich apartment Blondi had the run of the area; and when the end came in the Berlin bunker in 1945, Blondi died with her master. In the area reserved for Hitler's daily walk near his Wolfsschanze bunker, the German shepherd exhibited her repertoire of tricks. Hitler had her well trained, there was no question about that. Showing a patience that he lacked with humans, he would work with Blondi for hours to teach her a new trick. It gave him the greatest pleasure when she could jump a few centimeters higher than before or balance a few seconds longer on a narrow pole. He maintained that his association with his dog was one of his best means of relaxation.

It was impressive what Blondi could actually do. She sprang through tires, leaped a two-meter wooden wall, climbed a ladder, and sat up and begged on the platform above. One fringe benefit of the Blondi exhibition was that it offered some of Hitler's associates the only opportunity they had to get close to him. Since he was always in a good humor when the dog was showing off, he could sometimes be approached with subjects that he would otherwise ignore. Walther Horer, who was on the staff of Jodl, said, "I sometimes had the impression that the outcome of the Russian campaign depended more upon Blondi than the German general staff. When she did well Hitler would listen to his generals. Otherwise he usually ignored them."

Hitler had an abhorrence of personal correspondence. The only writing he did, except for letters to Eva Braun, were thank-you notes and letters of good wishes. These were usually dictated.

"Once he wrote a very short letter to his sister when he sent her some bacon which he had received from Spain," Christa Schröder, one of Hitler's secretaries, said. "He always emphasized that it was his great strength, even during time of war, to have written no letters because if he did and they fell into the wrong hands the letters could be used against him."

According to Schröder, who took dictation from Hitler for many years, he composed all his own speeches.

"Hitler dictated his major speeches into the machine," she explained, "and later made corrections and revisions. No one else, not even Goebbels, had any editorial influence on his speeches. Goebbels might supply statistical material, nothing else. Hitler did all his speeches himself, styled them and polished them."

At the recording studio in the Berghof, a room that was kept under lock and key at all times, Hitler always made several recordings before delivering a major address at a public gathering. One recording proclaimed martial law throughout Germany, another described a surprise attack on the Third Reich by a foreign government, while a third appealed to the Germans to stand steadfast in their loyalty to the Führer. Hitler made these recordings so they could be used in case he was assassinated while delivering his speech. The recordings were to be first transmitted to all military units and then broadcast over commercial radio channels at Munich and Berlin. The purpose was, of course, to conceal temporarily the fact that Hitler had died so that his Nazi associates could prepare to meet any internal revolt. Only his closest associates were aware of the recordings.

That he made them is strange, because Hitler was convinced there was no one in the NSDAP hierarchy capable of taking his place as Führer. It may have been an "inside joke" that gave him a great deal of personal pleasure. He told Schröder "there is no one who could take over the leadership."

"Neither Göring nor Himmler?" she asked. This was after Hess had made his infamous flight to England.

Hitler shook his head. "Hess has gone insane. Göring has lost the sympathy of the people. Himmler would be rejected by the party."

"Himmler is often mentioned by the people," Schröder reminded him.

"But he is completely nonartistic!" Hitler replied.

"But is that important during a war?" the secretary asked.

Hitler became very angry.

"It hurt his pride," Schröder explained, "that we who knew him and Himmler would compare him to Himmler."

"Don't worry your head any further about who should be my successor!" he shouted, and walked away.

Hitler's insomnia also affected many of his decisions. He rarely went to bed before three or four o'clock in the morning, after exhausting his guests and associates with hours-long monologues. But even then he couldn't sleep. Often he would get back up after an hour or two of tossing in his bed and telephone an associate. If Goebbels was at the Berghof, Hitler would drag him from his bed and discuss various schemes with the minister of propaganda until daylight. Sometimes Hitler would awaken his chauffeur, Erich Kempka, and they would go for a long drive on the deserted mountain roads. The kitchen at the Berghof had to be on a 24-hour alert in case Hitler wanted coffee or sweets in the early hours of the morning.

Experts from all over the world had been summoned to Germany to try to help Hitler overcome his insomnia, but all had failed. A Swiss psychologist had the most unusual scheme. He fitted a movie screen onto the ceiling of Hitler's bedroom,

Hitler watches as members of his staff dig his car out of the mud. An insomniac, Hitler often awakened his chauffeur to take him on long drives on deserted country roads. *(National Archives)*

and a color movie of a waterfall was projected onto the screen. Hitler was instructed to watch the water going over the falls and he would most certainly fall asleep. Unfortunately, after watching the waterfall for several nights, during which a few million gallons of water passed in front of his eyes, Hitler suddenly had to go to the bathroom every five minutes to relieve his bladder. After he had practically worn a path in the rug between his bed and the bathroom, he threw a shoe through the screen, and that ended that idea. Later he blamed Göring for suggesting the Swiss psychologist as a practical joke.

A Viennese specialist once induced Hitler to stand on his head in the corner of his bedroom until the blood rushed to his brain; then he was to leap into bed. The first time Hitler tried this procedure he became so dizzy that instead of leaping into bed he nearly jumped through his bedroom window. Nor did any of the other methods suggested by doctors from India, China, or Japan cure his insomnia. There was a good reason why the specialists were not successful—the secret R.R.

"R.R.," usually painted in red on a wall or written in ink on an envelope, was the signature of a group called Röhm's Revengers. Ernst Röhm, chief of the SA, was an intimate associate of Hitler during the early days of the NSDAP. He was a professional soldier, an obese man with a bullet-scarred face and a weakness for young boys. Röhm was at Hitler's side during the ill-fated Beer Hall Putsch of 1923, during which he was arrested. After Hitler became chancellor he appointed Röhm to the Reich cabinet, but their relationship began to deteriorate when Röhm insisted that his SA troops be incorporated into the German Army. Hitler, caught between the violent protests of the German generals and the demands of his close friend and unable to devise a compromise suitable to both, had to make a decision. He made it on June 30, 1934, when he purged the SA. Röhm at Hitler's insistence, was given the opportunity to commit an "honorable" suicide, and when he refused he was murdered. So were at least 77 other leading Nazis and 100 others who Hitler believed were in his way to complete dictatorship.

In the aftermath of the blood purge of June 1934, a secret group of Röhm supporters formed a vigilante team to avenge his murder. Hitler first became aware of the group when mail addressed to him began to appear with the letters *R.R.* written on the envelopes. Then the initials were found on a treaty that had been placed in front of him to sign. And one day the scarlet *"R.R"* appeared on the back of Hitler's trench coat! He ordered Himmler to investigate, and within a few days he learned that the letters stood for "Röhm's Revengers." From that moment his insomnia became worse.

Hitler knew that Röhm supporters were hidden throughout his political machine, that it would be very difficult to weed them out. The Gestapo tried, but even this feared organization was effective only periodically. On discovering that a former radio operator named Heinz Formis, a onetime close associate of Röhm's, was sabotaging Hitler's radio speeches, the Gestapo tracked him down. He fled Germany to Czechoslovakia, but Gestapo agents again picked up his trail in Prague. When they caught up to him they made short work of their mission. Formis's mutilated body was found the next morning on a back street.

At the Berghof, for example, Hitler's special bodyguard searched every nook and corner of the house before the Führer retired at night. Yet on several occasions the letters *R.R* appeared in bright red on the wall of his bedroom. It is no wonder that Hitler was afraid to close his eyes and go to sleep. Only a handful of the Röhm's Revengers were ever caught and executed.

Hitler had a strange preoccupation with blood. He revealed this facet of his psyche in many ways. He often stated his belief that "blood is the cement of civilization." During his desperate struggle to assume power, he had often vowed that his opponents would "drown in a bloodbath." The flag carried during the 1923 putsch was dubbed afterward the "Blood Flag," and those who marched with Hitler in Munich that day were his "Blood Order." And he said many times that the worth of a man depended on one factor alone: the purity or impurity of his blood. Dozens of his political speeches highlighted his concern. His speech outlining the Nürnberg racial laws, written by Hitler personally, was titled "The Laws for the Protection of German Blood and German Honor."

Not only in his public life did the word *blood* recur in Hitler's speech. In fact so obsessive was Hitler in a conversation he had one day with Otto Skorzeny, the 6 feet 4 inch adventurer whom Hitler assigned to direct secret agents in foreign and neutral countries and who won worldwide fame for his 1943 rescue of Mussolini from the Italian partisans, that Skorzeny emerged from the meeting with the impression Hitler was a modern-day Dracula.

"I couldn't believe the conversation," Skorzeny exclaimed. "Instead of talking about the war he spent all the time talking about blood. First he spoke about blood soup, which was popular in ancient times. That was strange, but then he told me that the struggle of one country against another really could be defined as one creature drinking the blood of another and that the death of one nourishes the other. I kept quiet although I was beginning to feel sick at my stomach."

Hitler apparently enjoyed having his own blood drawn from his body: He often had his doctors bring leeches to the Berghof for this purpose. Morell even drew Hitler's blood and put it into test tubes so the Führer could gaze at it. No wonder Skorzeny had told friends, "If I was a woman alone with Hitler,

I'd make certain my neck was covered. He is fascinated by blood."

Often at the Berghof he would wait until his guests were eating meat—while he ate his vegetarian fare—and then start talking about a slaughterhouse.

"When the German Army was in the Ukraine," Hitler said at the dinner table one night, "my people built the most modern and largest slaughterhouse in the area. It was completely mechanized, from pig to sausage including the bones, bristles and hide. Everything was so clean and orderly and beautiful girls stood around in high rubber boots . . . up to their thighs in fresh blood."

Those sitting at the table who had heard the story previously kept on eating, but this night Hitler found a victim. Otto Dietrich, the Nazi press chief, put his silverware aside and murmured that he wasn't very hungry.

As unpleasant as was his obsession with blood, the Führer's fascination with decapitation was hardly more cheerful. He constantly spoke of severed heads. Of his opponents he often said, "Heads will roll in the sand." Yet Hitler himself was in fear of decapitation. He told Goebbels on July 24, 1926, "My head will not roll in the sand until I have completed my mission."

One sight he said he would have liked to behold more than any other in England was the decapitations of wives of Henry VIII. He admired Cromwell because he'd had the courage to order a king beheaded and thought Frederick William I, the Prussian king who sired Frederick the Great, was a great man because he too had ordered decapitations.

Yet the same Führer who took delight in such gory visions could be very gentle and kind to children and almost overwhelmingly courteous with his secretaries. He spent many hours with the children of the inner circle who visited the Berghof or lived on the Obersalzberg, taking them for walks, giving them candy, or telling them stories. The two young daughters of Herta Schneider, Eva Braun's close friend, were always welcome on the Obersalzberg or in Munich. In fact Hitler and Eva spent so much time with them that it was rumored they were the girls' parents. Goebbels' six children adored their "Uncle Adolf" until the very end and had been speaking of him just before they were murdered by their mother in the Berlin bunker. One pretty young girl often walked up the mountain from Berchtesgaden to visit Hitler during the early days of his regime, and he always had candy or a gift for her. When Himmler told him that one of the girl's parents was Jewish and he shouldn't be seen with her, Hitler complained that even his small pleasures in life were denied him.

He greeted each of his secretaries politely when he saw her for the first time each day, often kissing her hand or commenting on her dress or hair. He closely watched Gerda Christian and Traudl Junge, the two youngest of the secretaries, and if they changed the color or style of their hair, he would examine the change critically and issue his opinion on it. He didn't like the secretaries or any of the other women around him to change their hairstyles.

"How would I look if I changed the way I comb my hair?" he asked Junge.

She had to admit that it would be a serious matter, since the world was accustomed to his dangling-lock coiffure.

Hitler had a routine procedure that resulted in his world-trademarked forelock. He would bend over forward and comb his hair down before his eyes, then make a part and loosely comb back the left side so that a jerk of his head would cause a lock to drop over his forehead. This happened all the time during his public speeches. His official photographs all showed this artfully disarrayed forelock as well as his caterpillar mustache. No one else in the NSDAP hierarchy was permitted to have a similar mustache.

Another quirk of the Führer's personality was his infatuation with wolves. He insisted *Adolf,* as a compound of *Athal,* which meant *noble,* and *Wolfa,* was an excellent description of himself; and he always used the pseudonym "Herr Wolf" when he didn't want to use his real name. The designations of all his military headquarters were connected in one way or another with the word *wolf: Wolfsschlucht* (Wolf's Canyon), in France; *Werwolf* (Werewolf), in the Ukraine; and *Wolfsschanze* (Wolf's Lair), in East Prussia. He asked his sister, Paula, to change her name to Frau Wolf; and he approved that the huge Volkswagen factory be constructed at Wolfsburg. His senior secretary was named Johanna Wolf; and one of his favorite tunes, which he often whistled was "Who's Afraid of the Big Bad Wolf?"

Was Hitler like a wolf? In many ways he was. He was a loner, cunning, independent, and resourceful. But he certainly wasn't a flesh-eater.

irony

Once, when the industrialist Otto Harz was visiting the Obersalzberg and Hitler likened himself to a wolf, Harz jokingly remarked, "But Führer, a wolf is long-legged, skinny, has a long nose, and eats meat."

Hitler reddened and walked away. A few minutes later Rudolf Schmundt, Hitler's chief armed-forces adjutant, suggested to Harz that he leave. The industrialist was never again invited to the Berghof.

"A wolf has courage," one hunter will say. "A wolf is a coward," says another. And Hitler? Like a wolf, he had courage and he displayed fear. His travels by airplane early in his career were an example of his courage, and that image helped in his political ascent. He embraced air travel when other politicians were afraid even to try a short ride in a plane. Only five years after Charles A. Lindbergh's 1927 flight across the Atlantic, Hitler was covering many more miles by aircraft than by automobile. Partly as a result of this exploitation of the airplane's potential, nowhere and at no time previously had any one person addressed as many people in person as he did. He covered 50,000 kilometers by plane, 25,000 kilometers by car. He spoke to over 10 million German citizens in 200 public meetings. If small party addresses and minor federal election campaigning are also included for that year, Hitler probably addressed more than 15 million people. This high visibility helped him conquer Germany.

Aircraft in 1932 were not the safest of vehicles, and much of the instrumentation and ground safety aids in use later were then unknown. Hans Baur, Hitler's personal pilot throughout the life of the regime, was a skilled flier, but at times he was confronted with situations that were extremely hazardous to both himself and his passengers. Often Hitler's foolhardiness was the problem.

April 8, 1932, was a very bad day at Mannheim. Heavy rain was pelting the airport and black clouds were rolling in very low. Hitler had a speech scheduled at Düsseldorf, and he had no intention of canceling it. He ordered Baur to prepare for takeoff despite the fact that the experienced pilot advised against the flight. Otto Dietrich also tried to discourage Hitler from taking such a chance, but Hitler waved aside the counsel of both his press chief and his pilot.

"It wasn't a flight," Dietrich explained. "It was a whirl. First we passed over a squall, then we tore into the clouds, then an invisible whirlpool sucked us down, then we felt as if we were drawn steeply upward by some lofty crane. Snow and hail pattered upon the wings of our D1720 and against the cabin windows. Sometimes we flew so low that our operator had to pull in the antenna to prevent it from catching in the treetops or in the telephone wires."

Throughout the wild trip Hitler studied his speech, to all appearances oblivious of the weather, the turbulence, and the danger. He made many night flights while on the campaign trail, all with the same disregard for danger. Yet by 1941 Hitler had developed such a pervasive fear about flying or participating in any personally hazardous movement that he saw very little of the country and nothing whatever of what was happening to it. The wolf turned coward.

Hitler's attitudes toward sex, so strange and so unconventional, are covered in a later chapter.

Hans Baur, Hitler's personal pilot, who, in late April 1945, assured Hitler he could fly him out of Germany.
(National Archives)

5

Hitler and the Actress

The crowd in front of the Ufa-Palast-am-Zoo, Berlin's most famous theater, pushed against the ropes holding them back on the night of March 28, 1935, when Adolf Hitler stepped from his Mercedes-Benz. Hitler raised his arm in the familiar Nazi salute, his right arm extended stiffly, and walked inside the movie house. He was followed a few minutes later by Goebbels and several other high-ranking NSDAP officials.

Inside the packed theater Hitler acknowledged the greeting of the enthusiastic crowd; but before he entered his private box with his entourage, he made his way to the front of the movie house, stopped in front of a smiling woman sitting there, and kissed her hand. He then turned and walked to his private box. The crowd cheered louder, an indication that they understood the Führer's high regard for the woman whose hand he had just kissed. The woman, Leni Riefenstahl, stood up and waved to the audience. She was wearing a white fur coat, and when she bowed slightly to acknowledge the acclamation of the crowd, her large breasts protruded from her low-cut dress. She too appreciated the Führer's thoughtfulness in showing his esteem for her in public, but she knew she deserved the gesture.

The audience that night had gathered to attend the premiere of Leni Riefenstahl's latest film, *Triumph of the Will,* the film she had made at the request of Hitler. The moviegoers were well familiar with her appearances as an actress in German films during the previous nine years, knew about her directing success in the movie *The Blue Light,* and were now settled in their seats to enjoy her latest production, a documentary about the NSDAP's sixth party congress, which had been held at

Nürnberg the previous fall. *Triumph of the Will* lasted 110 minutes and was an outstanding success. The audience viewed the action on the screen as good entertainment, and Hitler was delighted that it projected the image of the party and himself that he wanted the world to see. He knew that the time and effort he had expended purposely to make Riefenstahl one of his circle of intimates had been well worthwhile.

Leni Riefenstahl was one of the most popular German actresses of the late 1920s and early 1930s. The daughter of a Berlin merchant, she originally was a dancer. When she injured her knee Riefenstahl changed her artistic course and became an actress, a very good one. And a very brave one: She chose to appear in the then-popular mountain films. She convinced Arnold Fanck, the most famous director of such films, to allow her to appear in one of his productions, *The Holy Mountain.* All such movies before Fanck's were produced inside studios, for reasons of cost and safety. Fanck decided to make his mountain films on location, and this required actors and actresses who could ski as well as emote before a camera. Riefenstahl had not done either previously, but with the determination and talent that marked her entire career she accepted the challenge. She persuaded actor Luis Trenker to take her to Cortina d'Ampezzo, in Italy, to teach her to ski. The second day she broke a bone, and her foot was put into a cast. She was ordered to stay off it for four weeks. Fortunately for Riefenstahl, bad weather and an injury to one of the other actors slated to appear in the film gave her foot time to heal. Undaunted, she learned to ski and completed her part in the film without further problems. *The Holy Mountain* was a financial success, and Riefenstahl was a success with audiences and the reviewers.

She appeared in nine mountain films while Hitler was struggling to power. Despite his obsession with politics, however, Hitler attended many movies during the later 1920s and early 1930s, and Riefenstahl soon became his favorite actress. He was attracted to her for several reasons. She was a very beautiful, sensual woman. Hitler was one of the first politicians to recognize the importance of film as a propaganda medium. He understood that a properly scripted and filmed documentary

Film director Leni
Riefenstahl at the
premiere of *Triumph of
the Will* in Berlin.
(National Archives)

Leni Riefenstahl and
Hitler discussing plans
for *Triumph of the Will*,
the famous film about
the Nazi Rally of 1934.
(National Archives)

could project the desired image of himself and his party to the German people and to the world. Even before he became chancellor, he was searching for someone who could produce such films. Particularly fascinating to Hitler was the motif that dominated Riefenstahl's first work as a director. The film, *The Blue Light,* dramatized beautiful protagonists engaged in a heroic struggle against a mountain that was mystical, Wagnerian. The movie posited the vision of an ideal community victorious over a corrupted one. This worship of beauty, strength, and struggle was, in Hitler's mind, comparable with his vision of the Nazi party.

There was still another reason Hitler wanted Riefenstahl to be the party filmmaker. Hitler valued showmanship, appreciated what could be accomplished by a politician who was also a fine actor. He recognized his own limitations along these lines and was determined to overcome them by learning techniques of drama from Riefenstahl.

Hitler met Riefenstahl for the first time in February 1932. Hanfstängl verifies that they were acquainted that year. He attended a small get-together at the Goebbels' apartment one night during 1932 when both Riefenstahl and Hitler were guests.

"Riefenstahl was a very vital and attractive woman," he said, "and had little difficulty in persuading the Goebbels and Hitler to move on to her studio after dinner. I was taken along and found it full of mirrors and trick interior decorating effects but better than one would expect. Out of the corner of my eye I could see Hitler ostentatiously studying the titles in the bookcase. Riefenstahl, I must say, was giving him the works. Everytime he straightened up or looked around there she was dancing at his elbow, a real summer sale of feminine charm. Finally we made our excuses and left, leaving them alone."

Hitler insisted on keeping his personal life secret from the public, so only his inner circle was aware of his close friendship with Riefenstahl. When he became chancellor on January 30, 1933, their friendship continued, and she spent considerable time with him at his apartment and at the Berghof. It soon became impossible to keep their affair secret, and rumors throughout Germany became numerous. Riefenstahl was called "Hitler's sweetheart," "the sex symbol of the Third Reich," "Filmmaker of the Nazis." She was reputed to have danced nude for the Führer, and she was also linked with Goebbels, Streicher, and Bormann. Perhaps the most persistent rumor was that Riefenstahl was Jewish. According to a report circulated in Germany, Göring voiced his objections to Hitler about Hitler's association with Riefenstahl: She was a Jew, he said. The Führer told him to mind his own business. Göring, furious at the rebuke, went to Riefenstahl and warned her that if she did not agree to leave Berlin and stay away from Hitler, he would have her imprisoned in a concentration camp.

Riefenstahl, according to the report, simply smiled in his face and sweetly answered, "Just try to do any such thing and you will see what will happen to you."

Göring retreated.

When Goebbels heard that Riefenstahl was Jewish, he ordered an investigation into her background. The investigation proved to his and Hitler's satisfaction that the rumor was false.

Shortly after Hitler became chancellor, he very clearly hinted at his basic, practical reason for desiring the friendship of Riefenstahl.

"I want to exploit the film as an instrument of propaganda in such a way that the audience will be clearly aware that on such occasions they are going to see a political film," he said. "It nauseates me when I find political propaganda hiding under the cloak of art. Let it be either art or politics."

Hitler knew exactly what type of film he wanted when he asked Riefenstahl to produce the documentary of the 1934 NSDAP congress at Nürnberg. He wanted a propaganda epic that would convince everyone who saw it that he was in firm control of a united Germany and that he was going to lead his countrymen back to world power. Hitler needed such a film badly, because despite being chancellor he was *not* in firm control of Germany. The German General Staff and the German Army were still undecided whether they wanted to throw their support behind him. Many of the German people were still not willing to follow him. There were no home television screens at the time to flash his face and broadcast his words to all the outlying districts, and many Germans had only seen

Hitler in a newsreel or heard him on the radio. They wondered about this strange-looking new leader.

Hitler wanted to show the doubters that the labor force, the SA, the SS, the German Army, the youth, the women, people from all over the country were behind him. He had tried to have a film of the 1933 NSDAP congress made, but Riefenstahl had ended up with much less footage than he desired. It was then that he discovered he didn't even have complete control of his party associates, let alone all of Germany.

"I met with Hitler at lunchtime," Riefenstahl explained. "The place was crowded so he, Dr. Goebbels, and I went to a small room by ourselves and had coffee. I told him what had happened. Naturally, I was excited, but I noticed that as I talked to Hitler Dr. Goebbels' face was very white."

Riefenstahl explained to Hitler that the staff of the Ministry of Propaganda had not cooperated in her filming of the 1933 party congress.

"I told Hitler that filming the party congress was too difficult for a girl. I told him the men were jealous and that the problems I encountered affected my nerves. Hitler became very angry. He told Goebbels that when he gave an order, Goebbels was supposed to obey it."

Hitler then told Riefenstahl that he wanted her to film the congress at Nürnberg in 1934, but she protested, saying that the same thing would happen again. Hitler assured her there would be no interference, and he was absolutely correct.

Once she was committed to the film, which on Hitler's orders was titled *Triumph of the Will,* Riefenstahl showed why she was considered one of the most skilled filmmakers of the time. She planned every move in detail. She had pits dug before the speaker's platform to aid with camera angles, tracks laid so her cameramen could make traveling shots, elevators constructed so that filming could be done above the million-and-a-half people expected at the congress. She even arranged to have a camera crew on a dirigible drifting overhead. She had learned a lesson during her attempt to film the 1933 NSDAP congress. This time she outfitted many of her film crews in SA uniforms so that Goebbels would be foiled if he did ignore Hitler's order to cooperate. Rudolf Hess supervised the many projects

Riefenstahl planned and made certain her demands were fulfilled.

"I asked my husband for details of his talks with Leni
Riefenstahl," Elisabeth von Stahlenberg said, "but he told me
only bits and pieces. I gather there is antagonism towards her
because she is a woman and very demanding. It shows Hitler
has more common sense than most men, since he is the one
who asked her to make the film."

Her husband, Hugo, was on Goebbels' staff and obviously
wasn't overly fond of Riefenstahl.

Hitler and Riefenstahl together planned every parade, every
speech, every maneuver, every setting. It was not a spontaneous
filming of an event; it was an event planned for filming. Hitler
involved Speer in the production once he had decided that
more drama was needed when units other than the disciplined
ranks of the SA and SS were to appear before the cameras.
Speer suggested having these units march to the reviewing
stand in the darkness carrying torches while Hitler waited. By
Speer's plan, behind the fence surrounding Zeppelin Field
there would be thousands of flags, belonging to local groups, to
be displayed in groups of ten and spotlighted by 130 antiaircraft searchlights. At a precise moment the beams of the
searchlights would penetrate the darkness to a height of 26,000
feet, giving those assembled the feeling that they were in a vast
room, a "cathedral of light"—dominated by a godlike Hitler.
And so it was done.

"I imagine this 'cathedral of light' was the first luminescent
architecture of this type," Speer said, "but, after its fashion, the
only one that has survived the passage of time. For me, it
remains my most beautiful architectural concept."

Speer's use of flags fitted in very well with Riefenstahl's
desire to transfigure the events of the congress with the use of
motifs. She filmed the swastika from all angles; used shots of
ancient buildings and statues to contrast with the "new order"
in Germany; employed fire to support Hitler's declaration that
he had come to kindle a new movement that would liberate the
German people; and focused on various groups of people—
students, workers, soldiers, farmers—paying homage to the
Führer in confirmation that he was supported by the masses.

Hitler, after viewing the edited film, recognized its value immediately. He ordered the production shown all over Germany, knowing that it would strengthen his own position as well as enhance the status of the NSDAP. *Triumph of the Will* was so successful that the Wehrmacht was jealous. Field Marshal Werner von Blomberg, Minister of Defense and supreme commander of the armed forces, realized that the film glorified the Führer and the party but did little for the German armed forces. He was furious. He went to Hitler and demanded that additional footage of the military forces be shot and included in the film so the armed forces would get as much exposure on the screen as the SA and SS. This presented a problem for Hitler. He wanted and needed the support of the German armed forces; yet he didn't want to antagonize Riefenstahl, because he had further need of her talents. He tried to effect a compromise. He suggested to her that Blomberg and others of the German General Staff be assembled and filmed as a background for the title of the documentary.

"I told him no, I can't do it," Riefenstahl recalled.

That wasn't the right answer, she immediately discovered. It made him angry.

"He looked at me and said that I had forgotten to whom I was speaking. That was the first time I was really scared of him."

Riefenstahl changed her mind in a hurry and made a short film, *Tag der Freiheit (Day of Freedom)*, featuring the Wehrmacht. It too was an excellent production, and Blomberg was very pleased. Many historians credit this film for swinging the German armed forces to Hitler's side at the crucial moment in the early years of the regime. The only known extant copy of *Tag der Freiheit* was seized by the Soviet Union after the war.

Triumph of the Will won Riefenstahl the German National Film Prize of 1935, and, in June 1936, the Italian Film Prize. Even Goebbels, who was jealous of Riefenstahl's intimate association with Hitler, understood the great value to the NSDAP of *Triumph of the Will*. He also knew that Hitler was infatuated with the beautiful director and did not want to antagonize the Führer as he had done in opposing Riefenstahl's filming of the 1933 congress. Consequently the Ministry of Propaganda praised her skill and talents publicly as much as possible, and Goebbels made certain she was invited to all important gatherings of film notables sponsored by his department.

Riefenstahl basked in the praise of both the Führer and Goebbels, who was the most important man in the country's film world.

"Leni Riefenstahl loved the Führer deeply," says Anni Winter, Hitler's housekeeper in Munich. "She told me, 'You know the Führer is my great love. I would even stay with him as his friend.' I think he liked her, too."

But Hitler was playing the game with Riefenstahl that he played with so many persons during his career. He "liked" them until he had obtained all the help he could from their particular talents, then abruptly dismissed them from his plans. And Hitler had still more plans for Riefenstahl. The treatment of the Jews in Germany by his regime was being criticized around the world, and although he didn't care personally about the criticism, he realized that in 1936 he was not yet prepared militarily to antagonize his enemies. He expressed his views to American journalist H. V. Kaltenborn in an interview at the Berghof.

"You have a Monroe Doctrine for America," Hitler asserted. "We believe in a Monroe Doctrine for Germany. You exclude any would-be immigrants you do not care to admit. You regulate their number. You demand that they come up to a certain physical standard. You insist that they bring in a certain amount of money. You examine them as to their political opinions. We demand the same right. We have no concern with the Jews of other lands. But we are concerned about any anti-German elements in our own country. And we demand the right to deal with them as we see fit. Jews have been the proponents of subversive anti-German movements and as such must be dealt with."

Hitler was determined, however, that the Olympic Games of 1936, which were to be held in Berlin, would be used to create quite another impression of Germany. He asked Riefenstahl to film the Olympics, promising her the financial backing and all the equipment and personnel she needed. And he left no doubt in her mind that he wanted her to portray him and the party as she had shown them in *Triumph of the Will.* It is a tribute to

Riefenstahl's talent that at a time when the opposite was true, she was able to project the image of a strong, freedom- and peace-loving Germany united behind an all-powerful Hitler.

While Riefenstahl was making her plans for the filming of the 1936 Olympic Games, Hitler's Jewish policy weighed against her determination to show a liberated and happy Germany. Three years earlier Hitler had ordered that all Jews were forbidden to belong to gymnastic organizations. Gradually the restrictions spread. Swimming pools were off-limits to the Jews; all private and public practice fields were closed to them; and even the all-Jewish war veterans' athletic organizations were ordered disbanded. The ski resort at Garmisch-Partenkirchen had a sign bluntly stating: "Jews, your entry is forbidden."

Bruno Malitz, sports director of the SA, stated the NSDAP views on Jews in sports in a treatise that Goebbels declared should be read by every German.

"Jewish sports leaders, like the Jewish plague, pacifists, and other reconcilers," he said, in part, "have absolutely no place in German sport. They are worse than rampaging hordes of Kalmucks, worse than a burning conflagration, famine, floods, droughts, locusts and poison gas—worse than all these horrors."

Compounding the effect of such statements and lending further impetus to the increase in discrimination against the Jews was Hitler's decision to oust Dr. Theodor Lewald, the president of the German Olympic Committee, because his paternal grandmother had been a Jew. Following this action Captain Wolfgang Fürstner, director of the German army's athletic program and the man who had designed the Olympic Village for the 1936 Olympic Games, was suddenly replaced and dismissed by the army. Hitler had learned Fürstner had Jewish blood. A few days later Fürstner committed suicide.

Enough was enough. Count Henri Baillet-Latour, president of the International Olympic Committee, met with Hitler and told him that either the signs would be removed and Jewish athletes treated as other Olympic participants were treated or he would cancel both the winter and summer Olympic Games.

Hitler shook his head. "I cannot alter a question of the highest importance within Germany for a small point of Olympic protocol."

When Baillet-Latour was adamant, Hitler finally relented.

The signs were taken down ... until after the Olympic Games.

Despite these obstacles Riefenstahl managed to produce a film that, by consensus, remains unequaled among sports documentaries. *Olympia* was divided into two parts. Willy Zielke, a famed German cameraman, who later feigned mental illness to avoid working for Hitler, was hired by Riefenstahl to film the famous prologue. Nudes were featured in the prologue, and in one of these shots a woman on a bench, filmed full-figure from the rear, is Riefenstahl herself.

"When the film was first screened for Hitler he had the prologue rerun several times," says Hugo Müller, a former member of the Reich Film Chamber. "He was delighted with the nudes. Once I heard him say 'Leni' when a nude was flashed on the screen. If he actually recognized her from the rear he certainly must have been a very good friend of hers."

The Munich Olympics opening ceremonies that followed the prologue were representative of the Nazi propaganda the viewer could expect during the remainder of the production. The director had the long line of official cars heralding the arrival of Hitler to the Olympic stadium filmed both from the ground and from the dirigible *Hindenburg,* drifting overhead. Hitler, wearing his SA uniform and polished leather boots, was shown leading the NSDAP officials and guests to the place of honor in the stadium. He was followed by the king of Bulgaria, several crown princes of European countries, and the sons of Mussolini. Also in view for Riefenstahl's cameras were Göring, in his Luftwaffe uniform; Field Marshal August von Mackensen, in his army uniform; and Goebbels in a white suit. It was a well-staged piece of propaganda that pictured Hitler as a leader revered by royalty and the common people alike.

This subtle but effective propaganda was an integral part of *Olympiad.* The individuals upon whom Riefenstahl trained her cameras ranged from Germans to Americans to Japanese, without favor by race or nationality. The shots of the mass gymnastics and team sports, often accompanied by well-selected music; the marathon and the agony of the runners; the intently appreciative portrayal of American black Jesse Owens; and the marvelous diving scenes, one of the most famous sports sequences ever filmed, all established her as one of the outstanding film directors in the world. And her clever editing of the footage—during which she arranged the events in the sequence she desired and inserted propaganda shots that praised the NSDAP and Hitler—deserves equal professional acclaim. Her intuitiveness and skill kept the film from being obvious propaganda and permitted her to control the audience's emotions while she entertained them. Hitler had chosen well when he selected Riefenstahl to produce the party's films.

Erwin Goelz, a German film critic, expressed the value of *Olympia* very well in his review: "It had to succeed here because Germany created for the Olympic Games of 1936 a wonderfully perceived, symbolic framework that from the very beginning elevated the games above a mere sport report. Only in the ideological structure of National Socialism could this great documentary film have come into being as an artistic achievement."

Copies of *Olympia* were made in 16 languages, and the film, on Hitler's orders, was distributed around the globe. In 1938 Riefenstahl traveled to the United States hoping, through her fame as a film star and as a director (*Olympia* which was then being shown in the country), to improve relations between the two nations. It was a disastrous visit for Riefenstahl. When she arrived in New York aboard the *Europa,* on November 4, 1938, the first question asked her was about her personal relationship with Hitler. She denied any serious romantic interest existed between them, but her remark, "He is not difficult to see," gave her away. The reporters were well aware that except for members of his intimate circle, Hitler was all but inaccessible. Even his ministers and generals complained they could seldom get past Martin Bormann to confer with the Führer. From that opening interview it was all downhill for her. The American Jewish Congress, the Jewish Labor Committee, the Hollywood Anti-Nazi League, national syndicated columnists, and others spoke out against "Hitler's Nazi Filmmaker." Frustrated and defeated, in January 1939 she took the boat back to Germany and Hitler.

A "source close to the government"—probably Hitler himself—issued a statement when she reached Berlin:

Hitler meets with Olympic officials. He used the games of 1936 and Riefenstahl's film *Olympiad* to give the world a false impression of the Third
Reich. *(National Archives)*

These stills. by
cameraman Willy
Zielke. were included in
the prologue he filmed
for *Olympiad*, Leni
Riefenstahl's motion
picture of the 1936
Olympics. held in
Berlin. Hitler delighted
in the nude photographs
and obtained a set for
his private viewing.
(Willy Zielke)

(Willy Zielke)

(Willy Zielke)

(Willy Zielke)

Incessant agitation against the Third Reich in the United States, which among other things has hampered the showing of the Olympics film otherwise received throughout the world with the greatest applause, and which forced Hollywood film artists to sign an inflammatory declaration against Germany, has brought an understandable reaction in the film industry in Germany. It is pointed out that the American film industry stands under predominating Jewish influence and it may be stated that the number of American films in Germany has declined.

This failure of Riefenstahl to endear herself to the American people also marked the beginning of Hitler's own apparent disenchantment with her. She had served her purpose and served it well. With *Triumph of the Will* she had helped establish Hitler as a powerful dictator. Her *Olympia* had helped to lull the world into prolonged inaction against a Führer who had threatened doom to all Jews and who was building a powerful military machine with the full intention of going to

(Willy Zielke)

war against his neighbors. Now, in 1939, Hitler was ready. He was in complete control of Germany, and his military might was feared throughout the world. He had no further need of Riefenstahl. It was time for propaganda to give way to action. The German invasion of Poland on September 1, 1939, and the declaration of war on Germany by Great Britain and France two days later pushed Riefenstahl to the background. She never again played an important part in Hitler's life.

After giving up the attempt to make such films, as *Tiefland* and *Penthesilea* on her own, without the support of Hitler or the NSDAP, Riefenstahl returned to her home in Kitzbühel, Austria.

One day in 1945 there was a knock at the door of her mountain home. When she opened the door she was greeted by a Boston Irishman of the Forty-second ("Rainbow") Division of the U. S. Army. He told her that the army needed her home and she would have to leave. Later, when her identity had been established and her close association with Hitler became known, she was detained by the U. S. Seventh Army interrogators. Their report, plus investigations after the war by the German de-Nazification court and the French courts, led to a decision classifying her as a "sympathizer" of the Nazi regime. The stigma of this classification prevented her from making another successful film.

Hitler had used her and abandoned her.

Leni Riefenstahl at work on *Olympiad.* *(Bundesarchiv)*

6

Operation Seduction

"If Hitler walked through the door today, I would be just as glad and happy to see and have him here as ever."

Those words were spoken in 1975 by Winifred Wagner, daughter-in-law of the famous musical genius Richard Wagner and a close friend of Hitler for nearly a quarter of a century. She insisted that Hitler was not cruel, malevolent or megalomaniacal: To her he was the sort of man who could be tempted into cheating on his vegetarian diet with liver dumplings, a man with "immensely appealing eyes," a Führer who was "really touching with children."

Wagner even insisted that the Third Reich policy against the Jews was not Hitler's idea. "The main instigator was Streicher. Adolf should not have let himself be influenced so much and he shouldn't have given in to these radical demands."

That such statements could be made when irrefutable documentation of Hitler's actions during the Third Reich proves them false is a tribute to the power he had not only over men, but also over women. This power has been ignored or downgraded by many historians and biographers, who have overlooked the important role women played in his life. Wealthy and influential women helped finance the NSDAP in its early days. Women aided him in spreading the "word" first revealed in *Mein Kampf.* He was often seen in public with beautiful actresses in an effort to improve his image with the German public. He used women to convey political and military plans, some true, some false, to foreign officials when he thought it was to the advantage of his Reich. He enjoyed the company of women when he was relaxing and to fulfill his sexual demands. Women, individually and generally, were important instruments in the establishment, successes and ultimate failure of the Third Reich. Hitler knew how they could be used and was much more adept at appealing to women than Franklin Roosevelt, Joseph Stalin, or Winston Churchill, the other world leaders of the time.

Many writers and historians have suggested that all women in Hitler's life were substitutes for his mother. It is an interesting theory but, once his affairs are analyzed carefully, it is just not plausible. Except for one or two of his feminine companions, Hitler had a practical purpose in mind each time he became intimately associated with a woman. Going to bed with them was not his primary aim. Even when he coupled with older women, as he did early in his political career, the cause wasn't mother-fixation. It was financial need.

As noted earlier, one of the "older women" was Helene Bechstein, wife of the famous piano manufacturer Carl Bechstein. She was a tall woman, heavy, a matronly type at least 20 years older than Hitler. His friend Dietrich Eckart had introduced him to the wealthy Bechsteins during a stay on the Obersalzberg in 1922. It was a lucky move for Hitler, because Frau Bechstein took a great interest in the radical politician who was struggling to establish a political party and a name for himself. She gave him large sums of money, and when cash wasn't available she often gave him valuable jewels from her collection, paintings, or tapestries. In 1923, when Hitler needed money to keep his NSDAP active, he obtained a loan of 60,000 Swiss francs from Richard Frank, of the Berlin firm Korn-Frank. According to the agreement he used the following as collateral:

As security for the loan Herr Adolf Hitler will make over to Herr Richard Frank the undermentioned property presently in the keeping of Heinrich Eckert, Bankers, Munich ... A platinum pendant set with an emerald and diamonds ... A platinum ring set with a ruby and diamonds ... A platinum ring set with a sapphire and diamonds ... A diamond ring, a 14-carat gold ring with diamonds set in silver ... A piece of *grospoint de Venise,* hand-stitched, six and a half meters long and eleven and a half centimeters wide ... Spanish red silk piano runner with gold embroidery.

When Hitler was in Landsberg prison Frau Bechstein posed as his mother so that she could visit him, and she and Winifred Wagner provided the paper on which he began writing *Mein Kampf.* After his discharge from prison she helped furnish his bachelor home on the Obersalzberg, the home that eventually became the famous Berghof. She performed perhaps her greatest service to Hitler when she introduced him to politicians and industrialists who could help his career. Whether there was ever more than a platonic friendship between the two is not known for certain, but many persons believe Frau Bechstein was in love with Hitler despite their difference in age.

"When I worked for Frau Bechstein on the Obersalzberg," recalled Ilse Meirer, Bechstein's housekeeper, "Hitler often stayed at the Bechstein home all night when Herr Bechstein was in Berlin. They slept in the same room, but the door was always closed. I don't know if they made love or not."

Other "older women" with whom he associated at this time were Carola Hoffmann, the widow of a schoolmaster; Gertrud von Seydlitz, the widow of a Baltic German officer; and Elsa Bruckmann, the wife of a Munich publisher. Frau Bruckmann also introduced Hitler to selected industrialists and intellectuals whom she felt could help him and the NSDAP. Witty and wealthy, Romanian princess Bruckmann was able to teach the middle-class Hitler some upper-class manners that were of great value to him in later years. But with these women it was "use them and leave them," a policy he followed throughout his career.

His association with the older women involved a minimum of sex. But Hitler was certainly not immune from sexual desires. Based on information provided by some who should know, Hitler's sex life ran the gamut from weird to normal, depending upon who was involved and what the situation was. Today symbols such as leather coats, shiny boots, swastika jewelry, chains, whips, and motorcycles signify sexual adventurism to many. In designing these symbols for his SS Hitler was expressing his own private desires—desires that he fulfilled or attempted to fulfill in secret. Publicly he projected the image of a sexual conservative, as was evidenced by the great secrecy surrounding the fact he kept a mistress.

Privately, however, he was a man whose sex habits were

anything but conservative. He often invited striptease artists to the Brown House Nazi party headquarters in Munich, and their nude dancing delighted him. He often used opera glasses to get a closer look at the girls. Incidents at the Berghof were reportedly still more unusual. Pauline Kohler tells about going into the basement of the Hitler home on the Obersalzberg and seeing a room fitted for a gynmasium, a second room used as an extra office, and a third room that completely puzzled her. Its door, of iron bars, was like a prison cell door. Erik Keitner, the SS officer showing her around, saw her puzzled look and explained.

"Sometimes girls are brought here for questioning if we have any reason to suspect their racial purity. After a few hours with us they will usually talk very freely."

She learned later that the girls were stripped and made to stretch out on the vaulting-horse in the gymnasium, where the SS, and possibly Hitler, "inspected" and sometimes assaulted them.

Hitler was also fascinated by the feminine buttocks, and the entire anal-genital region was a sexual focus for him.

Otto Strasser, Hitler's intimate associate during his early political struggles, explained the nature of Hitler's perversion when he related the story Geli Raubal, Hitler's niece, told him.

"Hitler made her undress. He would lie down on the floor. Then she would have to squat over his face where he could examine her at close range and this made him very excited. When the excitement reached its peak, he demanded that she urinate on him and that gave him sexual pleasure. Geli said the whole performance was extremely disgusting to her and it gave her no gratification."

If one accepts this account, it is no wonder that many of the women with whom Hitler had intimate relations tried to avoid him after the first experience. Renate Müller, the actress, was one. Renate was a star of Ufa, Germany's leading moving picture company, when she met Hitler for the first time in autumn 1932. She was on location near the Danish coast, and Hitler visited the filming site. He watched the shooting all day and that evening stopped at the house where Renate was staying.

"It was really funny," she said. "He sat there, not moving at all, looking at me all the time and then he would take my hand in his and would look some more. He talked all the time—just nonsense."

But that wasn't all. Later she was invited to a party at the Chancellery. During the entire evening Hitler ignored her. Only when everybody was leaving did he take hold of her arm and detain her.

"I should like to show you the other rooms," he said.

Hitler actually did show her through the remainder of the Chancellery, boastfully telling her about the various changes he had made in it. Then he wanted her to admire his tails. "You know, I never had evening clothes before I came to power." He even showed her his silk stockings. And then suddenly, for no apparent reason, he sprang to his feet and raised his arm in the Nazi salute. "I can keep it up for hours at a time. I always laugh because Göring has so much trouble doing it."

"I wanted to laugh," Renate told a friend later. "He thought he was making an impression on me. He probably thought he wanted to show me how strong he was."

Her inclination to laugh at Hitler soon turned into an obsession to escape from him. In 1936 Renate confessed her fear and its basis to Adolf Ziessler, a film director she knew well. Instead of making love to her normally, to which she would not have objected, Hitler lay on the floor, after they were both undressed, and insisted she kick him. She refused; but he ordered her, and finally, afraid not to do as he wanted, she kicked him repeatedly. The more she kicked, the more excited Hitler became and the more disgusted Renate grew. Once he had induced her to satisfy his masochistic demands, he would not leave her alone. He kept inviting her to the Chancellery during succeeding months, and she did not dare refuse. His exotic sexual behavior in these encounters became more and more intense. Even the diamond bracelet, the flowers, the riding horse, and other expensive gifts could not make her forget the things he asked her to do and the things he did to her.

Eventually, after gratifying Hitler one long night, she asked his permission to go to London for a vacation. He granted her wish but asked Himmler to have the Gestapo keep a watch on her while she was in England. Himmler discovered that Müller spent most of her days with Frank Deutsch, a former lover, who was Jewish. When she returned to Germany, she was blacklisted from the Nazi-controlled movie industry. There were rumors that she was going to be put on trial for "race defilement," since it was a crime for a German woman to have an affair with a Jew. It was then she started to take morphine. Finally, because of the ensuing drug addiction and her fear of Hitler, Renate was taken to a sanatorium. Once, at the instigation of friends, she left the institution to try to see Hitler and clear herself. But Hitler refused to see her.

A few days later it was reported publicly that Renate Müller had died of a heart attack. The truth was that she had jumped to her death from a window of the sanitarium: She had just seen a car stop at the entrance and four SS officers get out. Renate Müller was 30 years old when she made her final escape from Hitler.

Another young woman who became involved with Hitler and afterward tried to kill herself was Mimi Reiter. He met her in Berchtesgaden, and for a while he spent a great deal of time with her. At first it was all innocent fun to the 16-year-old Mimi—walks in the woods, rides in Hitler's Mercedes, long talks. But gradually he became more and more possessive, more and more demanding. His strange behavior alarmed her despite the fact she was adventurous and willing—to a point. When that point was passed, Mimi Reiter tried to kill herself by hanging. She recovered, however, and later married the owner of a hotel. Yet it is a tribute to Hitler's attraction, as strange as it was, that when, several years later, Hitler sent Rudolf Hess to ask Mimi to visit him in Munich, she left her husband and spent the night with Hitler at his apartment in the Prinzregentenplatz. She later said, "I let him do whatever he wanted with me."

She didn't go into detail.

The acknowledged love of Hitler's life, in addition to his mistress whom he married during the last hours of his life, was Geli Raubal, his niece. Her name was Angela, after her mother, who was Hitler's half-sister. The nickname Geli, however, was used by everyone who knew her. The mother and Geli, lived with Hitler in his Munich apartment in Prinzregentenplatz in

1929. Geli was a very good-looking young girl, blonde, blue-eyed, the "Gretchen" type. Photographer Heinrich Hoffmann thought she was an enchantress.

"In her artless way," Hoffmann said, "and without the slightest suspicion of coquetry she succeeded by her mere presence in putting everybody in the best of spirits. Geli was worshipped by her uncle. To him she was the personification of perfect womanhood—beautiful, fresh and unspoiled, gay, intelligent, as clean and straight as God had made her. He watched and gloated over her like some servant with a rare and lovely bloom and to cherish and protect her was his one and only concern."

That was a misleading statement. Hitler protected her all right . . . from other men. He wanted her all for himself, and it wasn't just a typical uncle-niece relationship. When he discovered that Emil Maurice, his dark complexioned, well-built chauffeur, was fond of Geli and had been alone with her several times, Hitler was furious. He ousted Maurice from his position, and it wasn't until several years later that he relented and once again became friendly with him. This incident gave warning to Hitler's surprised associates that Geli was strictly a "hands-off" woman reserved for her uncle. Initially Geli was delighted by the attention her uncle paid her and enjoyed the comfortable life he provided at his apartment in Munich and at the Berghof, in the mountains of Bavaria. Hitler never insisted that she do any work, and he granted her every wish. When she decided that she wanted to be an opera singer, Hitler hired one of the best voice teachers in Munich, despite his knowledge that she didn't have a good voice. When she wanted to go swimming at the Königsee, Hitler went with her, although he dreaded being seen in a bathing suit. Picnics, long walks, new clothes, movies . . . whatever Geli wanted, Hitler provided. Except for one thing. Freedom.

He watched her closely when he was with her in Munich or at the Berghof, and when he was away he had others spy on her. He wanted her to stay away from other men, wanted her kept available for himself. What went on behind the closed doors? There is Strasser's description, as he said Geli had confided it to him. Hitler had her pose in the nude for pornographic sketches. When the sketches were later stolen from Hitler, he paid a small fortune from the NSDAP treasury to ransom them in order to save his political career from destruction. Geli's expressed distaste for the whip he quite often carried in public suggests to some that it was used during their sexual sessions. At any rate she paid dearly for the luxurious living Hitler provided her. Finally she could stand his absolute possessiveness no longer. She felt that she had to get away from Munich for a while. But when she told Hitler she wàs going to Vienna for a few weeks to take advanced voice lessons, he went into one of his tantrums. This was on September 18, 1931, as he was preparing to leave on a political campaign tour.

Just exactly what happened that day has remained a mystery. Officially Geli committed suicide, and at first most of Hitler's associates believed this word to be the truth. However as more facts were revealed over the years, other theories were advanced. Some thought Hitler murdered her. Some were certain that she was pregnant, that Hitler felt threatened, saw his political ambitions being thwarted over the looming scandal, and pulled the trigger on the Walther 6.35 pistol himself. (The gun was the Führer's personal pistol.) Others said that Geli was assassinated by associates of Hitler who feared that the incest-tainted romance might ruin his career.

According to Geli's mother, Angela, when her daughter mentioned over dinner that she was going to Vienna, Hitler leaped to his feet and gripped her shoulder so tightly she cried out in pain. Suddenly he rushed from the room and returned carrying his whip. That was too much for Angela. She stepped between her half-brother and her daughter and took the whip away. Without a word Hitler sat back down at the table and started to eat again. After the evening meal was over Angela took the train to Berchtesgaden—which was a mistake. The cook at the Munich apartment later told her that shortly after Angela had left to catch the train Hitler began again to bluster and shout. He disappeared from the kitchen, and a few minutes later the cook heard Geli scream. The cook said she hurried into the living room. It was empty, but she heard Geli moaning in her bedroom. When the cook tried to get into the room, she found the door locked. She went to hunt for the key.

Meanwhile Hitler took his bags and went outside to a waiting car to leave on his campaign tour. The cook saw him glance one final time toward Geli's room and then motion for the driver to move on. Everything was quiet until half past eleven that evening, when a shot was heard. The cook and the house-keeper, Anni Winter, both rushed to Geli's room and opened the door with Frau Winter's key. They found Geli dying beside the big leather armchair, her left hand clutching her chest. Frau Winter, loyal to Hitler, didn't call police. She called Rudolf Hess, who hurried to the scene and then notified Hitler, who was at the Deutscher Hof Hotel in Nürnberg. Hitler returned to Munich, and the cover-up began. Franz Schwarz, treasurer of the NSDAP, and Hess contacted Dr. Franz Gürtner, the Ba-varian Minister of Justice and a Nazi sympathizer, and through Gürtner's influence the legal investigation usually conducted in such deaths was waived. Gürtner officially termed the death a suicide. Within two years Gürtner was named Reich minister of justice in Hitler's first cabinet.

Geli's body was sent back to Vienna in a sealed lead coffin as soon as Gürtner had signed the papers declaring her death a suicide. As a Catholic her mother wanted her buried in the Central Cemetery in Vienna. The nature of her death would normally have prevented this interment; however church offi-cials decided that she "was in a state of mental aberration and confusion and therefore not wholly responsible for her act." Her funeral at the Central Cemetery was attended by Ernst Röhm, who would soon die on Hitler's orders, and Heinrich Himmler. Hitler was not permitted into Austria at the time.

And so another of Hitler's women died.

There were others. Count Galeazzo Ciano, Italy's foreign minister, was convinced that Hitler had intimate relations with Sigrid von Lappus, a beautiful woman 20 years younger than he. Perhaps it was Ciano's "loose tongue" about Hitler's alleged love affair that prompted the Führer to insist that Mussolini execute Ciano in the latter years of the war despite the fact that Ciano was married to Mussolini's daughter Edda.

In the name of Fascism and Nazism, lovely, slender Italian Countess Maria Magistrati made many conquests, including the Führer of Germany. She died from over-dieting.

Paul Joseph Goebbels and his wife. Magda, entertain Count Galeazzo Ciano. Mussolini's son-in-law. Ciano was convinced that Hitler had intimate relations with a beautiful woman 20 years his junior. Ciano's "loose tongue" on the subject may have prompted Hitler to insist later that Mussolini execute him. *(National Archives)*

Swedish-born Princess Ann Mari von Bismarck, wife of Prince Otto, who had an unlimited allowance from the German Embassy in Rome, did her part for Germany and Hitler, reportedly both in and out of bed.

Hitler also had an affair with a young married woman, Suzi Liptauer. After a rendezvous with Hitler in a Munich hotel one night, she hanged herself.

Inge Ley, wife of the leader of the German Labor Front, was infatuated with the Führer, and when she discovered that she couldn't have him despite her willingness to submit to any erotic demands he might make, she committed suicide.

There was an aura of desperation and death surrounding Hitler's romances. After she met Hitler for the first time, Emmy Sonnemann, the actress who later became Göring's second wife, said "I'm afraid of him. There is something in his eyes."

She met him in the summer of 1930 during the film festival at Lauchstädt. She also met Göring at that time, and she soon fell in love with him. At that time Göring was slim, dashing, and very handsome. With Hitler's encouragement Göring married Emmy, on April 11, 1935, in the first state wedding of the Third

Reich. She had no reason to fear Hitler any longer. In fact she thought she was in an enviable position.

"Well, after all, I shall be the first lady of the Third Reich. Every dynasty has its crown jewels. Everyone says Hitler won't marry. It will be up to me to bear the Third Reich an heir," she was said to have explained to her friends.

She didn't realize at the time she made the statement that she wasn't only impressing her friends but also accurately predicting the future. When her husband's addiction to drugs became so serious that he had to go to a sanatorium for a cure, she found out. It was in the spring of 1939. Hitler asked her to go to the Berghof with him, and she agreed. With Hitler and Emmy now both dead, there is probably no one certain about what happened. Probably Emmy went through the same traumatic sexual experiences with Hitler that many other women experienced. She didn't commit suicide, but on December 1, 1939, she arrived in Lausanne, Switzerland, where she checked into the Hotel Mont Blanc. A day or so later, according to reports, she checked into a hospital, where she bore a child. Contrary to Swiss law, the child was not registered.

The whole trip was a mystery. Why did Göring send his wife to Switzerland? Why is it this second child of Emmy's was never mentioned publicly? Why did Emmy seclude herself in the Göring house on the Obersalzberg when she returned from Switzerland. The child, of course, would be 40 years old now. One can only speculate about where he might be now, whether he knows of his suspected paternity, and what he plans to do about it.

Magda Goebbels saw Hitler for the first time on a spring evening in 1927, when he and Goebbels came to visit her and her first husband, Günther Quandt, an industrialist. She was beautiful, a golden blonde with a slender figure and dark blue eyes. Hitler was amazed when he met her, not having known beforehand that Magda was 20 years younger than her husband. At that time Hitler was seeking funds and support from Quandt, but later, after Magda left her husband, he switched his interest to her. Immediately after her divorce they were seen together quite often. When Hitler was in Berlin, Magda waited patiently at the bar in the Hotel Kaiserhof until Hitler left his

Hitler. whip in hand. greets his half-sister. Angela Hitler Raubal. right. and Magda Goebbels and her son. Harald. by a previous marriage. Hitler's sexual perversions with Angela's daughter. Geli. probably contributed to the young girl's suicide. *(National Archives)*

suite, and then she joined him. She often went to Berchtesgaden for the weekend. To avoid rumors Hitler made her private secretary to Goebbels, knowing that with Magda in this guise her visits to the Berghof would appear to be legitimate business. Later, he insisted that she marry Goebbels, which she did in December 1931. Quite appropriately, Hitler was best man.

After the wedding Hitler often found an excuse to visit the Goebbels' home. The food, the music, the conversation, the movies . . . all were used as a reason to get near Magda. Goebbels obviously was aware of the affair and started romancing actresses in an effort to forget that he was married to a woman who was in love with the Führer. Throughout the years of the Third Reich Magda Goebbels was loyal to Hitler. No more evidence is needed of her devotion to him than that when the end came in Berlin, she killed not only herself in Hitler's bunker but also her six children.

And what of Winifred Wagner, who in 1975 said she would be "glad and happy" to see Hitler again? Born in England eight years after Hitler was born in Austria, at 18 years of age she

Hitler spent some of his free time at Haus Wahnfried. the home of Winifred Wagner. at Bayreuth. *(National Archives)*

married Siegfried Wagner. the only son of composer Richard Wagner. Hitler was a fanatic devotee of Wagnerian opera and found in it some of his inspiration for Nazism. It was only natural, then, that he would attend the annual Bayreuth Festival. It was there in 1923 that he first met Winifred, and their mutual love for her father-in-law's music soon developed into a personal love affair. Winifred was an enthusiastic supporter of the NSDAP, but her husband was not. Consequently when Hitler visited Haus Wahnfried, the Wagner home, Siegfried usually managed to be away. That made the course of romance convenient for Winifred and Hitler. After her husband died in 1930, Hitler's visits became more frequent. In addressing the Führer Winifred used *du,* the intimate pronoun that only a very few of Hitler's associates presumed to use in speaking with him. Her children called him "uncle." The Nazi inner circle favored this affair, knowing the Wagner name gave Hitler status with the public, and many of his associates pressed him to marry her.

For a number of years the reason they didn't marry wasn't known, but gradually the truth leaked out. Winifred had visited

Dr. Kurt Krüger in Munich, supposedly to check on the physical condition of her daughter, who had earlier had an examination. During her conversation with Krüger it became evident to him that she had reservations about the way Hitler treated her when they were alone. She admitted she was shocked by his unorthodox approach to lovemaking. This was verified after the war by her daughter Friedelind, who told Allied intelligence agents that her mother had misgivings about Hitler once he had asked her to whip him. Winifred came to the conclusion that she could not control him. At times he frightened her.

Dr. Karl Brandt, another of Hitler's personal physicians, was puzzled by the Wagner-Hitler affair. "Whether relations between Frau Wagner and Hitler were consciously fostered by her in order to attain the fulfillment of her objective [revival of the Bayreuth Festival] is hard to say," Brandt said, "If that were the case, it would be indicative of Frau Wagner's cleverness rather than the nobility of her character. She did try to influence the political views of the Führer, but as she seldom saw Hitler in later years her influence was slight."

Winifred Wagner, left, was the widow of Siegfried Wagner, son of the composer Richard Wagner. Although Hitler and Winifred were very close and many of his associates encouraged him to marry her, she confided to her physician and her daughter her fear of Hitler's unorthodox approach to lovemaking, especially after he asked her to whip him. *(National Archives)*

Winifred Wagner was one of the women in Hitler's life to survive her affair with him. Two others who fought the Hitler "love battle" but who, like some others, failed to survive were Unity Mitford, the English beauty he betrayed, and Eva Braun, the mistress he married.

7

The Eagle's Nest

Both Eva Braun and Unity Mitford, who figured prominently in Hitler's life, were enthralled by the Eagle's Nest. In fact it seemed the entire world was fascinated by this unique retreat perched on the peak of the Kehlstein, where, supposedly, Hitler in solitary retirement communed with his Teutonic gods. The fascination was hardly without basis. The Eagle's Nest was a masterpiece of engineering, a paragon of mysticism, the apotheosis of determination.

The determination was Martin Bormann's.

Bormann had noticed that Hitler greatly enjoyed his after-dinner walks from the Berghof to the small tea pavilion on the first level of the Obersalzberg. Since he was constantly seeking ways to ingratiate himself with the Führer, Bormann decided he would construct a new teahouse unequaled anyplace in the world. He also had another reason for constructing this out-of-the-way building. He wanted a place where his meetings with Hitler would be disturbed less often than they were at the Berghof. More and more Bormann was controlling who saw Hitler and what they told him, and he thought that by creating the Eagle's Nest he could further isolate the Führer from others. Contrary to what some historians believe, the structure was not originally intended to shelter Hitler in case of extreme danger, nor was it built for military purposes. Later it was considered for both.

In August 1937 Bormann selected the peak of the 5500-foot Kehlstein as the spot for the Eagle's Nest; and he personally placed the marking pegs while watched by Fritz Todt, a construction engineer in private business who was then also Reich

minister for armaments and munitions. Placing the pegs was
easy. Building the road from the Berghof to the base of the
Kehlstein and then blasting a tunnel and elevator shaft out of
solid rock were the difficult tasks. These feats were accomplished by laborers who were exposed to extremes of weather.
At this level on the Obersalzberg the ground was free of snow
only between the middle of May until October, and during
these snow-free months the hot sun and pouring rain made life
miserable for the workers. Several lives were lost while the
narrow, mountainous road was under construction, when trucks
went over the mountainsides because of shifting loads or failing
brakes. It took several months to complete the road.

It was nearly five miles long, built of a rock base covered
with asphalt. It circled upward from the Hintereck, just above
Hitler's Berghof, in hairpin curves and through several long
tunnels, and ended at a parking lot at the base of the Kehlstein.
The parking lot had to be blasted out of rock-face. At the far
side of the parking lot, set against the mountainside and
guarded by SS sentries, were massive bronze doors that
gleamed in the sun or glistened in the rain or snow. When the
identity of visitors was verified and the signal was given, these
doors swung open to reveal a high-ceilinged tunnel leading into
the interior of the mountain. The tunnel was 170 yards long
and wide enough for two cars to pass. Special mortar mixtures
were used in its construction as protection against humidity,
and it was lined with large rocks. At the far end of the tunnel
was a circular room, where another set of glistening bronze
doors greeted visitors.

These doors opened into an elevator with walls of polished
brass, mirrors, upholstered chairs and benches. It was operated
by electricity furnished by the Berchtesgaden power station, but
for emergency use there was a power unit from a submarine.
The elevator moved so silently that it was difficult to tell when
it was ascending; only the effect of pressure change on the
eardrums alerted the riders. It took only seconds to traverse the
shaft that had been bored vertically 200 feet through the
mountain.

The elevator delivered its passengers directly inside the Eagle's Nest. The rooms in the building were not large. There was

Hitler, when going to the Eagle's Nest, atop the Kehlstein, passed through massive bronze doors and onward through a tunnel to a plush elevator, which took him 200 feet up, through solid rock, to the sky-high teahouse. The tunnel, the elevator shaft, and the Eagle's Nest itself were all protected by poison gas capsules that could be activated by remote control. *(Hierzegger)*

a dining room, a study, a tearoom (which comprised the largest area in the Eagle's Nest), a kitchen, a guard room, washrooms, rest rooms, and a basement. Most of the rooms were lined with stone, pine or elm paneling. The tearoom, however, was lined with Untersberg and Cararic marble, and the huge fireplace was decorated with bronze tiles.

The cost of Bormann's "Thousand and One Nights" retreat? Bills from the construction firms indicated it cost 30 million marks. This amount, of course, does not include the several lives lost. The Eagle's Nest was undoubtedly the most expensive teahouse ever built. It was the most mysterious one, too. Until the autumn 1938 visit of André François-Poncet, former French ambassador to Berlin and one of the few non-Germans Hitler liked, no foreigner had ever visited the Eagle's Nest. His report of the visit to Georges Bonnet, the French foreign minister, is revealing:

In inviting me on the evening of October 17 to go to see him as soon as possible, Chancellor Hitler had placed at my disposal one of his private planes. I, therefore, left for Berchtesgaden by air the next day in the company of Captain Stehlin. Arrived there, an automobile took me not to the Obersalzberg Villa where Der Führer lives and where he had already received me, but instead to an extraordinary spot where, when the weather is good, he loves to spend his days.

Seen from afar, this place appears to be sort of observation hermitage, perched 1900 meters (about 6000 feet) on the crest of a ridge of rock. One arrives by a winding road about five miles long, hewn boldly out of the stone, its daring construction paying tribute as much to the talent of the engineer Todt as to the intensive labors of the workmen who completed this gigantic task.

The road ends at the entrance to a long tunnel which thrusts into the earth; heavy, double brass doors guard the entrance. At the further end of this tunnel a large elevator with copper walls awaits the visitor. Rising up a vertical shaft of 110 meters cut out of rock, the elevator ascends to the level of the Chancellor's abode.

Here one's surprise reaches its highest point. In effect, the visitor sees before him a squat and massive construction, consisting of a gallery of Roman pillars, an immense glassed-in circular chamber with a vast chimney in which burn enormous logs of wood, and a table, surrounded by about thirty chairs, as well as several side rooms furnished elegantly with comfortable armchairs.

On every side, looking through the bay windows, one's gaze, as from a high, speeding plane, passes into an immense panorama of mountains. In the distance one sees Salzburg and its neighboring villages, above which rises, as far as the eye can see, a horizon of mountains and peaks and of pastures and forests which cling to their slopes.

Close to the house, which appears to be suspended in the void, and almost hanging over it, an abrupt wall of naked rock rears itself. The whole, bathed in the glow of an autumn evening, is glamorous, wild, almost eerie.

The visitor wonders whether he is awake or dreaming. He would like to know where he is. Is this the castle of Montsalvat, inhabited by the Knights of the Grail, a Mount Athos sheltering the meditations of a cenobite, or the Castle of Antinea, rearing itself in the heart of the Atlas?

Is it a realization of one of those fantastic designs with which Victor Hugo used to decorate the margins of the manuscript of *The Burgraves*, a millionaire's fantasy, or only a hideout where brigands take their rest and accumulate their treasure."

François-Poncet, a suave, worldly diplomat, clearly was overwhelmed by the Eagle's Nest. He also wondered about the man who would have such a place constructed.

Is it the product of a normal mind, or that of a man tormented by delusions of grandeur, haunted by a desire for domination and solitude, or simply the prey of fear?

One detail attracts attention and for those who seek to determine the psychology of Adolf Hitler it is of no less value than others: The roads of access, the entrance to the tunnel, the immediate surroundings of the house, all are organized along military lines and protected by nests of machine guns.

The Chancellor welcomes me amiably and with courtesy. His face is pale and tired looking. He is not in one of his excitable moods; rather, he seems to be in a state of relaxation. At once he drags me towards the bay windows of a large room; he shows me the scenery, he enjoys the astonishment and admiration that I do not seek to hide. Then he expresses his regret at my approaching departure. We exchange some courtesies and phrases of politeness. At his command, tea is served in one of the side rooms where he conducts me with [Foreign Minister Joachim] von Ribbentrop while the Nazis of his entourage remain separately in the other rooms.

For nearly two hours Hitler listens with good grace to my questions; he answers them without the least embarrassment, with simplicity and, in appearance at least, with frankness. But the moment has come to return him to his freedom. The Castle of Antinea is now drowned in the shadows that fall upon the valleys and the mountains. I take my leave. Der Führer hopes that I may someday return to Germany and visit him as a private person. He shakes my hand several times. At the exit of the elevator and the tunnel I find a car that has been awaiting me; it takes me via Berchtesgaden to the airport whence the plane carries me through the night to Berlin.

The Eagle's Nest undoubtedly impressed everyone who was favored with an invitation from Hitler or Bormann to visit the place. Speer went to the Eagle's Nest only when necessary, but even he, an excellent architect, stood in awe of the feat it embodied. The fact that Fritz Todt, and not he, had planned and built the Eagle's Nest didn't detract from Speer's admiration.

"It is a tribute to Bormann, Todt, and, of course, Hitler, that this mountain-peak tea pavilion was built," Speer said, "but most of all I admire the men who actually did the construction."

The laborers who built the Eagle's Nest lived in barracks, 18 to a room. Each worker had a bed with a pillow, blankets, and a small cupboard. Washrooms and rest rooms were provided in each barracks. Although the laborers were hired by the various construction companies building the Eagle's Nest and those firms were supposedly responsible for the welfare of the men, Bormann was actually in charge. The extra pay each worker received—one mark separation allowance for a day for being separated from their family and one-half mark Obersalzberg allowance—didn't make up for the suffering inflicted by Bormann when he was angry.

Any worker whose behavior deviated from the standards set

down by Bormann was punished. Wage deductions were the most lenient form of punishment. Ration cards good for tobacco and food were withdrawn. Many of the labor foremen were "little Hitlers," and their cruelty caused a great deal of misery. Since the workers were separated from their families for long periods, many went absent without leave, only to end up in prison when they had returned from their escapes. The construction firm officials often complained about the punishment meted out to their workers, but Bormann ignored the pleas. Despite the hardships and cruel treatment, however, the workers built a masterpiece that amazed all who saw it.

There are conflicting reports on Hitler's feelings about the Eagle's Nest. Some say that the altitude affected his breathing and made his heart throb so loudly that he was frightened. It has been reported that he was at the Eagle's Nest only a few times during his life. Others, however, vow that he used the secluded, well-guarded tea pavilion often when he craved solitude or wanted to conduct secret discussions.

The Eagle's Nest. Bormann's gift to Hitler. The public never knew what went on at this mountaintop retreat. *(Hierzegger)*

"The Führer often came to the tunnel entrance in his car in the middle of the night," said Anton Bose, an SS guard who was stationed at the doors that opened into the mountain tunnel. "He evidently had trouble sleeping at night. Sometimes he was accompanied by another man or a woman, but quite often he was alone. His driver would wait at the bottom of the elevator shaft for him to return."

Because of Hitler's sometimes unexpected, unscheduled visits to the Eagle's Nest, the staff had to be on call at all times.

"There were three cooks and about six SS men who worked at the tea pavilion on top of the Kehlstein in shifts," Bose explained. "One cook and two SS men were there at all times to provide whatever service the Führer might need, day or night."

When asked if any unusual incidents occurred while he was on duty at the tunnel entrance, Bose smiled.

"I was surprised a great many times by what happened."

Pressed for details, the former SS member explained that Hitler often appeared at the tunnel entrance late at night with women. Many were actresses sent to the Berghof by Goebbels, who, as head of the Ministry of Propaganda, was in charge of the German film industry.

"I heard a lot of talk about Goebbels playing around with the starlets," Bose said, "but I was amazed when Hitler began going up to the Eagle's Nest with some of the young women. Especially when the Führer complained that the altitude at the top of the Kehlstein was hard on his heart. It's a wonder a couple of those beauties I saw with him didn't give him a heart attack."

Bose also said that Bormann often took his secretaries, and occasionally his mistress, to the Eagle's Nest. Since his wife spent most of her time on the Obersalzberg, however, most of his womanizing was done in Berlin. Goebbels came three times that Bose can remember, and two of those times he had with him a woman not his wife.

"I think it would have been more appropriate to call it the Love Nest rather than the Eagle's Nest," the former SS member said.

Another former NSDAP party member who spent a great deal of time at both the Berghof and the Eagle's Nest was

Albert Hellmuth. Hellmuth was an electrician employed during the construction of the Eagle's Nest to oversee the installation of the elevator.

"That elevator was the finest one I have ever seen," Hellmuth said. "It had everything—mirrors, cushioned seats, a telephone, carpeted floor, and every safety device known to man at that time. After all, if the elevator stopped midway between the Eagle's Nest and the tunnel, the Third Reich would have been at a standstill."

Asked if it ever did stop and strand the Führer, Bose verified a rumor that had been told and retold in the Berchtesgaden area for years.

"There was a problem once, in 1939, after Hitler confined me to my small room for a week because I had been drinking too much. He would've sent me to a concentration camp, I suppose, except for the fact there was no one else who really understood the complex electrical circuits of the elevator," Hellmuth explained. "I even remember the day. August twenty-second. The Führer had all his senior commanders of the armed forces meet at the Berghof to tell them, as we learned later, that the invasion of Poland would start September first. For some reason he went up to the Eagle's Nest one hour before the meeting was scheduled, and when he tried to return, the elevator wouldn't move. The SS commander put in an emergency call for me to hurry to the tunnel powerhouse, but I refused to go. I told him I couldn't disobey the Führer, who had told me not to dare leave my room." Finally Hitler told the SS commander to run a telephone extension into the electrician's room so he could speak with him personally. This took nearly an hour.

"I knew the Führer was very angry, but when he talked with me on the telephone and told me that he suspended my confinement, he was in very good control of himself," Hellmuth said. "In fact he said that if I could get the elevator running in time for him to hold his meeting on schedule, he would be very grateful. I did, and the next day a very good bottle of whiskey was delivered to my room. Several times later I heard him tell one or more of his military officers that if they would obey his orders as well as I did the time I was confined to my room, the war would be over much sooner."

Other previously unpublished facts about the Eagle's Nest were revealed by Hitler's commando chief, Otto Skorzeny, shortly before his death in Madrid in 1975. The tunnel, the elevator shaft, and the Eagle's Nest itself were all protected by poison gas capsules concealed from sight and ready to be activated by remote control from a panel in the Eagle's Nest. Gas masks were stored in secret containers in the tea pavilion and the elevator. The idea was that, if necessary, the Führer would leave Berlin by plane, fly to Berchtesgaden, and make his last stand on the Obersalzberg. In case this battle at his Alpine redoubt appeared lost, Hitler would take the elevator to the Eagle's Nest and there, if followed by Allied troops, release the poison gas into the tunnel and the elevator shaft behind him.

Capping this desperate plan was the procedure proposed to get Hitler off the peak of the Kehlstein, where the Eagle's Nest was located. According to Skorzeny, a slow-flying German troop carrier plane equipped with an elastic towline would snatch a glider, with Hitler in it, off the peak! The towline attached to the glider, which sat on the high ground behind the Eagle's Nest—the same area from which tourists today look down at the surrounding villages and countryside—was stretched between two poles. The pilot of the troop carrier plane was expected to slowly swoop low, hook this line, and yank the glider into the air. Skorzeny said that during practice several men were killed when a glider was pulled over the side of the peak instead of being yanked airborne. However after some modifications were made to the equipment, he said, the procedure was perfected. In the end Hitler decided not to make a final stand on the Obersalzberg, not withstanding that the Nazi treasure had been transferred to that area. The transfer was made when it became evident that the war was lost, and many of the art treasures Hitler had gathered for his proposed hometown art museum were stored in nearby salt mines and castles. Other Nazis did use the Obersalzberg as a starting point for their escape to South America, while Hitler died in Berlin. As far as is known, the glider wasn't used at all.

Strangers were not welcome at the Berghof or the Eagle's Nest, and after the war began more and more guardhouses were set up along the winding road from Berchtesgaden. Without proper authorization it was impossible to get within two miles of the Berghof, let alone near the Eagle's Nest. Mines were set into the slopes around the Berghof and throughout the area leading to the tunnel passage where the elevator to the mountain-peak tea pavilion was located. There was even an elaborate smoke machine installed; and, during the latter years of the war, when enemy air raids threatened the Berghof area, clouds of smoke completely obscured the house from the bombardiers. Yet in March 1943, during a night raid on Munich, the Eagle's Nest had a surprise visitor. In that month the Bomber Command of the RAF made a series of raids on cities in southern Germany. On March 10, in good night-flying weather, a large force of heavy bombers using radar bombed Munich, with excellent results for the RAF. One plane, however, was badly damaged over the city by German antiaircraft fire and continued south while the pilot tried to extinguish a fire in the No. 1 engine. When he finally decided the flames could not be put out, he ordered his crew to bail out. The flight engineer, Flight Sergeant Harry Owens, from Norwich, was the last man out of the bomber. He pulled the rip cord on his parachute when he was clear of the plane and drifted silently through the darkness, completely unaware of his location. Incredibly, he landed on the peak of the Kehlstein only a few yards from Hitler's Eagle's Nest. Seeing lights in the teahouse and well aware that he was somewhere in enemy territory, Owens slipped from his parachute harness, hid the parachute under a large rock, and then concealed himself as best he could on a ledge a few feet below the peak.

When it became daylight, the amazed Owens discovered that he was on a mountain very close to an impressive-looking building, which SS men were constantly entering and leaving. He stayed in his hiding place until nearly noon, when he heard voices near by. Sneaking a look over the edge of the higher ground above his ledge, he was shocked to see Hitler and several other men sitting at a small table behind the building. It was then he realized that he was at the famous mountain-peak teahouse he had heard about in England. Owens was hopelessly trapped, and he knew it. But he stayed hidden until, two days later, hunger and thirst forced him to reveal himself.

The SS officer to whom he surrendered was completely flustered. He made a telephone call immediately, while Owens stood under heavy guard. Then, when the conversation was completed, the SS officer took Owens into the Eagle's Nest, where the Englishman was served a very good meal and given several glasses of beer. Owens believed that this was done on Hitler's orders, that the Führer thought Owens's feat was so unusual he deserved a treat before being taken to a prisoner-of-war camp. Owens spent the remainder of the war a prisoner, but one who had the "tallest" tale of all to relate to his fellow prisoners.

The social event at the Eagle's Nest was the wedding reception of Gretl Braun, the younger sister of Hitler's mistress. Gretl spent a great deal of time at the Berghof and in Munich with her sister Eva. Of course this meant she was well acquainted with Hitler. A blonde who was not too particular about the men with whom she chose to associate, she was much more outgoing than Eva. She was well liked around the Berghof and was always good for a laugh or two.

Another regular visitor to the Berghof was Hermann Fegelein, the SS general who was the liaison officer between Hitler and Himmler; Fegelein was also a good friend of Martin Bormann's. A tall, handsome man, Fegelein had his choice of the Berghof women, many of whom went out of their way to crawl into bed with him. Hitler, playing the role of matchmaker, which he delighted in doing, decided that Gretl Braun and Hermann Fegelein would be an outstanding married couple. His suggestion delighted Gretl because of Fegelein's physical prowess and his status with the Führer. Fegelein was not madly in love with Gretl Braun, but he quickly saw the advantage of becoming "almost" related to Hitler by marriage. (So far Hitler had not married Eva Braun, even though she was his mistress and closest female companion.)

So, on June 5, 1944, the 30-year-old Gretl and the 37-year-old Fegelein were married in a civil ceremony at the Salzburg town hall. Bormann and Himmler both attended the wedding, making it a Nazi social event. Hitler, at Eva's urging, arranged for a wedding reception to be held that evening in the Eagle's Nest; it was one of the few gala affairs held on the Obersalzberg. The elevator whisked more than 50 guests, including the Braun and Fegelein families, to the tea pavilion high above the city where the couple had been married a few hours earlier. There was an abundance of schnapps, champagne, and wine; a band made up of SS members entertained; and the chefs arranged an elaborate table. For the only time during the war, Hitler permitted dancing in one of his houses or apartments. He soon tired of the affair, however, and after giving a short speech, he retired to the Berghof below. Not Eva: She danced all night long with the male guests. Bormann drank too much and had to be carried first to the elevator and then from it to his car at the bottom of the elevator shaft. A "wine, women, and song" attitude prevailed among those at the reception; most of them knew that time was running out for the Third Reich. Allied bombers were in the area day and night, and the Russians were moving steadily toward the German border. Many of the high-ranking NSDAP officials at the reception in the Eagle's Nest that June night in 1944 were aware that the Americans and English were expected to invade Europe from the west at any minute. They tried to forget their problems for a few hours.

Hitler, however, had been too tense to stay at the tea pavilion in the sky and join in the merrymaking. He wanted to be near his radio and telephones, to keep in touch with the deteriorating situation. Ironically, when, that very night, the awaited code words came over the BBC network to alert the French Resistance that the Allied invasion was imminent and were monitored by the Berghof operators, Hitler was sleeping, and, as noted earlier, his aides were afraid to awaken him. If he had stayed at the Eagle's Nest and enjoyed the merriment, he would have known hours sooner about the enemy invasion forces; and perhaps the course of the war would have been changed entirely.

8

Hitler's Famous Visitors

Although Hitler preferred to be thought of as a wolf, independent and courageous, with people he was more often foxy. Unpredictable, wily. Often, what seemed to be a spur-of-the-moment tantrum was a carefully staged emotional display, an act that he intended would help his opinion prevail. When he wanted to, he could be charming and gracious. If he didn't care about his visitor's opinion of him, Hitler could be rude and brutal. When François-Poncet visited him at the Eagle's Nest, Hitler was a perfect host. With Dorothy Thompson, the famed American journalist, he was abrupt, possibly because he sensed she was disappointed with him.

"When I walked into Adolf Hitler's room, I was convinced that I was meeting the future dictator of Germany," Thompson said. "In something less than fifty seconds I was quite sure that I was not. It took me about that time to measure the startling insignificance of this man who had set the world agog."

Hitler had made her wait for an hour in the upstairs foyer of the Kaiserhof Hotel before having her ushered into his room. It was 1932, shortly before he became chancellor, but he was showing an arrogance that would become increasingly evident. He refused to give a direct answer to her questions but launched instead into a monologue on a subject of his own choosing.

"When I dared to interrupt the stream of eloquence by bluntly repeating my question," Thompson explained, "he replied rather coyly that he didn't intend to hand his program over to his enemies for them to steal."

Nor did he escort her personally to the door and kiss her

hand, as he always did with women he liked or wanted to impress.

In contrast to his impolite treatment of Dorothy Thompson was the royal reception he ordered for Japanese Foreign Minister Yosuke Matsuoka; it was planned to the most minute detail. Hitler made certain that his chief of protocol had everything organized, down to the very second that Matsuoka would arrive at the Anhalt Station in Berlin. Ribbentrop had to be properly placed in the floodlights for the hand-shaking ceremony so that the photographs would flatter the German. The front door of Matsuoka's train coach had to stop exactly at the red carpet that was spread over the station platform. To achieve this precision the entire train was measured at the last station before Berlin; then it was calculated how much each of the buffers of the individual cars would be compressed at a given speed and brake pressure. This information was passed on to the engineer, who could then stop his train of 10 or 12 cars at just the right spot. Without a jolt, too, as had happened once when Mussolini visited. The train bearing the Italian dictator had stopped so suddenly Mussolini bumped his head on the window frame, and his smile of greeting to Hitler was definitely forced. Within a week, the engineer of that train was at the front lines of the war.

There was a "princes' room" at the Anhalt Station, a waiting room where state visitors could rest a few minutes after their official greeting and the posing for still photographs and newsreels. After this pause Ribbentrop and Matsuoka reviewed the guard of honor. They looked like the Mutt and Jeff of the comic pages, since the German was tall and the Japanese short. The Japanese foreign minister was then taken to meet Hitler.

The conference had been arranged by Hitler to delicately warn Japan that while Germany's relations with Russia were "correct," there was no assurance that they would not deteriorate in the future. Hitler, of course, had already planned to attack the Soviet Union later that year—1941—and he wanted Japan on the side of Germany, not the Soviet Union. He wanted Japan to make a surprise attack on Singapore. Matsuoka, however, didn't give the answer Hitler wanted to hear.

"I can give no firm promise on behalf of Japan at the moment," he replied, although he reassured Hitler that he personally thought the German strategy was the correct one.

Hitler was disappointed, but he immediately put his "Plan 2" into effect. He sent Matsuoka to visit Göring at Karinhall. The Führer knew that the plush and intriguing environment of Göring's home, plus Göring's expertise as the gracious host, always softened up the most obstinate state guest or celebrity. In the case of the diminutive Japanese foreign minister, however, the beginning of the visit didn't go well. The massive furniture and the heavy beams overwhelmed Matsuoka and made him seem even smaller than he was. When he sat at the table, he sank so low in his chair that he could barely see over the edge. Göring, sensitive to the situation, quickly suggested a tour of the house. The Japanese foreign minister showed normal interest in the paintings, Gobelin tapestries, and antiques Göring owned, most of which he had obtained from countries overrun by the German military forces. But Göring saved the best for the last—his model railway.

Over a 300-square-yard area Göring had arrayed 1000 yards of track and 40 electric contacts and signals. He had several trains in the layout, and for the rest of the afternoon Göring and a delighted Matsuoka operated the passenger and freight trains. Several times Matsuoka had to stand on tiptoe to pick up trains that jumped the track, but instead of being embarrassed, he seemed happy to have the chance to handle the coaches and engines. Unfortunately for Hitler, though, apparently the Göring treatment didn't soften Matusoka utterly. There was no agreement that Japan would enter any conflict on the side of Germany against the Soviet Union—or was there? Later events suggest that there may have been a secret understanding between Hitler and Matsuoka.

It was neither the first nor the last time that Hitler used Göring to host famous and powerful visitors. As counterpoint to Hitler's serious talks with the guests, the antics of the Reich marshal of the Luftwaffe were relaxing, amusing, and productive.

One of the most celebrated Americans to visit prewar Germany was Charles A. Lindbergh, the "Lone Eagle" who had conquered the Atlantic in the single-engined *Spirit of St. Louis* in 1927. Lindbergh, for at least a decade after his flight, was the most popular hero in the world. Hitler knew that a visit to Germany by such a celebrity would add stature to the regime. Even in his wildest dreams, though, the Führer probably never thought Lindbergh's interest in the Luftwaffe would be as beneficial to the Nazi cause as it turned out to be.

It all began when Truman Smith, the U. S. military attaché in charge of army and air intelligence at the embassy in Berlin, was seeking some way to obtain information about the German Air Force. Reading about Lindbergh's visit to France, Smith decided to try to get him to make a trip to Germany, where he was certain Göring would invite Lindbergh to visit the Luftwaffe airfields and German aircraft manufacturing plants. Smith thought that in this manner Lindbergh would pick up valuable information about German aviation that could be passed on to Washington. So on May 25, 1936, Smith wrote to Lindbergh, who was living in England at the time, emphasizing that Göring extended "an invitation to visit Germany and inspect the new German civil and military air establishments."

Hermann Göring showing Charles Lindbergh a sword from his collection. Göring convinced the famous American flier that the Luftwaffe could defeat any air force in the world. *(National Archives)*

Lindbergh accepted the invitation for himself and his wife. Taking delivery of a new aircraft, they flew off to Berlin on July 22, 1936. Meanwhile Hitler was making plans to circumvent Lindbergh's plea that there be no publicity surrounding the trip. Hitler understood very well the propaganda value of the visit and was determined to have the world aware of the famous flier's interest in German aviation. The Führer orchestrated every move the flamboyant Göring made. The 1936 Olympics were scheduled to begin in Berlin during Lindbergh's visit, and Hitler instructed the Luftwaffe chief to bring the American flier to the opening day ceremonies as his guest. It was obvious to Hitler that visitors from around the world would be attending the Olympics and would see Lindbergh sitting in Göring's private box. Indeed, newspapers in several countries published accounts of "Lucky Lindy" with Göring and Hitler at the opening of the Olympics, and newsreels showed him in Göring's box.

In addition to making this public appearance Lindbergh, during his nine-day stay in Germany, spoke at the Air Club in Berlin, attended a reception given by the mayor of the city, had tea with Crown Prince Wilhelm at the Cäcilien Palace, and was guest of honor at a state reception given by Göring at his residence on the Wilhelmstrasse. Each of these affairs was milked for all possible publicity. Eventually Lindbergh did visit a few aircraft factories and was briefed about Luftwaffe capabilities by General Field Marshal Erhard Milch, Göring's deputy, but social activities took much more of his time. At Hitler's orders, however, the factories, airfields, and Luftwaffe units visited by Lindbergh were all abnormally busy during his inspection. Consequently Lindbergh returned to England with an analysis of the German Air Force that was far from accurate. Hitler had outwitted the famous flier.

When he reached England, Lindbergh did exactly what Hitler wanted him to do. He made an appointment with Sir Thomas Inskip, minister of defense, and at the meeting told him exaggerated stories about the Luftwaffe. His warning was alarming.

"There can be no defense against the bomber fleets Germany is building," Lindbergh stated. "All fortification is useless."

He did an excellent job—for Hitler! He frightened the British government.

In 1937 Lindbergh went back to Germany as guest of honor of the Third Reich at the Lilienthal Aeronautical Congress, in Munich. Hitler used this prestigious conference as an excuse to get the gullible American flier back to Germany, where he could fill him with more false information. Instead of once again choosing Göring to lead Lindbergh by the hand, this time Hitler chose World War I ace Ernst Udet, a popular pilot whom Lindbergh admired. Udet flew him around Germany, showing Lindbergh exactly what Hitler wanted shown—aircraft factories in full production, the new Messerschmitt 109 fighter plane, and several Luftwaffe units that were manned by the best pilots in the German Air Force. Udet talked to Lindbergh during the various inspection trips, feeding him inflated figures about the number of aircraft available to the Luftwaffe and the excellent training programs for the German Air Force combat pilots. Lindbergh believed Udet, just as he had believed Göring the previous year; but this time there was an added bonus for Hitler. The Lone Eagle became convinced the Führer had a powerful Germany. He told everyone who would listen in England, France, and the United States that Hitler and the Luftwaffe were, in his opinion, an unbeatable combination. Hitler had duped him again.

Lindbergh estimated that Hitler was building 500 to 800 planes a month and that the Luftwaffe already had an armada of 10,000 aircraft. Actually the Luftwaffe had less than half that number of planes—4665—and was building 125 planes a month. The German Air Force was not prepared to fight a war. Hitler used Lindbergh to convince the West that the Luftwaffe was invincible; the dictator might gain his conquests without a war. Lindbergh's preaching made a believer of Joseph P. Kennedy, the American ambassador to England, and Kennedy decided he would try to influence Prime Minister Neville Chamberlain to appease Hitler. Chamberlain had been to Berchtesgaden to meet with Hitler, and another meeting of the two men was scheduled for September 22, 1938, at Godesberg, Germany. The night before the meeting Kennedy had Lindbergh put in writing his evaluation of the German Air Force, and the ambassador gave Lindbergh's letter to Chamberlain as the prime minister boarded his plane the next morning for Germany. Lindbergh said, in part:

Without a doubt the German air fleet is now stronger than that of any other country in the world. The rate of progress of German military aviation during the last several years is without parallel. I feel certain that German air strength is greater than that of all other European countries combined and that she is constantly increasing her margin of leadership.... I do not believe civilization ever faced a greater crisis. Germany now has the means of destroying London, Paris and Prague if she wishes to do so.... I am convinced that it is wiser to permit Germany's eastward expansion than to throw England and France unprepared into a war at this time....

Chamberlain was already frustrated and worried. This was his second trip to see Hitler within a week's time. The first trip had been on September 15, and he had not yet recovered from that ordeal. He flew from London to Munich, landing at 12:30 P.M., and then boarded a train for Berchtesgaden. Hitler, who had already decided to occupy Czechoslovakia, was prepared for the English prime minister. A 30-man SS guard of honor awaited at the Berghof for Chamberlain to arrive in the car Hess had sent to the station in Berchtesgaden. When he arrived, Hitler greeted him as an honored guest, although secretly he had no intention of permitting Chamberlain to dissuade him from moving into Czechoslovakia. He listened patiently while the prime minister stated that he personally had always worked for an Anglo-German *rapprochement* and was, as ever, on the lookout for opportunities to put his intentions into practice. At present, however, he said, the tension between the two countries was very great, and he had undertaken the journey to Germany in order, by direct conversation with the Führer, to attempt to clarify the situation.

Although Hitler was impatient to get the meeting over with, since he had to attend to other important matters connected with the occupation of Czechoslovakia, and time was running short, he was very gracious with the older man.

"I am well aware of the significance of your journey," he

said. "The whole German nation welcomed this journey, as you, of course, have gathered from the demonstrations of sympathy which you received from the German population on your arrival in Munich and on the way to Berchtesgaden."

After this opening statement Hitler got tougher. He angrily told Chamberlain about the terror campaign of the Czechs, during which, he claimed, 300 Sudeten Germans had been killed. He didn't mention that most of the terror campaign was planned and executed by Nazis in Czechoslovakia. Finally Hitler told the prime minister that talks between England and Germany could continue if Chamberlain would agree' to the secession from Czechoslovakia of the German-populated Sudetenland by the virtue of the right of self-determination. Chamberlain promised he would take the matter up with his government and with the French, although in his own mind the secession was acceptable under those terms. A second meeting would be needed once he had obtained answers from the British and the French governments. Now Hitler was the perfect, thoughtful host.

"I would gladly spare the Prime Minister a second trip to Germany," Hitler said, "for I am much younger and could undertake journeys of this kind but I am afraid that if I come to England anti-German demonstrations would complicate rather than simplify the situation. I am willing to shorten the Prime Minister's journey somewhat by proposing the next meeting be held in the Lower Rhine district, Cologne or Godesberg."

Chamberlain was pleased with this concession from the Führer and agreed to meet with him at Hotel Dressen in Godesberg on September 22. However he wanted assurance from Hitler that during the intervening days the situation would not deteriorate further. Hitler's bluff was masterful.

"The danger of such a deterioration in this situation exists," he told Chamberlain, poker-faced, "with the result that our military forces might have to be set in motion. If further major incidents such as cases of frontier violation and the like occur the danger will be increased to the utmost." He smiled and continued: "But even at the risk of this being interpreted as weakness, as perhaps the British press will interpret it, I am prepared to give an assurance that, if at all possible, I will not

give the order to set our military machine in motion during the
next few days, unless a completely impossible situation should
arise. In that case, of course, all future discussions would be
useless."

Hitler sent an apprehensive Chamberlain back to England;
and when the Prime Minister returned to Godesberg a week
later, he was met by an honor company of Hitler's own SS
troops and the Führer's announcement that the secession agreement discussed at the Berghof was no longer enough. Five days
later at Munich both England and France did exactly what
Lindbergh had recommended. Both nations signed the infamous Munich Pact, which was Czechoslovakia's death war-
rant, on September 29. So did Hitler and Mussolini—cheerfully.

Chamberlain flew home and happily reported at the airport,
as he waved his copy of the agreement, "I have brought peace
in our time."

Meanwhile, back in Munich, Hitler muttered to Ribbentrop:
"Ach, don't take it so seriously. That piece of paper is of no
significance whatever."

Two weeks after the Munich Pact was signed, Lindbergh was
back in Berlin to receive the Service Cross of the German Eagle
(Ver dienstkreuz der Deutscher Adler), one of the highest German decorations, by order of the Führer.

After this coup Hitler was ready for other visitors.

Sometimes his carefully laid plans for visiting dignitaries
went astray, however. In June 1941 Hitler and Mussolini met at
the Brenner Pass, between Austria and Italy, to discuss future
military plans. Paul Schmidt, Hitler's official Italian-language
interpreter, was dispatched to meet Mussolini at the pass and to
stay with him until the Duce returned to Italy. Since Hitler was
extremely busy with his plans to attack Russia later that month
and Mussolini wanted to inspect an Italian military unit, the
two dictators met only periodically in Hitler's special train or
plane or at one of his field headquarters. Hitler led the world to
believe that they were constantly together, but this was a fantasy, as were many of his other propaganda ploys. The meetings had to be organized very carefully.

"Everything had to be worked out to the minute," Schmidt
said. "Mussolini's shaving time during which his special train

would stop; staffs behind the front where Mussolini visited had to stop important work to stage a show for the visiting dictator; special train schedules had to be arranged so there would be delay of Mussolini's or Hitler's trains; and a hundred other details were required."

During the meetings many communiqués were issued, one of which stated, in the last paragraph, "In the military and political conversations there also took part, on the German side, General Field Marshal Keitel and Reich Foreign Minister von Ribbentrop." On the train back to Italy that very day Schmidt received a curt message to relay to Mussolini.

"The German foreign minister has withdrawn the agreed-upon communiqué."

Mussolini was furious. "Have the train stopped at once!" he bellowed to Schmidt, his lantern jaw sticking out several inches.

The official interpreter explained that they would have to stop at a station that had a telephone line connected to the main network. They did, and Schmidt immediately called Hitler's headquarters in an effect to learn what was wrong. Mussolini stood at his side, waiting for the reply, threatening and muttering to himself. It was a childish peeve that nearly terminated the friendship of the two nations.

What had happened was that after the communiqué had been agreed upon, Ribbentrop boarded his own train for the trip home. A few minutes later, while rereading the communiqué, he realized his name had been placed after Keitel's. He immediately called his press representative and told him to withdraw the release until the sequence of the names was changed and his name placed ahead of Keitel's. Hitler, in his private train, was notified, and he was infuriated. So while Mussolini, standing beside Hitler's interpreter, angrily cooled his heels at the railroad station, Ribbentrop pouted and Hitler had a tantrum. Finally calming down, Hitler agreed to the change. The matter was settled—or so the Führer thought. When Ribbentrop's press representative returned to the foreign minister's train and told him that Hitler had agreed to change the sequence of the names but that the Führer was angry, Ribbentrop suddenly had a change of heart.

"I withdraw my request," he said. "It shall stay as it was."

After an hour of waiting for an answer, the message finally reached Schmidt at the railroad station and was passed on to the ill-tempered Mussolini. Only then did Mussolini's train move again.

When the Duke and Duchess of Windsor visited Germany in 1937, not all went well with Hitler's plans. Since the former King Edward VIII of England had long shown pro-German sympathies, Hitler felt that he should be treated with great respect. The fact that the duke had recently abdicated his throne for the duchess, the former Wallis Warfield Simpson, didn't mean that his influence in England was not still considerable. Hitler had not forgotten what had happened a year earlier when German troops occupied the Rhineland, breaking the Versailles Treaty. England had been on the verge of declaring war on Germany, but the duke, then still king, had spoken in the Third Reich's behalf. He had called Leopold von Hösch, the German ambassador to London, to reassure him there would be no war. Fritz Hesse, the representative of the German News Service (DNB), was with Hösch when King Edward VIII telephoned.

"I sent for Chamberlain the prime minister and gave him a piece of my mind," the king said. "I told the old so-and-so that I would abdicate if he made war. There was a frightful scene but you needn't worry. There won't be a war."

When he did abdicate the following year, it was because of his love for a woman. Trying to establish a new stature then, as Duke of Windsor, he decided to go to Nazi Germany and study labor conditions. He knew that if there was one nation in the world that would welcome him, it would be Germany. Hitler was delighted and arranged for Dr. Robert Ley, chief of the German Labor Front, to greet the Duke and Duchess of Windsor and show them around the country. Ley had long been an alcoholic and was very unstable. His family life was irregular: He had divorced his first wife, and his second had committed suicide. Now he lived with a young Estonian girl without benefit of clergy. He was unable to carry on a coherent conversation even when he was sober, which was seldom, and he lived in a world removed from reality. Predictably, the reserved and sophisticated Duke and Duchess of Windsor were horrified at the behavior of their escort.

"Ley had a powerful black Mercedes-Benz," explained Hans Sopple, one of Ley's former aides. "The more he drank the faster he would drive. Sometimes his chauffeur would convince Ley that as an official of the Third Reich it was below his status to drive his own automobile, and when sober Ley would agree. But let him get a few drinks and he wanted to grab the wheel. I was with him when he decided the Duke and Duchess of Windsor should definitely visit the workers' barracks at a factory on the outskirts of Munich. He was drunk, of course. He drove the car through the locked gates and then raced up and down at full speed between the barracks, scaring hell out of the workers and nearly running over several. The next day Hitler told Göring to take charge of the duke's visit before Ley killed him."

Göring was an old hand at soothing the feelings of famous guests. He would be just right to get them into a suitable frame of mind to meet Hitler. Göring invited the couple to his home, Karinhall. For the slim, attractive duchess he had the ideal exhibition—his elaborate weight-reduction equipment and massage apparatus in the basement of the manor house. Göring wanted to show her how the rolls took weight off his body, but he got between the rollers while wearing his white uniform. He forgot that all his medals were pinned on his chest, and when one of the medals got caught in a roll, it wrapped his uniform jacket around his neck and nearly strangled him. That ended the exhibition.

Of course no tour of Karinhall was complete without a viewing of the elaborate model train layout. Like Japanese Foreign Minister Matsuoka, the Duke of Windsor was fascinated by the trains and spent a great deal of time playing with them.

Göring had another surprise for the duke. He sent a toy airplane, attached to an overhead wire, flying across the room, dropping small wooden "bombs" in its course. Two years later Göring's Luftwaffe planes were dropping real bombs on London.

Despite Ley's drunken reception and tour and Göring's brush with strangulation in the rolls of the weight-control equipment, the duke and duchess went back to England convinced, as Lindbergh had been, that Hitler and National Socialism were good for Germany. Hitler saw to that. He invited them to the Berghof and gave them the Third Reich's "royal" treatment. Hitler was amiable toward the duke and said of the duchess, "She would have made a good queen."

Hitler's success in hosting and wooing the Duke and Duchess of Windsor was noticed worldwide. On October 23, 1937, *The New York Times* reported:

The Duke's decision to see for himself the Third Reich's industries and social institutions and his gestures and remarks during the last two weeks have demonstrated adequately that the Abdication did rob Germany of a firm friend, if not a devoted admirer, on the British throne. He has lent himself, perhaps unconsciously but easily, to National Socialist propaganda. There can be no doubt that his tour has strengthened the regime's hold on the working classes. The Duke is reported to have become very critical of English politics as he sees them and is reported as declaring that the British ministers of today and their possible successors are no match for the German or Italian dictators.

Hitler had won again. The man whom much of the world thought of as just a paperhanger, a man who supposedly chewed on rugs and frothed at the mouth when angry, proved time and time again when hosting foreign visitors that the world had underestimated his talents and charm. His "secret" personality was so effective that he was able to convince kings, prime ministers, and other assorted celebrities that he and his Third Reich were paradigms of efficient and fair government and leadership. And he was able to accomplish this despite the concentration camps and Nazism's brutal policy toward the Jews.

On May 9, 1941, the citizens of Berchtesgaden, deep in the mountains of Bavaria and far from the sea, were amazed when a company of Nazi marines appeared. It was the first time a naval unit had visited the city, and it was evident that Hitler was planning some special event on the nearby Obersalzberg, where his mountain retreat was located. The French tricolor was hoisted at the airport, and within an hour a Junkers transport plane appeared in the sky, escorted by three Messerschmitt 109 fighters. When the aircraft landed it was obvious why the marines were in Berchtesgaden. Vice-Premier Admiral Jean François Darlan of France stepped from the transport and was greeted by Foreign Minister von Ribbentrop. As they clasped hands, the marine band played the "Marseillaise" and "Deutschland über Alles." A large tricolor waved alongside a slightly larger swastika banner.

Darlan was taken in Ribbentrop's car from the airport to the Berghof, where Hitler greeted him effusively. There was a reason for the warmth. He wanted Vichy France to be more active in its support of Nazi Germany. Since July 10, 1940, when Marshal Philippe Pétain obtained the authority of the French National Assembly at Vichy to rule France under the armistice agreement he had signed with Hitler a month earlier, the situation had changed. Pierre Laval, the vice-premier before Darlan, had been dismissed because of his intrigues in behalf of Germany, and Darlan had been appointed in his place. Hitler now wanted to convince Darlan to take up where Laval had left off.

After a 45-minute lunch, during which Hitler was jovial and communicative, he and Darlan went to the Führer's private

Hitler invited many foreign dignitaries to his home at the Berghof for secret talks. Here Vichy France's vice-premier, Adm. Jean François Darlan, arrives in early May 1941. He will be forced to collaborate with the Nazis. *(National Archives)*

study. They discussed the European situation in general, and then Darlan asked the key question: What terms might France expect for full collaboration?

Once again Hitler was shrewd. He declared that he had no terms to offer; that the warm reception accorded Darlan at the Berghof should have convinced the guest that Germany was prepared to deal with vanquished France as an equal. He quickly added that immediately after the dismissal of Laval as vice-premier he had considered annexing to Germany all French territory north of the River Somme, including the channel ports of Dunkirk, Boulogne, and Calais as well as the industrial cities of Lille, Armentiéres, Arras and Canbria. But, he implied, he had decided to wait until he determined Darlan's attitude toward the Third Reich. This statement, of course, placed Darlan and the collaborationist Vichy regime in a precarious position. Before Darlan left Berchtesgaden the next morning to return to France, the bargain had been made that Vichy France would work hand-in-hand with Nazi Germany.

While it was marines for Darlan, it was a prayer stool and a crucifix in the room of Madame Horthy, wife of Admiral Miklós von Horthy, Regent of Hungary. Madame Horthy was a devout Catholic and had a great deal of influence on her husband, whom Hitler was trying to convince to support Nazi Germany during the trouble with Czechoslovakia. He also made certain she had a large bouquet of lilies of the valley in her room each morning after he learned that was her favorite flower. For Yugoslavia's Prince Regent Paul and his wife, Olga, it was a gala performance of Wagner's *Meistersinger* at the Prussian State Opera. Unfortunately, conductor Herbert von Karajan, who always conducted without a score, lost his place and the baritone had to quit singing. The curtain was promptly brought down until everyone was organized again. Hitler was so angry that he vowed Karajan would never again be allowed to conduct at Bayreuth.

Model trains, toy airplanes, flowers, and falderal—no person or thing was beneath consideration if it could lend itself to the Führer's purposes. Every tool of persuasion was a weapon in Hitler's arsenal.

9

Sex Under the Swastika

Where women and sex were concerned, the public Hitler was entirely different from the private Hitler. He vowed to the German people, through the measures he ordered, that moral purity would be enforced and that those who violated his stringent orders would be severely punished. A report issued in 1944 by the Reich Bureau of Statistics, *The Development of Criminality in the German Reich from the Outbreak of War until 1943*, indicates that Hitler did penalize sex offenders. There were 238 castrations in 1939, 198 in 1940, 153 in 1941, and 152 in 1942. In the first quarter of 1943 60 castrations were added to the total. Offenses under paragraph 75 of the penal code, the law on homosexuality, totaled more than 7000 in 1939, and nearly 10,000 more violations were noted during the next three years.

Hitler absolutely forbade sexual intercourse between a German woman and a foreigner, but with the influx of prisoners of war and foreign laborers, this order was continually violated. With most of the German males in military service and away from home or, as in many instances, killed in action, many lonely German women soon were willing to bed down with lonely prisoners or laborers who longed for wives or girl friends back home. The relevant paragraph 4 of the Ordinance for the Safeguarding of German National Military Potential suffered 4300 recorded violations in 1941 and 9100 in 1942. Complaints about the number of German women and girls having intercourse with foreign males became more and more frequent as the war continued. In most cases the female was punished with a jail term, had her hair cut off, and was paraded through the streets with derogatory signs on her body. The "guilty" foreign

male was usually executed without trial. These punishments
bolstered Hitler's public image as a champion of sexual virtue.
Wasn't he the Führer who was "married to Germany"? The
man who kissed women's hands and bowed to them and
treated them like fragile works of art? Didn't he require the
highest standards of morality among his NSDAP associates so
that they would be inspiration for the average German citizen?
  No.
From the top down, the Nazi regime was riddled with sex
scandals, broken marriages, and all manner of sexual escapades—both "normal" and aberrant. Indeed, it was probably
inevitable that the Third Reich, revolving as it did around
Hitler's concept of a mythic, heroic, Pan-Germanism, revolved
around sex.
  Werner von Blomberg, whose availability for minister of
defense helped deliver the chancellorship to Hitler in January
1933, later found himself deposed from that office by the
Führer because of a woman. When President Paul von Hindenburg decided to give Hitler a chance to govern, it wasn't because the old field marshal trusted the demagogue; he didn't.
He considered Hitler a radical, a man who might destroy Germany were he to gain control of the German military. Consequently Hindenburg would not appoint Hitler chancellor until
his trusted friend Werner von Blomberg was assured the post of
minister of defense in Hitler's cabinet. Hindenburg was certain
that Blomberg would maintain control of the armed forces,
preventing Hitler's use of the Wehrmacht for some wild scheme
that might prove detrimental to the nation. Blomberg previously adjutant general of the Reichswehr was a man of imposing presence, sometimes called "a Siegfried with a
monocle." In 1933, at the beginning of Hitler's regime, he was
55 years old, a staid, conservative military officer and a widower who wouldn't have walked the same side of the street as a
prostitute.
  But in 1936 Blomberg, a widower since 1932 and the father
of five children, suddenly found an interest other than military
affairs, a very attractive young secretary, Fräulein Erna Gruhn.
For quite some time they had been meeting secretly at the
Goldener Hirsch hotel in Berlin. Gruhn would book a double

room for the weekend, and Blomberg would join her. Despite the difference in their ages—Erna Gruhn was 24—their romance progressed steadily; and finally the minister of defense—who was now also commander-in-chief of the armed forces—tired of the "back street" aspect of the affair. He decided he wanted to marry the secretary. But because of his and Gruhn's differences in age and social status, he wondered what Hitler would think.

Blomberg's opportunity to find out came shortly after the funeral for General Erich Ludendorff, Hindenburg's chief of staff in World War I and the man who had walked beside Hitler during the 1923 putsch. It was three days before Christmas, 1937, when Blomberg, dressed in his familiar leather greatcoat, peaked cap, and high boots joined Hitler, Göring, and other NSDAP officials in Munich for the state funeral. As soon as the last notes of "The Faithful Comrade" had died away and the 19-gun salute had been fired in memory of Ludendorff, Blomberg got Hitler off to the side and asked to see the Führer in private as soon as possible. Hitler invited him to his apartment on the Prinzregentenplatz.

Blomberg was frank and to the point. He explained to Hitler that he wanted to marry a secretary 35 years his junior, a woman of modest status whom he loved. Hitler immediately agreed to the marriage. He was aware that Blomberg had been having an affair and was happy to have it legalized before a scandal erupted. Besides, Blomberg still dominated the armed forces and Hitler preferred to be on his good side. The Führer wanted no interference from Blomberg in the implementation of NSDAP policies. Hitler sought personal control of the armed forces himself, but an overt move to oust Blomberg at that moment might have toppled the Nazi regime.

On January 12, 1938, Blomberg and Erna Gruhn were married in the Defense Ministry in Berlin. Hitler and Göring acted as witnesses; Göring even abandoned his own birthday celebration to attend. The pair left for a honeymoon, but on January 20 Blomberg received news that his mother had died. He immediately left for Eberswalde, where she had lived, and stayed four days. When he returned to Berlin he discovered that a terrible shadow had fallen over his new marriage. Despite the youthfulness of his new bride, she had allegedly packed those years with a wide variety of experiences. Göring told the Führer on January 24, when Hitler returned to Berlin: "Blomberg has married a whore!" The police took out her personnel folder when the new Frau Blomberg registered her change of address after her marriage. When they opened the folder, they discovered some "facts" about the former Erna Gruhn they thought Hitler should know.

"It turns out Fräulein Gruhn was the daughter of a brothel owner and had herself been convicted for prostitution and posing for a certain kind of photograph," Elisabeth von Stahlenberg wrote in her diary on February 12, 1938. "How everyone loves the gossip."

According to the Nazi version of the incident, Erna Gruhn's mother had operated a massage parlor for years, one that was known rather better for the delights of the flesh it afforded its customers than for the physical fitness its regimen enhanced. At 18 years of age, after years of helping her mother, Fräulein Gruhn left home and moved into an apartment on Wilhelmstrasse, in Berlin, with a much older man. Her companion hired a photographer to take pornographic pictures of her to sell, but when he tried to hawk them in Berlin he was promptly arrested, as was Fräulein Gruhn. She was released and the incident was forgotten . . . until Hitler saw the file. He immediately recognized his opportunity to get rid of Blomberg and take control of the German military apparatus. Hitler elaborated on the so-called crimes of Fräulein Gruhn, calling her a prostitute, a woman unfit to be the wife of a German General Staff officer. Accusing Blomberg of bringing shame upon the entire Wehrmacht, he suggested that the field marshal commit suicide as the honorable way out of the scandal. Blomberg didn't relish a confrontation with Hitler, but there was no way he was going to kill himself and leave his attractive young wife for the wolves of the Nazi hierarchy to hound. He met with Hitler in the library of the Chancellery, bade him farewell, took his bride and moved to a small cottage in the mountains. Later the two went into exile on the island of Capri. Blomberg was still living after the death of Hitler.

But the ousting of Blomberg in 1938 was very important to Hitler. It gave him an efficient and seemingly aboveboard way to get control of the armed forces. Yet he still had to overcome those who believed that Werner Freiherr von Fritsch, commander-in-chief of the German army, should be appointed to fill Blomberg's position. Fritsch was the logical successor, the man most of the other military officers wanted in the slot. Hitler, however, was determined to add the title of minister of defense and its authority to his own so that he could personally command the armed forces. He would find a way to rid himself of Fritsch as he had Blomberg.

Himmler came to his aid this time. Himmler showed Hitler a dossier indicating that Fritsch once had been an associate of a homosexual blackmailer.

"It's all scandal at the moment," Stahlenberg continued in her diary. "The commander-in-chief of the army is supposed to have had an affair with Bavarian Joe, a notorious homosexual. There are many versions and many stories, of course."

The entrapment and ouster of the pathetic Fritsch by Hitler was carefully planned and executed. Five years earlier the NSDAP had appealed for each of those able to give assistance to the poor to feed one less-fortunate Berliner during the winter. Fritsch had volunteered, and his charge had been Fritz Wermelskirch, a young factory worker. Later the boy had become a thief and bragged to his associates that he had as a friend a high-ranking military officer who would protect him from the law. When Fritsch heard this, he severed all relations with Wermelskirch, who later joined the Hitler Youth. Then, in 1937, a homosexual blackmailer named Otto Schmidt was arrested and testified that one of the men who had had sexual relations with him was Fritsch. Shown a photograph of the commander-in-chief of the army, he verified that Fritsch was the man he was talking about. When Fritsch was told about Schmidt's accusation, he was furious. He said it was a lie.

Hitler summoned Fritsch to the same library in which he had fired Blomberg. Fritsch's own notes on that encounter were obtained from Soviet sources long after the end of the war.

"I was eventually called in at about 8:30 P.M. The Führer immediately announced to me that I had been accused of homosexual activities. He said he could understand everything, but he wanted to hear the truth. If I admitted the charges against me I was to go on a long journey and nothing further would happen to me. Göring also addressed me in the same vein. I emphatically denied any kind of homosexual activities and asked who had accused me of them. The Führer replied that it made no difference who the accuser was. He wished to know whether there was the slightest ground for these allegations."

Fritsch, racking his brain to think who might make such a false charge, fell right into Hitler's trap.

"It must've been that Hitler Youth." He meant Wermelskirch.

Hitler was basing his flimsy charge, his excuse to get rid of Fritsch, on the testimony of the homosexual Schmidt. When he heard Fritsch mention a boy in the Hitler Youth, he didn't bother to ask any further questions about the meaning of the officer's statement. He just added the charge of homosexual activity with a member of the Hitler Youth to Schmidt's accusation. After that Fritsch never had a chance. Following further rigged questioning by the Gestapo, he was dismissed as commander-in-chief of the army and as a potential candidate for Blomberg's position of minister of defense. Disgraced, he volunteered for front-line duty when the war started and was killed near Warsaw on September 22, 1939. He had courted death.

And his replacement as commander-in-chief of the army? Hitler decided he would appoint General Walther von Brauchitsch to the position and summoned him to the Chancellery to announce his decision. Trouble again. Brauchitsch was grateful for the appointment, but he had a problem, he told the Führer. He wanted to marry a divorced woman, Frau Charlotte Rüffer. Go right ahead, Hitler said. But, Brauchitsch continued, he was financially embarrassed and his present wife wanted a sum of money before she would give him a divorce. By this time Hitler was growing tired of women, homosexuals, prostitutes, and German generals. Angrily he agreed to pay the first Frau von Brauchitsch 1500 marks a month if she granted the divorce quietly. She gave her consent when the general added to this stipend the lump sum of 20,000 marks, which he borrowed from the Nazi treasury. So Hitler bought himself a new commander-in-chief of the army.

It was much easier and cheaper to fill Blomberg's position. He appointed himself supreme commander of the armed forces.

Of course army men didn't own exclusive rights to sex scandal in the Third Reich. The navy managed to hold its own. Lieutenant Commander Alwin-Broder Albrecht was Hitler's naval adjutant in 1938. The 35-year-old naval officer was married to a young schoolteacher from Kiel who didn't crawl between the sheets of her husband's bed exclusively. According to several letters received by Erich Raeder, commander-in-chief of the navy, she was a very familiar figure around the navy garrison where her husband had formerly been stationed, and in 1938 she was living with a wealthy civilian. Raeder, always protective of the German Navy's reputation, ordered Albrecht to go on leave. Hitler wasn't informed of Raeder's order and was upset when he discovered his adjutant missing. After several inquiries he learned the reason and immediately summoned Raeder to the Berghof to explain the situation.

Instead of agreeing with the naval commander-in-chief that Albrecht should be dismissed because of his wife's actions, Hitler demanded to see Frau Albrecht. Undoubtedly he was curious, and since he too enjoyed meeting young women, Hitler's motives were probably as much personal as official. Raeder reacted angrily, and the argument lasted for more than an hour. Finally Hitler bellowed, "How many of the navy wives now flaunting their virtue have had affairs of their own in the past. Frau Albrecht's past is the concern of nobody but herself. The Blomberg case was quite different. He deliberately married a woman who committed immoral acts for cash and other considerations."

The stiff-backed Raeder didn't change his mind. He told Hitler that the Führer would have to choose between Albrecht and Raeder. Hitler shrugged his shoulders and told Raeder to do what he wanted. The following day Frau Grete Albrecht was brought to a guest house on the first level of the Obersalzberg, near the Berghof. Hitler was driven to the guest house, where he stayed with Frau Albrecht for nearly two hours. What went on there isn't known, but after the private meeting Hitler decided that his naval adjutant had made a fine choice of a wife. Just how she had convinced him wasn't revealed.

In an effort to effect a compromise and save face for the angry naval commander-in-chief, Hitler dismissed Albrecht as his naval adjutant but then immediately appointed him his personal adjutant. Raeder retaliated by refusing for several weeks to appoint a new naval adjutant. Relations between Hitler and Raeder deteriorated after the Albrecht escapade until Raeder was retired on the Führer's orders on January 30, 1943.

Raeder seemed to have a knack for getting involved in the sexual adventures of Hitler's henchmen. Reinhard Heydrich, head of the Reich Security Service and a specialist in Nazi terror, was earlier a naval lieutenant. While he was an outstanding officer, he was also an outstanding womanizer with an insatiable sexual urge. He had female friends in every port, every city, according to one of his fellow officers, in every farmhouse—quite an accomplishment for a man usually stationed near the water. In 1930 Heydrich became engaged to a young woman, Lina Mathilde von der Osten, whom he had rescued when a boat overturned. His engagement raised strong protest among his other lady friends, especially one blonde whose father was a friend of Raeder's. Since the father was also on the board of directors of I.G.-Farben the giant chemical cartel and had a great deal of influence beyond his friendship with Raeder, Heydrich was tried for conduct unbecoming an officer before a naval court of honor. Raeder was judge and jury in the case, and the good-looking, arrogant Heydrich didn't have a chance. He was kicked out of the navy . . . but he didn't marry the IG-Farben director's daughter. Six weeks later he was hired by Heinrich Himmler and began his reign of terror as head of the Reich Security Service. The misfired love affair that resulted in Heydrich's being cashiered from the German Navy ultimately cost thousands their lives. Heydrich's brutality became legendary.

Hitler had a standing order that his staff obtain his permission before marrying, but as the Blomberg affair indicated, this order could mean many things. He insisted on seeing photographs of the prospective brides and spent a great deal of time studying the pictures, presumably with pleasure. He seemed also to operate on a principle he expressed early in the summer

Reinhard Heydrich, head of the Reich Security Service and a specialist in Nazi terror, was involved in sex scandals. *(National Archives)*

of 1933: "In making Germany great, we are also entitled to think of ourselves. We have no need to cling to bourgeois notions of honor and reputation. Let these well-bred gentry be warned that we do with a clear conscience the things they do surreptitiously with a guilty one."

One of the few times that Hitler denounced a bride selected by a staff member without outsiders first having registered complaint was when his trusted chauffeur, Erich Kempka, married. Although he had given Kempka permission to marry, Hitler had never met the prospective bride. When he did meet her, he was furious. He berated Kempka for marrying a woman who was "too little German," too modern, and too well acquainted with Italian and Hungarian embassy personnel.

"I'll give you some good advice," he told Kempka. "Get a divorce. I, the Führer, am not sure anymore who is my friend and who is my foe."

Kempka knew that if he didn't divorce his new wife, Maja, he would be sent to the front lines. Yet he was deeply in love with her. With a 24-hour deadline set by Hitler for him to make his decision and to get Maja out of the Reich Chancellery area, Erich came up with a solution. He divorced his wife, moved her into a home near by, and continued to live with her when he was off-duty. Hitler never said another word about the matter. He was satisfied. In his mind this illicit arrangement was preferable to marriage.

Two of the men closest to Hitler were among the greatest womanizers in the country. Joseph Goebbels and Martin Bormann were Hitler's intimates until the end. Each assumed a work load at least as great as that of any other NSDAP official. But neither permitted his responsibilities or ambition to thwart his sexuality. The styles under which Bormann and Goebbels operated, however, were very different. Bormann was discreet. Goebbels didn't give a damn about discretion and incurred the wrath of Hitler on several occasions.

Martin Bormann was often called Hitler's "evil genius" and "the brown eminence" behind the Führer's throne. His rise to power began with the death in 1931 of Hitler's niece, Geli Raubal, under mysterious circumstances. Bormann took charge of the potentially explosive incident and made sure it didn't blow up Hitler's political career. He suppressed all evidence connecting Hitler with Geli's death. It was Bormann who arranged for her body to be buried in a Catholic cemetery in Austria despite the fact that her death was officially listed as a suicide; and it was also "the brown eminence" who helped keep Hitler from ever again becoming entangled in quite such an affair. After Hitler, Bormann was undoubtedly the most mysterious of the Nazi leaders, and he was certainly one of the most important. He achieved his power through his close daily association with Hitler and by reason of the wall he gradually built around the Führer. Only those whom Bormann permitted were able to get through to speak with Hitler. And mystery surrounds Bormann yet. Even today it is not certain whether he is alive or dead.

It is known, however, that Bormann had one of the most unorthodox marriages of any in the Nazi hierarchy. His wife, Gerda, was the daughter of Walter Buch, who had been chairman of the NSDAP court that Hitler had set up in 1926 to maintain party discipline. Frau Bormann was a devoted Nazi, in theory and in practice. She agreed wholeheartedly with Hitler's belief that German women should provide the Third Reich with as many children as possible. She bore "the bull," as she called her husband, ten offspring, more than any other wife in Hitler's inner circle. But she wasn't satisfied that she had done her part, and she encouraged Bormann to produce more children out of wedlock in order to help Germany outpopulate the despised non-Aryan people. A letter of January 21, 1944, from Bormann to Gerda details an affair with his mistress, whom he identifies as "M." Most husbands, if involved in such an adventure, would go to great lengths to keep it secret from their wives. Not Bormann. He states, in part:

You can't imagine how overjoyed I was. She attracted me immensely. And in spite of her resistance I kissed her without further ado and quite scorched her with my burning joy. I fell madly in love with her. I arranged it so that I met her again many times and then I took her in spite of all her refusals. You know my strength of will, against which M. was of course unable to hold out for long. Now she is mine, and now—lucky fellow!—now I am, or rather, I feel doubly and unbelievably happily married.

Frau Gerda Bormann, Martin Bormann's wife, was overjoyed that he kept a mistress. She pleaded with "the Bull," as she called her husband, to impregnate the mistress too. *(National Archives)*

Such a letter to a wife could be considered motive for murder
or, at least, the instigation of a divorce suit. To Gerda Bormann, it was an inspiration. Her January 24, 1944, response to
her husband's letter contains this thought:

You will have to see to it that one year M. has a child and the next
year I so that you always have a wife who is mobile. Then we'll put
the children together in the house on the lake and live together and
the wife who is not having a child will always be able to come and
stay with you in Obersalzberg or Berlin.

The strange relationship that ensued between the Bormanns
and M., Manja Behrens, continued until the end of the war. If
Hitler was aware of the arrangement, he didn't interfere, probably because Bormann was so circumspect in his private affairs
that there was no public embarrassment to the Führer.

Joseph Goebbels, on the other hand, flaunted his love affairs
for all to see; and he had a wife who, although a devoted Nazi,
was not so liberal minded as Gerda Bormann. In addition,
Hitler was very fond of Magda Goebbels, and Magda Goebbels loved the Führer. Goebbels' affairs with women were notorious throughout Germany, and his house in the Paulsbor-
nerstrasse in Berlin was known to Berliners as "the love nest."
Although Eva Braun was once invited to a luncheon with
Goebbels at the house, by Eva's account Goebbels was wise
enough not to make a play for Hitler's mistress.

"The room in which so many actresses have lost their virtue
does not look depraved," she said. "More like a woman's. If
you are alone with Joseph there is no service. He has arranged
that quite shrewdly for his many private adventures. He merely
presses a button and the circular table disappears through a
trap door in the floor very slowly. Down below they put the
next course on it and the table appears again. Most practical,
especially if you want to be alone."

Goebbels was very frequently alone with his women in the
luxurious house in Berlin, but actually he was wholly indifferent to the notoriety of his amours. "Affairs of the heart are
the least dangerous because they're the most natural," he often
said. "I have no need to bow down before the false bourgeois
morality."

Sometimes Goebbels allowed his increasing influence with Hitler to overshadow his good judgment. Pauline Kohler was a witness to one such incident at the Berghof.

"I saw Goebbels arrive, but out of the car there stepped not his wife, but a very attractive blonde with an exciting figure," said Kohler. "She was a Viennese and a very minor star, but also the star of Goebbels' life for the moment. She wore a long sable coat that must have cost thousands of marks. She entered the Berghof and was taken to a room adjoining that of Goebbels. Neither of them saw the Führer until dinner that evening. As they entered the dining room Goebbels led her up to where Hitler was standing and introduced her. Hitler ignored her."

Hitler demanded to know where Magda Goebbels was that night, and Goebbels said she had been too ill to make the trip. Hitler went to his study immediately and called Berlin to check on Magda Goebbels' health. When he discovered that she was fine, he insisted that she fly to Berchtesgaden the next morning. He told her his private plane would be waiting for her in Berlin.

"That done, he went back to where Goebbels was shifting about uneasily and announced that the Viennese would find an excellent meal served in her room in a few minutes," Kohler explained. "She left after breakfast the next morning and Magda arrived shortly afterwards to be greeted by an effusive Hitler and a sulky husband."

Goebbels' most serious "error of love" was his decision that he preferred a stylish young Czech actress, Lida Baarova, to Magda. The very beautiful Baarova had been on the rise to stardom since her appearance in the film *Barcarole* in 1934. Goebbels, as dictator of the German film industry, had noticed her. By 1937 he decided that she was the woman he wanted most of all, he laid siege to the young actress. At first she thought she was just another romantic interlude in his life and acted accordingly, without qualm: She was accustomed to sleeping her way to opportunity. It surprised her to discover that the relationship was to be serious and lasting.

"Sometimes he played the piano for hours and I listened to him," she said. "No man ever brought me such a feeling of undiluted romance and fascination."

By this time all of Germany was aware of the love affair and, because of Goebbels' inner-circle status, relished the gossip. All except Hitler. He clamped down on Goebbels for two reasons. First, Hitler was very fond of Magda Goebbels; second, he didn't want one of his top officials publicly tarnishing the reputation of the NSDAP hierarchy. Hitler felt that his Nazi intimates could do what they wanted privately, but in public they acted as "model" Nazis or paid the consequences. Of course a character reference from Hitler would hardly qualify the subject for model citizenship in most countries of the world; but in his Germany it was his definition that counted. When Hitler discovered that Goebbels' affair was not going to burn itself out, he acted. He met with Magda Goebbels at the Eagle's Nest on October 21, 1938, and listened as she revealed her view on the Joseph-Magda-Lida triangle. Two days later both Magda and her husband were summoned to the Eagle's Nest. Very bluntly he told them he wanted them to remain man and wife and he wanted an immediate end to the Baarova affair. He assigned his aide Julius Schaub to break the news to the film star, to tell her the affair was over. Hitler also arranged for Mussolini to offer Baarova, through the Italian film industry, a role in a movie to be shot in Italy.

The Goebbels had no choice but to agree to Hitler's edict, but neither Joseph nor Magda was happy. Magda had fallen in love, or so she thought, with Karl Hanke, a handsome official of the Ministry of Propaganda; she too had an affair to break off. A short time later, when the Nazi inner circle attended the Wagner festival at Bayreuth, Hitler forced the Goebbels to share the same bedroom. This upset Hanke, who went in tears to Albert Speer. That night at the opera house the production was *Tristan and Isolde,* and Magda cried throughout the performance. The next day a disgusted Hitler told them both to leave.

The reconciliation ordered by Hitler in 1938 lasted until the end of the war, when Joseph Goebbels, Magda Goebbels, and their six children died with Hitler in the Berlin bunker.

Hitler was surrounded by men who often placed sex a close second on their priorities list. Indeed, some let it creep ahead of their Nazi party responsibilities.

Heinrich Himmler, the stern Reichsführer of the SS and leader of the Gestapo was as devoted to Third Reich doctrines as Hitler himself. He also seemed devoted to his wife Marga. Heydrich's wife described Marga Himmler as "a narrow-minded, humorless blonde female, always worrying about protocol. She ruled her husband and could twist him around her little finger. Size 50 knickers. That's all there was to her."

If true, that was masterful "twisting": Himmler's cold cruelty and self-devised methods of mass murder and terror gave him a reputation as a man without sentiment. Pauline Kohler, who saw Marga Himmler once at the Berghof, said, "She was a woman of rather faded prettiness with an acid tongue and severe narrow lips. I did not see her smile. I doubt if she can. But Heinrich obviously found her to his taste."

Not exclusively. Most of his entourage were certain that Himmler was under the thumb of his wife, but they were wrong. Himmler had a mistress, a pretty young secretary from Cologne named Hedwig Potthast. He even considered divorcing his wife and marrying Fräulein Potthast, but on observing the Goebbels fiasco, which had so angered Hitler, Himmler had second thoughts. Instead of divorcing Marga, he established a second home. On February 15, 1942, his mistress bore him a son; two years later there was a daughter. Borrowing 80,000 marks from Bormann, Himmler built his mistress and their two children a home at Berchtesgaden-Schönau, not far from the Berghof. Since Himmler was discreet, Hitler never disturbed either of his two families.

Another problem-Nazi for Hitler was Robert Ley, although he felt the fellow provided some humor at times. Ley, who headed the German Labor Front, stuttered and drank excessively. The combination often produced effects that caused Hitler to laugh so hard tears came to his eyes. In fact Hitler learned to mimic Ley very well and often amused the inner circle around the fireplace at the Berghof with his mocking portrayal of the drunken labor chief. But it bothered Hitler to hear about Ley's habit of ripping the clothes from his pretty wife to show others her firm body. She called him a wild beast and told one group of party-goers as she stood nude: "He treats me outrageously. He'll end by killing me one day."

A year later she committed suicide. If Ley was remorseful, he didn't show it. He promptly moved in with a pretty young Estonian girl. Hitler said nothing.

Julius Streicher, the notorious Jew-baiter, was famous among Nazi officials for his huge collection of pornographic literature;

Left to right: Japanese Foreign Minister Yosuke Matsuoka; Inge Ley, wife of Robert Ley; Robert Ley, Labor Front chief. Ley habitually ripped the clothes from his wife at parties to show others her firm body. She eventually committed suicide. *(National Archives)*

the sexual gratification he received from horse-whipping prisoners, especially women; his affairs with young actresses; and his country house, with its special love chamber for his mistress, Anni Seitz. He paid for the house by melting down golden wedding rings confiscated from non-Nazis in his district.

Ernst Udet, the famous World War I flier whom Göring appointed chief of the Technical Office of the Air Ministry, was so busy drinking and chasing women—including Leni Riefenstahl, the beautiful actress and director who was Hitler's favorite filmmaker—that he permitted the Luftwaffe to deteriorate. Some have viewed this deterioration as an important reason for the Luftwaffe's defeat by the Allies, a defeat that opened the path for the invasion of the continent.

One of Hitler's cronies even managed to get the Führer to threaten to change the divorce laws in order to extricate him from a complex romantic entanglement. Hermann Esser, Hitler's first minister of economics after the Nazis came to power and later a senior official of Goebbels' Ministry of Propaganda, had two sons by his wife Therese before he decided one woman was not enough. He promptly took a mistress, a

Frau Strassmeir. Unfortunately she didn't satisfy all his needs either, and during one of his excursions outside her bed and his wife's bed, he contracted gonorrhea. The mistress was thoughtful. She immediately notified Frau Esser of the situation, thereby forcing Hermann Esser to look elsewhere for comfort. He became acquainted with Anna Bacher and moved in with her. She bore him three children. About this time Esser became aware of the problems his superior, Joseph Goebbels', had had with Hitler over the Baarova affair, and Esser became frightened. He filed for divorce, and on December 23, 1938, it was granted. However Frau Esser dissented, and the entire case was reviewed by the Berlin Court of Appeal.

Worried, Esser appealed to Hitler, who reminded the Reich minister of justice of paragraph 55 of the new Nazi marriage law. This paragraph explained that if a marriage was deemed broken and its restoration unlikely because the petitioner declined to be reconciled with his wife, then the divorce was not only morally justified but consistent with the interests of the

Left to right: Third Reich pornographer Julius Streicher. Gauleiter of Franconia. headquartered in Nürnberg: Robert Ley: and Heinrich Himmler. SS chief. Himmler built a home near the Berghof for his mistress and their two children. *(National Archives)*

national community—especially if there were illegitimate children and the petitioner wished to marry the mother of the children. When the court still hesitated to rule in Esser's favor, Hitler sent a warning.

"Should the courts, in applying paragraph 55, not concur with this interpretation, on which the Führer based his original consent to the law, there would be no alternative but to consider a change in the wording of the ordinance." In addition Hitler reminded the court of an earlier decision by Reich Legal Director Hans Frank, a decision obviously inspired, if not dictated, by Hitler himself: "Judges have no right of review over decisions by the Führer which take the form of a law or ordinance. Judges are also bound by other decisions of the Führer insofar as they express an unequivocal determination to make legal rulings."

That was clear enough for the court. Esser was granted his divorce immediately.

It is little wonder that the Führer was also called the "love dictator."

10

The Mysterious Doctor

Given the sexual wonderland in which the ruling Nazis lived, it is little wonder that Hitler selected as his personal physician a specialist in skin and venereal diseases.

Dr. Theodor Morell, Hitler's "Liebarzt," has been the subject of a great deal of controversy since the end of the Third Reich, just as he was during the years he served the Führer. Most observers considered Morell a "quack." His habits of personal hygiene were sickening. He was an alcoholic, and his speech was inarticulate. Why did Hitler surrender his person, against virtually unanimous advice, to such a man? Did Morell gradually reduce Hitler to a mental and physical wreck, a man who couldn't make decisions, whose judgment was seriously impaired, whose sex life was destroyed? If so, why? These and many other questions have perplexed historians since 1945, and only now, as formerly classified information has become available, is it possible to answer many of these queries.

Morell was born in Traisa, a small village in upper Hesse, in southwest Germany, on July 22, 1886, three years before Hitler was born. his father was a local schoolteacher, and his mother came from a well-to-do farm family. Morell attended a preparatory school at Lich and a teachers' seminary at Friedberg. He taught school for one year at Bretzenheim, near Mainz. When he decided that he wanted to become a physician, Morell attended the University of Giessen, the University of Heidelberg, and, later, the University of Grenoble, in France. After graduation he studied at l'Institut d'Accouchement Tournier, in Paris. One of his first jobs was ship's doctor for the Wöehmann Line. He also served in this capacity with the Hamburg South American and North German Lloyd lines.

Morell entered private practice at Dietzenbach but he closed his office there on entering the German Army as a surgeon during World War I. When the war ended, he decided he had had enough of small-town medical duty and went straight to Berlin. There he opened an office where he specialized in electrotherapy and treatment for diseases of the urinary system. Morell treated many patients who were members of the Inter-Allied Commission overseeing defeated Germany, and his success soon made his name well known throughout the Berlin area. So well known was he that he was offered a post as physician at the court of the Shah of Persia and a similar position with the King of Rumania. He declined both in favor of staying in Berlin. By this time, however, he discovered that there was real money to be made by treating celebrities and other wealthy persons suffering from venereal diseases—far more money than by continuing his former speciality of electrotherapy and urinary system disorders—especially if he kept secret the names of the his clientele and their problems. Before long he was prospering through his discreet treatment of appreciative patients whom Morell had spared both the ravages and the stigma of their disease. The doctor had geniune business acumen, too. He was an expert in foreign currency exchange rates and made a small fortune in such money-changing.

When Hitler became chancellor in January 1933, however, Morell suddenly discovered he had a problem. In appearance he somewhat resembled the Nazi stereotype of a Jew, and the fact that he treated so many Jewish patients in his office, which was located on the fashionable Kurfürstendamm in Berlin, made him suspect by those now in power. He therefore joined the NSDAP during the latter part of 1933, knowing that before he would be issued a membership card, his background would be investigated thoroughly. He was correct. He was cleared of all suspicion that he was Jewish and became a Nazi of good standing.

By this time he had quite a following among Berlin stage, film, and NSDAP people,—all of which groups suffered high rates of venereal disease. So Morell wasn't surprised when he was summoned to Munich to treat Heinrich Hoffmann, the Führer's photographer, in 1935. Nor was he surprised when he discovered that the Nazi had gonorrhea. Morell had soon cured the photographer with sulfonamides and returned to Berlin, where he promptly forgot about the matter. Hoffmann didn't forget, however. He was extremely grateful, since he had re-married a short time before he discovered he had the disease, and the discovery had rendered him frantic. His cure so amazed and pleased him that when he visited the Berghof, he related to Hitler how skilled he thought Dr. Morell was—with-out, of course, telling the Führer the nature of the disease he himself had suffered. But Hitler was uninterested in Morell, until May 1936, when his longtime chauffeur, Julius Schreck, died of meningitis. Hitler was at Hoffmann's home in Munich, discussing the sad turn of events, when Morell stopped for a visit with the photographer. Hoffmann introduced the doctor to Hitler, and during the ensuing conversation Morell intimated that if he had been summoned to treat Schreck, he could have saved his life.

This statement aroused Hitler's interest, not so much because of the lost opportunity to save his chauffeur's life, but because of his worry about his own health. For a long time he had been convinced that he was seriously ill. He had a constant stom-achache, slept badly, and thought his heart often beat too fast and too hard. When his throat began bothering him, he was certain he had cancer. And he suffered from flatulence, which was embarrassing and worrisome. Hitler periodically studied medical dictionaries in search of a folk cure of his various ailments. Ultimately he decided that a vegetarian diet would probably help. It didn't. Finally, on May 5, 1935, Professor Carl von Eicken operated on Hitler's throat and removed a polyp from his vocal cords, assuring Hitler after the operation that there was absolutely no indication of cancer.

Hitler still wasn't convinced. Nor was he convinced when Professor von Eicken reexamined him in the Chancellery, two days before Hitler met Morell for the first time. Eicken's report stated:

Consultation at the Reich Chancellery in conjunction with Dr. Brandt. (Führer suffering from) a roaring in the ears for several days, with high-pitched metallic sound in the left ear at night. Ears: no abnormalities observed. Hearing: more than six meters to each side. Obviously overworked. Preoccupied (chauffeur Schreck). Sleeps very little—can't get to sleep. (I recommend:) evening strolls before retiring to bed, hot and cold foot baths, mild sedatives. Time off. Always feels better at the Berghof.

After talking with Morell at Hoffmann's house, the Führer had decided to permit Morell to examine him; perhaps the Berlin physician would be able to help him with his various health problems.

Hitler had given up on the other doctors. He told Morell: "You are my last hope. If you can get rid of my stomach pains I'll give you a fine house."

Morell wasn't modest. "I'll have you well and fit again within a year."

Morell was a type of man who usually disgusted Hitler. He was much too fat, had a swarthy complexion and slick, black hair, and wore thick-lensed glasses. Worse than his physical characteristics, which were the opposite of Hitler's Nordic model, were Morell's personal habits. He was filthy and evil smelling, and his eating habits were disgusting. But Morell had one thing going for him: By late 1937 his treatments had made Hitler feel well for the first time in years. Hitler decided he could overlook the faults of the doctor if Morell could cure the ailments that had plagued him for so long.

Two days after New Year's, 1937, at the Berghof, Morell first examined Hitler thoroughly. He decided that the Führer "was suffering acutely from gastrointestinal disturbances and had difficulty with his diet. A swelling was noted in the [lower] portion of the stomach, the left lobe of the liver was found to be enlarged, and a region of the right kidney was causing pain. An eczema on the left leg was noted which apparently was related to the upset digestion."

Morell immediately had a fecal examination made by Professor Dr. Nissle, director of the Bacteriological Research Institute, in Freiburg. The report from Nissle laid the intestinal problem to the presence of dysbacterial flora in Hitler's intestinal tract and explained that it should be replaced by an emulsion of a strain of coli communis bacillus that had the property

Hitler at the Brown House, Nazi headquarters, in Munich. Until Dr. Theodor Morell treated the eczema on Hitler's left leg, the Führer was for many months unable to wear boots. *(National Archives)*

of colonizing the intestinal tract and that, incidentally, Nissle himself sold under the commercial name of Mutaflor. Morell promptly prescribed 1 to 2 capsules of Mutaflor, to be taken by mouth after every morning meal. Hitler's digestive system began to function more normally, the eczema disappeared within about six months, and he began to gain weight. He was delighted. In September he made Morell guest of honor at a NSDAP rally, to which for the first time in months, Hitler could wear boots.

The Mutaflor caused very little controversy in medical circles when Morell described it, but some of the doctor's other remedies raised a great many eyebrows. To relieve the accumulated gas in the Führer's stomach and intestines and the embarrassing flatulence, Morell prescribed "Dr. Koster's Antigas Pills," two to four every meal. The contents of these pills were a matter of great controversy among the other doctors and may have changed the course of history by their cumulative effect on Hitler. In 1937, however, the Führer was grateful for the relief the pills gave him. In his estimation Morell was the greatest physician in the Third Reich; and throughout the next eight years, despite increasing criticism of Morell from all corners of Germany, Hitler didn't change his mind. Wherever Hitler went, Morell also went. The more pills Morell gave him, the happier he was. And he never tired of telling his intimates that Morell was one man who lived up to his promises. He had told Hitler he would cure him within a year, and he had done exactly that. Hitler didn't realize though, that the treatment that initially made him feel so much better was ultimately to aid in his downfall.

Morell was also a help to Hitler in other ways at the beginning of their association. In March 1939, when Czechoslovakian President Emil Hácha met with Hitler at the Chancellery in Berlin, Morell was present. Hácha had flown to Berlin for medical consultation about his heart condition; but after the niceties of protocol, Hitler ignored the Czech President's health and told him bluntly that German troops were poised to invade his country. He pressured the old man to sign a surrender document, telling him that if he didn't, hundreds of bombers would be over Prague at daylight the following morning.

Hácha resisted, but the strain was too much. Around 3:00 A.M. he had a heart attack. Hitler summoned Morell immediately, fearing the Czech President would die on his hands. Morell gave him an injection, and Hácha began to recover within minutes. In fact he revived so quickly that Hitler had little trouble getting him to sign the surrender and to telephone Prague with instructions not to oppose the invading German troops. Hácha was so grateful for Morell's help that he remained friends with him for years and often sent the pudgy doctor presents. He also acquired a supply of the prescription with which he had been injected at the Chancellery that fateful morning, and he used it the remainder of his life. He outlived Hitler.

Eva Braun and Albert Speer both visited Morell with their health problems, but not often. Both thought he was much too dirty and careless. During the Führer's state visit to Italy in 1938, Eva Braun accompanied the official party, but she was rarely in personal contact with Hitler during the visit. He didn't want the Italians to know he was keeping a mistress. Morell and his wife were in a group with Eva Braun the day they visited an Italian sloop to watch a parade. The crowd was large, and in boarding the vessel Eva received a serious shoulder injury. Whether the injury was an accident or an attempt upon her life is still conjecture, but Morell treated her immediately. He also stayed with her in Italy for nearly two weeks after Hitler and the remainder of the official Nazi party had returned to Germany. Hitler was very appreciative of Morell's tender care of his mistress, and the doctor's position in the Führer's inner circle was now more secure than ever.

The Morell-Unity Mitford case was the beginning of a strange episode that has never been revealed fully. Unity Mitford was an English aristocrat and a close friend of Hitler's. Some historians believe she was in love with the Führer and thought that through her efforts she could aid both Hitler and England. Others think she was spying on Hitler for English officials. When, on September 3, 1939, war was declared by France and England on Germany and she realized she had failed, Unity Mitford went into the Englischer Garten in Munich and shot herself in the head. She didn't kill herself, but the severe temple wound paralyzed her nervous system. For months she lay in coma. Hitler sent the best available doctors to Munich to treat her, including Morell, but the effort was useless. Finally Hitler made arrangements to send her back to England via neutral Switzerland, and Morell was ordered to accompany her. This December 1939 trip to Switzerland was a turning point in the life of Adolf Hitler, although neither he nor Morell was aware of it at the time.

After Unity Mitford had been placed under the care of a waiting English doctor in Switzerland, Morell took a short vacation. Zurich was a beehive of intelligence agents, both Axis and Allied, but the doctor ignored that. He decided that while in Switzerland he would make certain that Swiss medical circles were aware he was Hitler's personal physician. A Swiss physician who learned his identity tipped off Allen W. Dulles, who was already involved in counter intelligence for the U.S. and spent considerable time in Switzerland. Fearing that Morell would be suspicious of an American, Dulles had a former German police officer from Munich, who had escaped from Nazi Germany after denouncing the NSDAP in 1935,

Members of the Berghof "gang." Eva Braun. Hitler's mistress. is at his left: Bormann is at the far right of the photograph: in the back row Speer is second from left. and Dr. Morell is the man with glasses. Allied agents managed to incorporate ever larger doses of strychnine into the pills Dr. Morell gave Hitler. *(National Archives)*

make friends with the unsuspecting doctor. The German defector learned about the antigas pills that Morell prescribed for Hitler and discovered that Morell was interested in opening a firm in Switzerland, officially or unofficially, to produce the pills. Morell wasn't satisfied with purchashing them from another firm at a discount; he wanted to make a profit. Dulles arranged for the German defector to open a small pharmaceutical firm in cooperation with the greedy doctor.

From the company's opening day the slow poisoning of Hitler was undertaken. A trace amount of strychnine properly belonged in the pills, but the amount of the poison was increased gradually with each shipment. Not until late 1944, when Dr. Karl Brandt and Dr. Erwin Giesing became suspicious and had the pills analyzed, was the secret discovered. Hitler disbelieved the charges made by Brandt and Giesing, and they were lucky to escape with their lives.

At least one other person was suspicious of Morell. In an interview at Rupoldingen, Germany, on September 4, 1948,

Frau Franziska Braun, Eva's mother, told about her visits to the Berghof.

"One day we were having pork," she said. "I was pleased because I had not eaten pork for a long time and I told the Führer. He said that he was sorry that he couldn't eat it too but Dr. Morell didn't allow him. Everybody hated Morell and even Eva tried to get rid of him. She didn't want him to touch her after her first visit to him. She called him the 'injection quack.' I often heard her tell the Führer that the injections Dr. Morell was always giving him would poison him, but Hitler didn't agree. He always said that he felt so wonderful after the injections. In my opinion Dr. Morell was a British agent who wanted to dope Hitler so he couldn't think properly."

Frau Braun had come close to the truth. Morell was a dupe of the Allies. The test he gave each shipment of Anti-gas Pills from Zurich was not thorough enough to detect the slight increase of strychnine that was effected each time. The anti-nazi agent also added atropine to the pills, and when conferring in later years with Morell in Switzerland, he encouraged the doctor to use still other drugs to treat Hitler. By 1944 Morell was prescribing 28 different drugs for the Führer. Some were used every day, while others were administered only when needed. Some of the substances took effect rapidly. Glucose, for example, was absorbed quickly and produced a feeling of

Dr. Karl Brandt, left, tried to warn Hitler in 1944 that Dr. Morell was slowly poisoning him, but Brandt was lucky to escape with his life when Hitler disbelieved the charge. *(National Archives)*

well-being in the Führer. It also caused him to deal with situations very differently than he would have done without the injection. Constant medication over a period of years, encouraged by the German defector and others in Zurich, upset Hitler's physiological balance to such an extent that he became dependent upon drugs that are normally harmless and none habit-forming.

"After the effect of the injections wore off," Frau Braun explained, "he would flop more and more. One could notice that they harmed him. The last year he was not normal anymore in his thinking and reasoning."

Traudl Junge, his secretary, was with him at the Chancellery, the Berghof, the Brown House, and the various military headquarters, and she was amazed at the number of drugs administered to Hitler by Morell.

"The Führer took an unbelievable number of drugs," she said. "We had to give him five different pills either before or after meals. The first pill was to stimulate the appetite; the second to stimulate the digestion; the third was to stop flatulence; and so on. Besides, every day Dr. Morell came moaning and groaning to give the Führer his customary wonder-working injections."

Hitler seemed to ignore the fact that Morell himself had several health problems that the doctor wasn't able to control. He suffered from a bad heart, but none of his injections helped discernibly. He was extremely heavy, but his injections for slimming were a complete failure. At the daily afternoon tea he would eat much more than anyone else; then, as Hitler gave one of his usual monologues to those assembled for the snack, Morell would go to sleep. A soft snoring would be heard, and it stopped only when Hitler addressed him. Morell would awaken with a jerk and assure Hitler that the Führer's remarks were certainly accurate and important, although he hadn't heard a word said. Hitler was never angry with the fat doctor, as he would have been with other members of his circle if they had dared to fall asleep while he was talking. Instead he treated Morell as a child. He always spoke about him with sympathy and kindness. He trusted him explicitly and often said, "Without Morell I would already be dead."

One episode can be deemed to suggest that Morell may indeed have been aware that the drugs he injected into Hitler and gave him orally were dangerous. When Morell himself became very ill in 1944, he had to take to his bed and couldn't treat Hitler. His assistant had to take over. It was a severe blow to Morell. He seemed almost insanely jealous and continually checked with his assistant to make certain that there was no change in the Führer's daily treatments. Hitler, instead of being suspicious, was gratified that Morell felt so distressed over his inability to personally treat his master. Hitler even tried to comfort him. Within a short time, however, Morell was back on his feet and busily following Hitler around with his pills and needles.

Morell disagreed at least once with Hitler, but only Eva Braun was aware of it; Morell didn't have the nerve to tell Hitler. The Führer often conjured up harebrained schemes, some of which may have been brought on by Morell's drugs. In this particular instance he had devised a method by which Eva Braun could retain her youth and beauty. Twice a week she was to use a night-pack of raw fresh veal and once a week take a bath in warm olive oil. Hitler told her that she should take special care of her breasts and hips. He banned massages and also expressed a dislike of paraffin packings; he was convinced both caused cancer. When Eva Braun told Morell about Hitler's home remedy for aging, the doctor said it was pure nonsense. She suggested he tell that to Hitler, but he didn't have the courage . . . and neither did she.

Morell's treatment failures with other members of Hitler's circle didn't faze the Führer. As Eva Braun complained, "I don't believe Morell. He is such a perfect cynic. He experiments with all of us as if we were guinea pigs." This was evident in a second case involving Heinrich Hoffmann. Hitler enjoyed having Hoffmann with him because of the photographer's storehouse of jokes and his generally pleasant conversation when he was sober. When Hoffmann became ill in the autumn of 1944 and went to Morell for an examination, the obese doctor informed him that he had paratyphus B, a dangerous typhus bacillus, in his blood and that he would have to stay away from Hitler indefinitely. Hitler had a horror of germs and quickly concurred in Morell's decision. So Hoffmann wasn't able to visit Hitler for several months despite the fact that Hoffmann went to three different hospital laboratories and each verified there was no trace of paratyphus. Hitler just shrugged his shoulders and defended Morell when the error was disclosed.

Albert Speer had been troubled with a pain in his knee for some weeks in 1944, and finally he was admitted to a hospital. Morell was consulted, and he promptly recommended Vitamultin-Calcium injections. The following day Speer was near death, and it took the efforts of three other doctors to save him once they had diagnosed his main problem—a pulmonary embolism.

This was the medical expert on whom Hitler depended. And Morell's questionable medical theories and treatments, encouraged and augmented by the subterfuge of Allied agents in Switzerland, slowly and inexorabably took their toll. The Führer, who had once valued longtime friendships and associations, became more and more unapproachable. He became enraged when opposed. His handwriting deteriorated until it was very difficult to read. He reached a point at which his memory began to fail and he was no longer in control of his intellect. Major achievement seemed beyond him. "The outstanding commander of the early part of the war," said Field Marshal Gerd von Rundstedt, "has become a second-rate architect where military planning is concerned."

As early as 1938 Hitler was seriously worried about his physical condition. He drew up a private testament in May 1938 and put all his papers in order. He was concerned about his health despite the "improvement" in his condition that he credited to Morell. When he ordered the September 1, 1939, invasion of Poland, Hitler was suffering from fatigue and mental disorientation. If he had been in full control of himself at the time, it has been suggested, he might have adhered to his original plan to start the conflict in 1941, when the German armed forces would have been better prepared.

On December 21, 1940, while he was secretly preparing his attack on the Soviet Union, Hitler felt so bad that he underwent a complete examination by Morell. He hated such examinations and permitted them only when he was seriously concerned about his health. His blood pressure was too high, and he had an enlarged left ventricle and a heart murmur. Despite the Morell drugs and injections, he still had his digestive problems and intermittent stomach pains. Early in 1941 he developed edema in his calves and shins, for which Morell prescribed ten drops weekly of Cardiazol and Coramine. These drugs were stimulants, aggravating Hitler's heart problems and strongly influencing his general behavior. He became more aggressive and argumentative, made ridiculous remarks, and issued promises that were outside the bounds of possible fulfillment. It was while he was in this physical condition that Hitler launched Operation Barbarossa, the invasion of the Soviet Union. The move led, ultimately, to his defeat. In July 1941, one month after launching the invasion of Russia, he had to break off a conversation with Ribbentrop because of a severe pain in the area of his heart. The following month he was still suffering from nausea, shivering spells, diarrhea and dystentery. When Smolensk fell to Hitler's troops that August, he had a real reason to be elated, but under Morell's drugs he was so sedated that he showed no emotion whatever.

By 1942 it was quite evident to his generals and his inner circle that Hitler was changing physically and mentally. Himmler no longer considered him "normal" and even queried his own personal physician, Dr. Felix Kersten, whether he considered the Führer mentally ill. Around this time Hitler's associates noticed a bronzing of his skin, and doctors who saw him became suspicious of Morell's injections and pills. Morell stated that the discoloration was a result of Hitler's being afflicted with gastroduodenitis complicated by an obstruction of the bile flow. Hitler took his word, and the matter was not investigated again until 1944. By that time it was much too late for Hitler. During much of the African campaign of 1942 his irrational military orders may be traceable to his condition. Many feel that his interference resulted in Rommel's defeat by Montgomery at the gates of Egypt, a defeat that cleared the way for the American invasion of Algeria and the subsequent Allied victory in French North Africa.

Only those who were with Hitler daily were fully aware of

the change in the man, and they did not know the reason for it. Some days he was completely "normal," the old Hitler. Other days he was a thoroughly changed man, and they feared him. Even Eva Braun was confused. She noticed that more of his hair was turning gray, that he seldom stood straight, as he always had during his early years in power, and that his energy was waning. One day when she and Traudl Junge were alone, Eva asked, "What do you think about the Führer's health, Frau Junge? I don't want to ask Morell. I don't trust him and I hate him."

Traudl Jung didn't commit herself. "I know less about him than you. You can deduce things he doesn't tell me."

Later that day Frau Junge heard Eva Braun reproach Hitler because he was so bent in posture. Hitler shrugged and said he had heavy keys in his pocket.

He continued to deteriorate mentally and physically during 1943 and 1944. At a conference of his leaders on May 20, 1943, attended by Erwin Rommel, Walter Hewel, Rudolf Schmumdt, Wilhelm Keitel, and others, he completely ignored verified data about the strength of Allied forces in the Mediterranean area. When asked about transferring the Hermann Göring Division from Sicily, he considered only two factors, which in the end were really irrelevant: ferries and willpower.

"It's not the ferries that are the decisive factor; the decisive factor is willpower," he declared.

The Allied troops he ignored destroyed the division and captured all of Sicily by August of that year.

During the summer Morell doubled the hormone injections and added another drug, Prostakrin. When Hitler didn't improve, the doctor went back to his old reliable, the antigas pills, and increased the dosage by one third. Soon afterward, if Hitler stood too long, his knees would tremble noticeably, and it was difficult for him to hold a cup of coffee without spilling it. His nerves were very bad. When he met with Admiral Miklós Horthy, regent of Hungary, at Klessheim Castle, near the Berghof, he completely lost control of himself. He insulted Horthy, his forced collaborator, accusing him of planning to surrender his country to the Allies. The aged Horthy hurried out of the castle, and Hitler ran after him, urging him to return.

Only by faking an Allied bombing raid and laying down a smoke screen, which prevented Horthy's private train from leaving, did the unstable Führer get the regent back to the castle for further, more productive discussions.

A few days later Hitler withdrew military divisions from the western front where his commanders were expecting the Allies to invade, and from the Ukraine, as the Russians massed for an offensive. His generals protested, but Hitler took no advice from anyone . . . except medical advice from Morell.

The attempted assassination of Hitler on July 20, 1944, at Wolfsschanze, his military headquarters, in East Prussia, was to affect Hitler's health the remainder of his life. The plot to kill Hitler enlisted several high-ranking military officers, including General Henning von Tresckow, chief of staff in the army group center on the Russian front; General Erich Hoepner, commander of an armored force, who had been dismissed by Hitler in 1941; General Friedrich Olbricht, head of the supply section of the reserve army; General-Karl Heinrich von Stuelpnagel, military governor in France; Colonel Hans Oster, chief of staff of the Abwehr; and Field Marshal Erwin von Witzleben. Younger officers involved included Lt. Colonel Claus Schenk Graf von Stauffenberg, the man who actually carried the bomb into the military headquarters. Field Marshal Erwin Rommel, the popular German officer; General Adolf Heusinger, operations chief of the army high command; and Field Marshal Günther Hans von Kluge, army group commander in France, were aware of the plot but did not take an active role. Some civilians also helped.

Shortly after 10:00 A.M. on July 20 Stauffenberg was admitted through the heavily guarded gate at Wolfsschanze. He had been summoned to give Hitler a report on replacements for the troops. Inside his briefcase he had a bomb, its timer set for several minutes after the conference was scheduled to begin. He placed the briefcase underneath the table as near to Hitler's position as possible and then excused himself to make a telephone call. Stauffenberg kept right on going, trying to put distance between himself and Wolfsschanze. Back in the room, as the conference began, Colonel Heinz Brandt couldn't find a comfortable spot for his legs because of Stauffenberg's brief-

case, so he kicked it to the side of the table farthest from Hitler
... and saved the Führer's life.

When the bomb went off one of the 24 men present was
killed outright, three died later, and several were seriously
wounded. Hitler's hair was set afire, his right arm was injured,
his right leg was burned, and his eardrums were damaged.
Morell, who was with Hitler at the conference, was uninjured.
Hitler could barely hear, and his balance was affected. That
evening while walking, he twice strayed off the path through
the woods. Morell told him that the ear problem was minor and
would clear up in a day or so. Instead, the pain became severe,
and Dr. Erwin Giesing was summoned from a nearby field
hospital to look at the ear. He reported that the right eardrum
was badly ruptured and the inner ear had also suffered damage.
Morell was furious when he discovered another doctor had
been called, but Hitler patted him on the shoulder and told him
to calm down. Morell wanted to insert a hemostat, but for once
Hitler listened to someone else and did as Giesing suggested.
He had a drum cauterization the next day to stop the bleeding.
Meanwhile Morell treated Schmundt, Hitler's chief adjutant to
the armed forces, who had been seriously injured during the
assassination attempt; but the adjutant died.

Hitler's condition became progressively worse after July 20.
His right hand trembled continuously, he had an incessant
earache and a feeling of pressure in his head, and his voice
became hoarse. Dr. Giesing warned Hitler that many of his
problems, especially his severe stomach pains, were probably
caused by Morell's injections and pills. Hitler didn't agree, and
instead of reducing the number of injections and pills, he once
again increased the number of antigas pills he took daily.
However, Hitler didn't completely ignore Giesing's advice and
agreed to his prescription of a 10 percent cocaine solution to
help his head pains. By September, when he was planning the
Ardennes offensive, which became known as the Battle of the
Bulge, Hitler was so dizzy he had trouble standing. He also had
several spells during which his pulse was rapid and weak and
he broke out in a cold sweat. Morell was quick to give him
injections, which did provide temporary relief, but by the
middle of the month it was obvious that further treatment was

needed. He consented to Giesing's suggestions that he have X-rays taken of his head. The X-rays revealed nothing serious—except the fact that Morell couldn't read them. In front of an amazed Giesing he identified the cheekbones as the sinuses. This incident started the "doctors' revolution."

Finally one morning, when Hitler couldn't get out of bed, the four doctors who had attended Hitler at various times—Giesing; Karl Brandt, another personal physician of Hitler's; Dr. Hanskarl von Hasselbach, Brandt's deputy; and Karl von Eicken, the throat specialist who had operated on Hitler earlier—decided that the Führer should be told Morell's treatments were killing him. When Giesing noticed that the

Hitler and Dr. Brandt. in friendlier times. sitting in the winter-garden room of Haus Wachenfeld. (*Bundesarchiv*)

Führer took the antigas pills by the handful and that his skin and eyes were turning yellow, he had the pills analyzed. It was then that it was discovered the antigas pills contained two poisons, strychnine and atropine.

Dr. Brandt had been with Hitler's circle since he had saved the life of the Führer's niece, Geli, and a companion when they were in an automobile accident, and he was elected by the four doctors to present the truth to Hitler. He did so on September 29, 1944. Instead of being grateful for the warning, Hitler was angry. He dismissed Brandt immediately, and he was also furious with the other three doctors when he discovered through Bormann that they were involved. He retained Giesing for a time, because he believed the doctor had acted "professionally," but later he too was sent packing.

The "doctors' revolution" had its affect on Hitler, however. His trust in Morell began to waver, although he continued to take the injections and pills because of his dependency upon them. Finally, the day after Hitler's birthday celebration in the Berlin bunker on April 20, 1945, the strange patient-doctor relationship abruptly ended. Morell went as usual to Hitler's room in the bunker to give him his injections. Suddenly Hitler leaped to his feet and pointed toward the door.

"Morell, leave my room at once. You want to drug me so you can forcibly take me away from Berlin. That's what all of you want but I'm not going."

He ordered the shaken Morell to take the next airplane out of Berlin, which the doctor did. For the few remaining days of the Third Reich Hitler went without the injections and pills upon which he had depended for eight years.

11

Eva: The Secret Mistress

Eva Braun was the mystery woman of the Third Reich, the beauty Hitler kept hidden from most of his associates and the public. Even though they had spent many long hours at the Berghof conferring with the Führer, many of his generals first became aware of Eva Braun's existence on learning of her death. Yet for 16 years she was the most important woman in Hitler's life, a woman he frequently abused and ignored, a woman he loved as much as he could love any person. It was a strange romance, one of the most intriguing love affairs in history.

Eva Braun was born in Munich on the morning of February 7, 1912. Adolf Hitler was 23 years old at the time, a bohemian living at a hostel in Vienna and struggling to make a living by painting picture postcards. Eva's father, Fritz Braun, was a schoolteacher; and her mother, Franziska, known in the neighborhood as Fanny, was one of the more beautiful woman in Munich. When Eva reached the age of 15, Fanny Braun decided she should attend a convent school to acquire the education and social graces that would fit her for later life. Eva was sent to the English Sisters, a Catholic order in the small town of Simbach, approximately 60 miles east of Munich.

Eva, however, disliked the rigid rules of the convent school; she found the routine repetitive, dull, and, ultimately, unbearable. In the fall of 1929 she left and never returned. Since the only subject at which she had excelled was dancing, the English Sisters were not sorry to see her go. Back in Munich, Eva convinced her father that she should seek a job. Her personal appearance was now important to her; this meant new clothes, which her father could not afford. It was then she took the fateful step that led her to a life-and-death affair with Adolf Hitler. She accepted a job at Heinrich Hoffmann's photography shop, at 50 Schellingstrasse in Munich.

Heinrich Hoffmann was an excellent photographer who had apprenticed under his father and his uncle, both of whom had many patrons among royalty. He himself had worked with Hugo Thiele, court photographer to the Grand Duke von Hessen, in Darmstadt, and had also been associated with the prestigious studios Langbein, in Heidelberg, and Theobald, in Frankfurt. He was also a friend of Hitler's and the first photographer Hitler permitted to take pictures of him after his release from Landsberg prison. Hoffmann eventually became Hitler's personal photographer. In 1929, when the NSDAP was still years from power, this post didn't mean much. Later, however, it meant millions of Reichmarks and worldwide fame for Hoffmann.

Hoffmann was delighted to hire Eva, because she was young and attractive. He had another responsibility besides pho-

Eva Braun. her sister Ilse. and friends visiting Innsbruck. *(National Archives)*

tographing Hitler; he also provided him with female companionship. He maintained a list of women whom he could introduce to his friend Adolf whenever Hitler was lonely and bored, hoping that this favor would be remembered when Hitler assumed power, as Hoffmann was convinced he would. He plotted every move in his progressing friendship with Hitler. Hoffmann made certain that all photographs he showed him were flattering, and he destroyed the negative of all others. He often traveled across the country on a moment's notice if Hitler requested it. If Hitler was in Munich, Hoffmann made certain to go to the Café Heck, Hitler's favorite restaurant, in time to eat lunch with him. So when Hitler appeared at Hoffmann's studio one day not long after Eva came to work, the photographer made certain they met. Eva's mother, wanting to correct rumors that had arisen, later explained how Hitler and her daughter had met.

"All the stories about Eva's meeting with Hitler are quite wrong," Frau Braun said. "I know of a witness who worked with Hoffmann and who volunteered to testify in behalf of Eva if she ever needs such testimony. One day Hitler came into Hoffmann's office, which Hitler used for his work since he didn't keep his own office then. Eva was standing on a high ladder getting something from a high shelf. Hitler watched her and when Hoffmann saw he was watching, he introduced them as soon as Eva came down from the ladder."

According to Hoffmann, Hitler's eyes moved slowly up her long legs, appraised her hips, and finally stopped on her neatly brushed hair. He knew at that moment that his new clerk interested Hitler. He was disappointed, however, when he introduced her to "Herr Wolf," as Hitler wanted to be called at the time. Eva just smiled at him and turned away. He had anticipated that she would be overjoyed to meet the celebrated Hitler, and when she hardly changed expression, he was puzzled. After Hitler left, Hoffmann called Eva aside and asked, "Do you know that man?"

"Only that he is a friend of yours."

Hoffmann shook his head. "I mean, don't you recognize him? His name is not Herr Wolf. That is Adolf Hitler!"

"Who is Adolf Hitler?"

Hoffmann was mystified that anyone in Munich—or in all of Bavaria, for that matter—could be ignorant of the importance of Adolf Hitler. Frustrated with his new clerk, he walked away.

That evening at the dinner table Eva asked Fritz Braun about Adolf Hitler. That was the wrong question to ask in the Braun apartment in 1929. Fritz Braun considered Hitler a fanatic and opposed most of his political program. A personal matter made Eva's father dislike Hitler and the Nazi party even more: He had been proposed for promotion to assistant master of the school where he taught; but when the school officials, all Nazis, learned that Braun didn't belong to the NSDAP, they refused to recommend him for the advancement. So when Eva innocently mentioned Hitler's name that evening, her father became very angry.

"Hitler? I would not walk on the same side of the street with him. He is a fanatic."

Her father's comments made Eva curious to learn more about Hitler. The next day she studied the photograph file on him in Hoffmann's studio. The pictures fascinated her. Some showed women trying to break through guard lines to touch him, throwing flowers in his path, reaching for him as he passed in his Mercedes-Benz. There were photographs of him at the opera and the theater with glamorous actresses and fashionably dressed society matrons. Sometimes he was pictured in his uniform and highly polished boots; other times he had exchanged his slouch hat for a top hat. By the time she had finished examining the file, she had changed her opinion about "Herr Wolf." She hoped he would come to the studio again.

Because he was busy with his political activity, Hitler saw little of Eva for several months. Besides, he was spending much of his free time with his niece, Geli Raubal. When he did come back to Hoffmann's studio, however, Hitler was very friendly with Eva, and when he had left, Hoffmann joined her at the counter.

"I would like to have you come to the house tonight, Eva," he said. "Hitler is going to stop by and he asked that you come too."

After their first meeting in Hoffmann's home, Hitler often asked the photographer to arrange other meetings with Eva. As

Hoffmann told Hitler's personal adjutant, "I think he is interested in the young girl. Often when he intends to stop at our
house for an hour or so he suggests that I ask Eva to come over
because she amuses him."

Despite his ongoing affair with Geli Raubal, Hitler continued to see Eva and send her flowers, candy, and trinkets of
modest value. Hoffmann concentrated on promoting Eva as the
woman Hitler needed. He knew that if she became his mistress,
he would get a reward from his idol. The death of Geli Raubal,
in September 1931, moved Eva to the forefront of Hitler's
private life. Eva was quick to realize that with Geli out of the
way she had an opportunity to ingratiate herself more deeply
with Hitler. But despite the removal of the biggest obstacle to
her becoming Hitler's favorite woman, she still had a problem.
Her parents were very strict and continually checked on her.
Eva knew that if her father and mother learned she was associating with a man 23 years older than she and that the man
was Adolf Hitler, they would be furious. Because her father still
thought Hitler was a radical who would destroy Germany if he
ever came to power, Eva didn't dare even mention Hitler's
name at home. Only her older sister, Ilse, was aware of Eva's
feelings toward Hitler.

The strain of keeping her romance secret from her parents—
plus the frustration of learning the hard way that for Hitler no
woman had priority over the pursuit of power—began to tell on
her. She soon realized that loneliness and the waiting, always
waiting, for Hitler to visit her were an ordeal that could result
in personal tragedy. The summer of 1932 was a miserable one
for both Eva and Hitler. Hitler felt that he had lost his battle
for power, and Eva felt that she had lost Hitler. On the night of
November 1, 1932, Eva's depression got the better of her. Alone
in the Braun apartment, sometime after midnight she opened
the drawer of the night table beside her parents' bed, took out
her father's 6.35-mm pistol, stretched across the bed, and shot
herself. Her aim was poor. The bullet lodged near an artery in
her neck. Still conscious, Eva decided she did not want to die
after all. She telephoned Heinrich Hoffmann's brother-in-law,
Dr. Plate. The physician had her taken to a private clinic, where
the bullet was removed.

Hitler received the startling news from Hoffmann and hurried to the clinic, where Eva, for the first time in months, now had the full attention of the man she loved. He was properly concerned, and it was obvious that he was flattered she would do such a thing to prove she loved and missed him. This tragic gesture of love strengthened his ego when he most needed it strengthened. Eva was in the clinic for only a few days, and the wound healed completely, leaving no scar. Her desperate gamble paid off: Hitler now felt he had to watch over her.

"She did it for the love of me," he told Hoffmann. "I must look after the girl."

Her parents were, of course, upset, but Eva's explanation satisfied them. As Fritz Braun related the incident to his curious friends: "She got hold of my Browning and it accidentally went off. I asked her how it happened and she said that she wanted to see what a gun like the one Geli had used looked like. While she was examining it, the gun went off. That's all there is to it."

Eva was taking a nap on January 30, 1933, when her mother knocked on her bedroom door.

"Eva, wake up. I have news for you. Herr Hitler has come to power."

Eva was delighted with the news, but she had to be careful. Her parents realized that she was acquainted with Hitler through his visits to the Hoffman studio, but they did not suspect that Hitler and Eva were having an affair. Now Fanny Braun was quick to tell the neighbors that "Eva knows the chancellor" and to garner any prestige that news might bring to the Braun family, but she was completely unaware of the personal relationship. And Eva was worried about how she was going to break the news. She needn't have been concerned that publicity would come from Hitler, because he had no intention of allowing the citizens of Germany to find out about her. As he told Hoffmann, "The *chère ami* of a politician must be quietly discreet." Certainly, however, he thought about Eva on the night of his victory. Even though the scene in Berlin was hectic, with crowds jamming the Kaiserhof Hotel, where he was meeting with his party officials, and thousands of telephone calls lighting the hotel switchboard, Hitler placed a personal telephone call to Eva in Munich.

Yet his demand for secrecy about the relationship didn't solve Eva's problem concerning her parents. As soon as he returned to Munich, for example, Hitler insisted that she come to his apartment and stay all night.

"He received many women but none of them ever stayed overnight," Frau Anni Winter, his housekeeper, explained. "Eva Braun was the first."

This overnight stay and many other visits left Eva more and more entangled in her attempts to conceal her true relationship with Hitler. Her father could not understand her irregular hours and why she "stayed overnight at a friend's house" so often. Nor did he understand why Eva insisted on having her own telephone in her bedroom and allowed no one to answer it but herself. Gradually the web of deception became too complicated, especially when Hitler invited her to the Berghof for extended stays. She finally decided she had to bring Fritz and Fanny Braun face-to-face with Adolf Hitler. Patiently waiting for an opportunity, she was rewarded one Sunday when she heard her father suggest to her mother that they drive to Berchtesgaden and look at Hitler's mountain home on the Obersalzberg. Eva had already planned to accompany Hitler and his entourage to the Berghof that day. She knew that her parents often stopped at the Lambacher Hof, in the small town of Lambach, for tea and a snack. If she could get Hitler also to stop there, perhaps she could finally introduce him to her parents.

Eva's plan worked out very well as far as the "chance" meeting was concerned. The Brauns decided to stop in Lambach on the return trip to Munich. At the town, however, they learned that the road was guarded by SS troops checking all automobiles. The troops explained that the Führer was traveling through Lambach and strict security measures had been ordered. The Brauns were permitted to drive to the Lambacher Hof to get tea and a snack. They had just finished their tea and were about to leave when a shiny Mercedes-Benz drove up to the main entrance of the café and Eva stepped from the back. Fanny Braun could not believe her eyes. She hurried over to the automobile to make certain. "Eva, you?"

When Fritz Braun joined them, he demanded, "What does this mean?"

The intimacy of Hitler and Eva Braun is evident as they walk near the Berghof. Eva once complained. "Sometimes he doesn't even take his boots off. and sometimes we don't get in the bed. We stretch out on the floor. On the floor he is very erotic." *(National Archives)*

Very calmly Eva said, "I have just come from the Berghof." Without another word to her parents she went into the café. A few minutes later another Mercedes-Benz stopped at the Lambacher Hof and Hitler got out. As the townspeople cheered and crowded around Hitler's car, Fanny Braun edged away. Now she understood. Eva was more than just a casual friend of the Führer's. Fritz Braun had stayed by Hitler's car, and when Hitler neared him, Braun extended his hand.

"I am Eva's father."

He expected an explanation from Hitler, but the Führer gave none. All he said was, "Where is your frau?"

While Fritz Braun searched the crowd for his wife, Hitler walked into the café. When Herr Braun finally located his wife, she insisted that they leave immediately. Just as they reached their automobile, however, Hitler's aide came onto the porch of the Lambacher Hof.

"Where are the Braun parents, please?"

Frau Braun turned her back on the inquiring aide and whispered, "I don't want to go inside."

Fritz Braun convinced her it would be best if they did. They were ushered into the private dining room where Hitler and Eva were eating. Hitler immediately stood up and motioned for Frau Braun to sit next to him. After they sat down, Hitler immediately began talking, but only about trivial subjects, not about Eva and himself. Frau Braun was very attentive and waited patiently for Hitler to speak about her daughter, but he never did. When it came time to leave, Hitler took her hand and kept her in the dining room after the others had left.

"He squeezed my hand and looked straight at me as if he could see into my soul," she told her husband later. "He never said a word."

Frau Braun had the impression he was trying to comfort and reassure her but didn't know how to express his feelings. Eva and Hitler got into his Mercedes-Benz and drove off. It was obvious that Eva was indirectly telling her parents she intended to live her life as she pleased.

When she returned home that night, her father was waiting for her. "Is it true that you are the Führer's mistress?"

Eva didn't answer the question. She merely asked, "If you want, I'll leave."

Fritz Braun turned and walked away.

The Braun parents slowly became accustomed to the fact that their daughter was the mistress of the most powerful man in Germany. At first they didn't like it, but it soon became apparent there were certain advantages for them in Eva's status. They were invited to the Berghof, Fritz Braun became a paymaster in the German army, and, as Hitler made certain, Eva's parents were treated properly by his associates.

As for Eva, Hitler still ignored her completely for long periods and exhibited all the characteristics that women detest in a lover who puts his ambition ahead of his romance. Fanny Braun understood her daughter's frustrations and tried to comfort her. In May 1935 Eva was desperate. She hadn't seen or talked with Hitler for three months, although she had seen photographs of him going to the theater or the opera with other women. On May 28 she sent him a letter, which she mentioned in her diary for that date.

May 28, 1935—I have just sent him a letter, one that is decisive for me. Will he consider it as important as I do? Well, I'll see. If I don't get an answer by ten o'clock tonight I'll take my twenty-five pills and lie down peacefully. Is it a sign of the terrific love [of] which he assures me that he hasn't spoken a kind word to me for three months? Agreed, he has been busy with political problems but haven't things eased off? And how about last year when he had lots of worries with Röhm and with Italy and still found time for me? True, I'm not in a position to judge whether the present situation isn't much worse but after all a few kind words at Hoffmann's would hardly have taken much time. I fear there is some other reason. It's not my fault. Certainly not. Perhaps it is another woman although I doubt that it is the Walküre. But there are many others. What other reasons could there be?

Lord, I'm afraid I won't get an answer today. If only someone would help me. Everything is so hopeless. Maybe my letter reached him at an inopportune time or maybe I shouldn't have written it at all. Whatever it is, the uncertainty is much worse than a sudden end would be.

Dear God, please make it possible that I speak to him today. Tomorrow will be too late. I have decided on thirty-five pills so as to make it dead certain this time. If he would at least have someone call up for him.

The ultimatum wasn't answered by the deadline to which Eva had committed herself. Early on the morning of May 29 she swallowed two dozen Phanodom tablets. Within a few minutes she was unconscious. Fortunately, her sister Ilse decided to return an evening gown she had borrowed, and when she found Eva prostrate on the bed she immediately called her employer, Dr. Marx. Within two hours the doctor had purged Eva of the drug and she was safe.

This second attempt at suicide completely changed Hitler's attitude toward her. He arranged for Eva to move into a small apartment on Wiedermeyerstrasse, in the Bogenhausen district of Munich, so that he could see her without her parents supervising her every move. Later he purchased her a villa across the river Isar from his own apartment in Munich, and he provided her with an automobile and a chauffeur. He even bought her two Scottish terriers, which she named Stasi and Negus. For the first time since her affair with Hitler had begun six years earlier, Eva was truly happy. Hitler's private show of affection made up for the "back street" secrecy of the affair. She was never seen in Munich society but lived in complete retreat, amusing herself by reading; studying her paintings by Midgard, Gallegos, Popp, Fischbach, and Rosl; sunbathing; caring for her beloved dogs; and exercising. She was careful not to gain weight—much to Hitler's dislike, because he preferred voluptuous women. She also spent a great deal of time applying cosmetics, tinting her medium-blond hair different shades, and manicuring her nails. She had plenty of time to do all this, because Hitler's visits were not frequent during this period.

When she became "queen" of the Berghof, however, she saw Hitler much more often and more intimately. During her early visits to the Obersalzberg, Angela Raubal, Hitler's stepsister and mother of Geli, was hostile. Eva said little, realizing that she could alienate Hitler if she was not careful. She bided her time and waited for an opportunity.

It came in 1935 at the Nürnberg rally. Eva stayed at the

A laughing Hitler and a pensive Eva with Hitler's dog. Blondi. on the
Obersalzberg. *(National Archives)*

Hotel Kaiserhof, as did Frau Raubal and the wives of high-ranking Nazi officers. Frau Raubal was openly insulting. She called Eva a "disgraceful blonde" who openly chased the Führer and accused her of being worse than a streetwalker. Eva remained silent, hopeful that at least one of the other women would tell her husband about Frau Raubal's overt hostility and the matter would be relayed to Hitler.

It was. When Hitler asked Eva what Frau Raubal had said to her, Eva at first refused to tell him. He insisted. She began to cry and then related the abusive statements Frau Raubal had directed at her in front of the other women. Hitler was furious that his stepsister would dare meddle in his private affairs. As soon as the rally ended, he had his chauffeur drive him directly to the Berghof, where he told Frau Raubal to pack her belongings and leave immediately. He then hired Frau Endres, of Munich, to take care of the Berghof. Afterward Eva was definitely the queen of the Berghof, and everyone knew it.

Why didn't Hitler and Eva marry then? The expulsion of Frau Raubal from the Berghof sharply upgraded Eva's status. Those of the inner circle who had previously sided with Hitler's stepsister now found themselves in an uncomfortable position. One such person was Julius Schaub, Hitler's longtime adjutant. He decided he would find out just how well he should treat Eva, the woman he had previously ignored or derided. During one of their intimate conversations, he mentioned to Hitler that the others at the Berghof thought he planned to marry Fräulein Braun.

Hitler stared at Schaub for a moment, then said, "I will never marry her. I don't have the time. I am always away and cannot behave to a wife as a married man should."

Schaub was delighted with Hitler's answer . . . until Hitler added: "I am very fond of her."

Eva's real value to Hitler was her ability to comfort him, to soothe his shattered nerves, to calm his anger, and to divert his thoughts to more pleasant subjects when he was upset over a political or military matter. Eventually Hitler would not visit the Berghof unless Eva accompanied him. Before one of his periodic visits to the Obersalzberg, he would arrange for his plane or car or train to take Eva from her villa in Munich to the

Berghof, where she would be waiting for him. In addition Hitler arranged quarters for Eva in Berlin; she had an apartment in the so-called Führer—dwelling in the Wilhelmstrasse, and one in the Chancellery. She also began to accompany him to places other than Berlin, Munich and the Berghof. She stayed with him at Victoria Hostel in Stuttgart, the German House in Nürnberg, and the Hotel Dreesen in Godesberg. Of course, if Hitler was on official business she had to stay out of sight or pretend she was a secretary on his staff.

Hitler took care, as the years passed, to make certain Eva was recognized and respected properly within his inner circle. He personally gave orders that she should receive the salute reserved for the highest dignitaries and assigned bodyguards to accompany her everywhere. He also made certain she had money enough to buy whatever she wanted; and since Eva was obsessed with clothes, she was soon the best-dressed woman in the inner circle.

Sometimes the secrecy of Eva's status caused her annoyance. One day she and her younger sister, Gretl, went to the famous leather store Lederer, in Berlin. Eva was looking for a handbag, but an arrogant clerk, judging her less than affluent, showed her only the cheapest ones. When Eva pointed out a bag she liked, one that was in the window, the clerk shook his head and told her it was much too expensive. Eva became angry and demanded to see the manager. When the manager arrived, she bought everything in the display window.

"I want it delivered to the Chancellery this afternoon," she said, "and give the bill to the Führer's private secretary."

The frightened clerk and the stunned manager watched silently as Eva and Gretl walked out of the store and got into Eva's Mercedes-Benz, with its uniformed SS driver. The purchases were delivered promptly that afternoon, with a large bouquet of flowers from the manager.

It is easy to understand how Eva could handle Hitler. She was so much younger than he; a naturally passionate woman, she had virtually no inhibitions; and she had a good deal of time to prepare for Hitler's visits, since he was constantly beset by problems brought on by his ambitions. If, as some evidence indicates, Hitler was exotic in his sexual behavior, there is no

Hitler and Eva with the daughter of Eva's friend Herta Schneider. Because she was seen so often with Hitler and Eva, many persons thought the girl was their daughter. There is evidence that Hitler did have a child, born December 1, 1939, by Göring's wife, Emmy. *(National Archives)*

suggestion that this troubled Eva deeply. However, early in the
affair she honestly believed that she was merely a sex object to
him. The last paragraph of the entry in her diary for March 11,
1935, indicates her feelings:

He is only using me for very definite purposes. When he says he loves
me he takes it about as seriously as his promises, which he never
keeps. Why does he torture me so much instead of just putting an end
to the whole thing?

It is known that Hitler often asked Morell for injections to
make him more virile, so obviously he was having trouble
keeping up with his mistress sexually. Eva explained, in another diary entry, that Hitler always wanted to undress her
himself. His strong hands made her "quite crazy," she admitted, but he couldn't really undress her because he simply was
not skillful enough. When they went to Achensee or Chiemsee
in Bavaria to relax, sometimes Hitler would have his SS troops
block off an area from the public and then insist that Eva swim
in the nude. Hitler himself never went into the water or wore a
bathing suit. Once, when Eva was undressing at the Chiemsee
he noticed she wasn't wearing any underclothes, and he roared
at her that she was behaving like a whore. Then he said, "It
must never happen again. You might fall down. How would
that look?"

Hitler enjoyed watching Eva take baths. He would sit beside
the tub fully dressed and observe her closely, "as if he wanted
to memorize every movement." Nudity fascinated him. Once
Eva was sunbathing at the Berghof on the upper balcony when
she noticed Hitler stepping out onto the balcony. She pretended
to be asleep. Hitler stood for a long time, very still, staring at
her naked body. Then he sat down by her side and caressed her
smooth skin very gently and softly. A few minutes later he
stood up and took a photograph, back view, explaining to Eva
later that he wanted such a view so that if the picture accidentally fell into the wrong hands, no one would recognize her.
Eva, however, was aware that Hitler collected photographs
such as the one he had just taken of her, that he used them as
sexual inspiration to help overcome any tendency to impo-
tency.

According to both Speer and Skorzeny, Hitler's lovemaking was "normal." Skorzeny explained that after the 1943 rescue of Mussolini from the Italian partisans, an operation Skorzeny personally led, Hitler invited him to the Reich Chancellery to receive the Führer's personal congratulations. He awarded Skorzeny the Knight's Cross and promoted him on the spot. Then he "rewarded" him in another manner.

"You have been away from your wife too long, Skorzeny, preparing for this rescue," Hitler said. "It is not good for a man to be away from his woman's bed that length of time. Go home and enjoy yourself and make your wife happy."

Later, when Skorzeny related these remarks to Eva, she nodded her head. "He understands. He understands," she told Hitler's commando chief.

Yet later, during an intimate conversation with Skorzeny, she admitted that Hitler was not *entirely* conventional when in bed with her. Sometimes he was discreet, other times direct and blunt. When they were talking and he asked if she wasn't "too hot in her clothes," Eva knew what he meant and they would go to his bedroom.

"But sometimes he doesn't even take his boots off," she complained to Skorzeny. "And sometimes we don't get into the bed. We stretch out on the floor. On the floor he is very erotic."

She gave no details.

As the war turned against Hitler, he became more and more gentle and protective with Eva and more and more brutal and violent with others. He forbade Eva to go to Munich as the Allied air raids increased, fearing she would be injured or killed. He didn't want her to go skiing, a sport she loved, because she might break her leg. Thinking she might slip and hurt herself, he even forced her to stop taking her long daily walks when the snow was deep. On July 20, 1944, when the attempt was made on his life by some of Hitler's military leaders, he demanded that Eva be notified immediately that he was all right. He didn't want her to worry. At the same time he demanded that his attempted assassins be found and executed.

Eva, of course, worried constantly about Hitler. She was concerned as a woman who had few material or political demands but continued the association with Hitler because she truly loved him. On December 10, 1944, when Hitler told her he was leaving the Berghof to go to Adlerhorst, his field headquarters near Ziegenberg, she tried to change his mind. Hitler's health was deteriorating fast. His hands shook; he had just had an operation on his throat in October; and Morell's drugs were slowly poisoning him. But Hitler insisted that he personally had to give his orders to the generals, because otherwise they would ignore his directives. When Eva told him his health was much more important to her than another victory on the war front, Hitler smiled.

"You are the only one who would say that. You are the only one who cares."

This was one of the most affectionate remarks Hitler ever made to her in public.

After the German counteroffensive had been beaten back in the Ardennes Forest, Hitler returned to Berlin to make his final stand. When Eva heard that he was at the Chancellery, she joined him.

"This time you will stay with me," she told Hitler. "I will take care of you. We will not part again."

On February 8,1945, after making up his mind that he would stay in Berlin to the end rather than go to the Berghof and try to escape, Hitler arranged for Eva to be driven to the Berghof. He had not told her of his decision to stay in Berlin but pretended he wanted her on the Obersalzberg to greet him when he arrived there later. Eva was reluctant to leave Hitler, but suddenly she changed her mind. Judging by her actions, she had learned or guessed that Hitler was never again going to the Berghof, that he was using a pretext to get her out of the besieged city to safety. Taking her two dogs and some of her personal belongings, including her jewelry and photo albums, Eva went to Munich. She put her villa in order, arranged for friends to care for her dogs, and visited her parents. She also made a special trip through the badly damaged city to spend a few hours with her close friend Herta Schneider and Herta's children, whom Eva loved.

Both Herta Schneider and Eva's mother told Eva that they would join her at the Berghof within a few days. Eva smiled but said nothing. Frau Braun said later that Eva was more quiet than usual during this final visit and that her farewell kiss was long and very affectionate. Franziska Braun's final words to her daughter were: "A stay on the Obersalzberg will cheer you up. It will be nice and quiet after Berlin."

Eva nodded and left the Braun apartment without another word. She didn't tell anyone that she had no intention of continuing south to the Berghof. She was going back to Berlin, back to Hitler.

12

A Day at Hitler's Berghof

On the Obersalzberg, more strikingly than anyplace else, Hitler led a double life. Part of the time he was the amiable, country host who came to the mountains to relax; the remainder of the time he was the commander-in-chief directing military and political wars on many fronts.

The Berghof, on the Obersalzberg was considered home by Hitler and he spent as much time as possible at this mountain retreat. What was it like to be invited there by him, to spend a day or so as his guest?

Traudl Junge, the private secretary to whom the Führer dictated his last will and his political testament when the end of the Third Reich was imminent, was first invited to the Berghof during the winter of 1941–1942. It was an exciting time for her and also a period during which she and other invited guests learned a great deal about Hitler's habits when he was "at home" and out of sight of the public eye.

She and Christa Schröder traveled on the Führer's private train from Hitler's field headquarters, at Rastenburg, East Prussia. The newest and youngest of Hitler's secretaries, Junge was briefed by her companions during the train ride. She was told that Eva Braun was the mistress of the Berghof and was to be acknowledged as such by all guests. Junge had heard a great deal about Eva Braun but had never seen her and was looking forward to the visit. She was also told that the Berghof was Hitler's private household and that all on the Führer's personal staff, including secretaries, were to consider themselves guests. They would eat with Hitler and be expected to conduct themselves in accordance with his daily routine. This was a privilege and a responsibility accorded only those on Hitler's personal staff. The remainder of the staff were housed in neighboring buildings on other sections of the Obersalzberg; and the departments of the Reich Chancellery and the army command were quartered in Berchtesgaden.

The private train stopped at a small village near Salzburg, where Hitler immediately transferred into his black Mercedes-Benz. Junge and the others got into cars waiting behind the Führer's vehicle, and the long line of official automobiles moved off in the night toward the snowy peaks in the distance. Hitler's Mercedes-Benz quickly raced off by itself, leaving the rest of the convoy far behind. As Junge's car neared the Berghof, she saw a long line of spotlights that reached up to a thousand-meter height, giving the entire mountainous area a spectacular appearance. Finally she saw the famed Berghof in the distance, its large windowpanes shimmering, reflecting the snow. Two lamps lighted the wide front steps of Hitler's home, and as the young secretary walked up the steps she was apprehensive, wondering what she would see and how she should act inside the Berghof.

"Hitler had arrived several minutes before we did," Junge said, "and had already disappeared into one of the rooms. His coat and his hat hung on the hooks in the wardrobe in the hall, and for the first time I realized that this was really and truly Hitler's home."

She was greeted by Frau Margaret Mittelstrasse, a pretty, small, resolute woman from Munich who was housekeeper of the Berghof. Frau Mittelstrasse escorted Junge through a wide, roomy entranceway that led to a small staircase. This staircase connected the new part of the Berghof with the older section that had been Haus Wachenfeld. The housekeeper showed Junge into a small, charming bedroom, painted blue and white, that contained a dressing table, a desk, and a bed. Fräulein Schröder, the other secretary, was given a room, done in red, directly across the hall. Near by was a large common bath.

The following morning Junge awakened early, dressed, and then tried to discover where she could eat breakfast. No one had told her where or when it was served. She cautiously went down the stairs she had climbed the night before. On the first

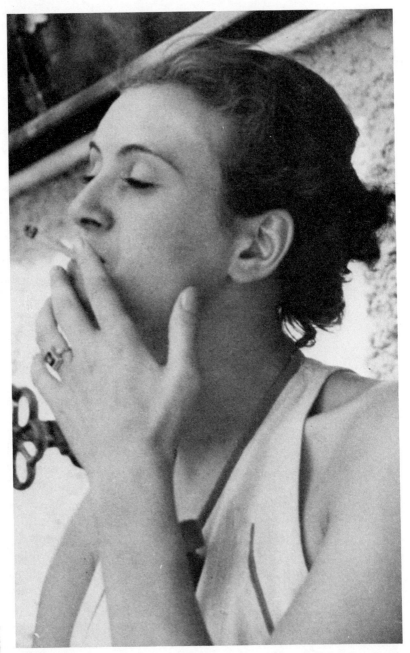

Hitler. who abstained from liquor and tobacco. didn't want his mistress to smoke. but Eva smoked anyway. *(National Archives)*

landing she found a door; behind it she heard the voice of Rudolf Schmundt, chief adjutant of the armed forces to Hitler. Since she feared she might interrupt a military meeting, Junge continued down the steps. At the bottom she found, to the left, a glass-windowed door. To the right was an exit to the court-yard. The glass doors led to a rustic living room containing a gigantic stove. Junge quickly backed out of the room, since there was nothing to indicate breakfast would be served there. She felt nervous, afraid she might accidentally wander into Hitler's study.

The forecourt at the bottom of the steps narrowed into a corridor illuminated by large windows. She walked down the corridor, turned, and found herself in the large vestibule through which she had entered the Berghof the night before. Seeing a large semicircular folding door, Junge opened it slightly and saw the famous conference hall, with its massive picture window. She decided to continue farther down the corridor. Passing the wide marble steps that led upstairs to Hitler's quarters, she came to another folding door and heard voices behind it. She entered the room and discovered that she had finally found where breakfast was served at the Berghof.

"No one had thought about my being at the Berghof for the first time," Junge said, "and for that reason I had to find my way to the dining room alone. It was an elongated room which took up a large part of the left wing, which had been added when Haus Wachenfeld was remodeled. The entire right side of the room was made up of large windows which afforded a view far into the Salzburg countryside. In the center stood a long table with armchairs. There was room for about twenty-four persons. At the front end the room widened to the right side to form a semicircular alcove and in the alcove stood a rather large table set for breakfast. And by this time I was hungry, very hungry."

The walls, furniture, wall lamps, and even the chandelier were made of pine wood of matching grain. A built-in cabinet with glass doors covered the wall opposite the large windows. A few expensive vases colorfully accented the predominant gold-yellow of the room. At the breakfast table Fräulein Schröder motioned for Junge to join her, Rudolf Schmundt, Karl-Jesco

von Puttkamer, Hitler's naval adjutant, and Walther Frentz, the
Führer's documentary photographer. There were tea, coffee,
cocoa, and fruit juice to drink; and different types of bread,
such as cracked wheat, whole wheat, and ordinary black bread,
were available. White bread was reserved for those with stomach problems. Marmalade was provided.

Smoking was not permitted in the breakfast room, so as soon
as the guests were finished eating, they quickly left to have an
after-breakfast cigarette or cigar outside. Junge ventured off
with Fräulein Schröder and Otto Günsche, another Hitler adjutant, to familiarize herself with her new surroundings. First
they climbed the wide marble steps to the first-floor corridor,
which was so broad it resembled a room. There were several
large windows and many valuable paintings on the walls of the
corridor, and fine sculptures and many beautiful gifts from
foreign statesmen were displayed along its course. A heavy
carpet deadened the footsteps of anyone walking in the corridor; the carpet had been placed there so Hitler would not be
disturbed. At the top of the steps a door to the left led to a two-
room apartment occupied by the servant on duty and the
chauffeur. Opposite this apartment was the small ironing room
of Eva Braun's maid.

Stationed in front of the next door to their right were two
Scottish terriers, sitting so still Fräulein Schröder at first
thought they were ornaments instead of real dogs. Stasi and
Negus were Eva Braun's beloved pets.

"They will sit there without moving until Fräulein Braun
awakens and greets them," Otto Günsche explained to the two
secretaries. "It is the same every day."

The next room was Hitler's bedroom. Between Hitler's bedroom and Eva Braun's was a bath, which had an entrance from
each of the bedrooms but none from the corridor. A large
folding door on the opposite side led to Hitler's study. The
adjutant motioned for the two secretaries to be very quiet as
they tiptoed past the study. Hitler didn't welcome distraction
while he was working.

The trio went back downstairs, and Junge found herself in
the rustic living room she had come upon before eating breakfast. Günsche explained that it was Hitler's previous living

The door on the left leads to Hitler's bedroom at the Berghof. A door in Eva Braun's bedroom also led. via a shared bath. to the Führer's room. *(National Archives)*

Hitler's library at the Berghof. Any guest was permitted access to the books. *(National Archives)*

room. Furnished in middle-class fashion, it reminded Junge of many homes in Munich. It was the only room in the Berghof that Junge and Schröder considered pleasant. The large stove had an inviting bench around it, while a square table, placed beside the window, offered a pleasant setting for a meal. The tablecloth was made of the same rustic pattern as the drapes and the upholstery of the bench, contributing to the cozy, lighthearted atmosphere of the room. At the opposite side of the room was a large bookcase. Junge and Schröder looked at the books inside, but none intrigued them. There were dictionaries, copies of literary masterworks that seemed never to have been opened, and, of course, a leather-bound copy of *Mein Kampf.* Junge learned later that any Berghof guest could borrow any book from Hitler's library.

A heavy velvet curtain separated the rustic living room from the large conference hall. To the two secretaries it looked just as it had on the picture postcards they had seen before their first visit to the Berghof. It was very large, monumental, like everything the Führer built. And it was austere, despite the thick carpet, the Gobelin tapestries, and the many other valuable articles that decorated the walls and the furniture. The room seemed too large for normal-sized persons. Through her many subsequent evenings spent in the room, Junge verified this initial impression. No matter how many persons were present, the room still appeared to overwhelm the guests.

Next to this large conference hall was the winter-garden room, through which one had to go to reach the terrace. The women loved this room. There were many flowers in it, brightly colored upholstered chairs and sofas, and little round tables. It was a fairly small room, about three-by-three meters, and two sides were glass.

Every guest, including Junge and Schröder, agreed that the most beautiful part of the Berghof was the terrace. It was a large, flat area paved with flagstone, and there was a stone rampart around it. Guests could look one way from the terrace and see Salzburg, the other and see Berchtesgaden. Straight ahead was the Untersberg, and in clear weather the cross on its peak was easily visible. The terrace ran around the entire winter-garden room and ended at the living-room window in a

The winter-garden room at the Berghof was a favorite with the female guests. It had many flowers and plants, brightly colored upholstered chairs and sofas, and little tables. *(Bundesarchiv)*

small paved court. This court extended around the back of the building and had as a natural wall the rocks of the area. It was a place where the women guests rested, talked, and sunbathed while waiting for Hitler to finish his conferences or his work in his study upstairs.

The secretaries used the rear entrance of the Berghof to go to the adjutants' offices, which were in a small building nestled against the rock-face just west of Hitler's home. On the lower floor there was a small office for the Führer's press chief and an office for Walther Hewel, Ribbentrop's liaison with Hitler. The upper story held office space for the chief adjutant on duty. This second floor also contained a rustic apartment consisting of living room, bedroom and bath for use by the adjutant. It could be reached by an outside wooden staircase that was picturesque but exceedingly treacherous when coated with ice in winter. A long, low building was connected to this small house; it contained several offices used by Hitler's staff. The secretaries' office was there, and neither Schröder nor Junge thought much of it.

"It was an extremely dull, ugly room," Junge said, "with very shabby furnishings. I think it was never furnished well because Hitler himself never entered it."

A wooden walkway ran the entire length of the building. It shut off the sunlight, contributing to the general gloom of the atmosphere inside.

Next to the secretaries' office was the dental clinic, commanded by Dr. Hugo Johannes Blaschke, Hitler's dentist. Blaschke had studied dentistry at the University of Pennsylvania, in the United States, and at the Royal Lental Hospital, in London, and had afterward opened his own office in Berlin. He often treated Göring, and in 1934 he was called to do some dental work for Hitler. He remained the Führer's personal dentist until the end of the Third Reich. The Berghof dental clinic had the utmost in modern equipment; and when Hitler needed dental attention he would usually have the work done at the Berghof, even if he had to return there from one of his other official residences or military headquarters. There was also a dental clinic at the Reich Chancellery, however, in case of emergency. Blaschke wanted to examine Hitler's teeth at three- or four-month intervals, because he felt their condition required constant supervision. The dentist didn't always have his way, though.

"In the years 1938–39 I didn't examine his teeth for more than a year. Whenever I called I was told that treatment was not possible at the time and that I should wait until notified. When I was finally called in the Führer was in pain because his upper left central incisor had an extensive caries. It was a difficult session because he was very concerned about the pain of the drill and he always demanded that I be cautious. I think he often took drugs to keep his teeth from hurting him and so he would not have to call me."

There was a barber in the building too, but he had very little equipment. There was also a large area that was used by the SS on watch at the Berghof for sleeping during their off hours.

Above the Berghof, toward the Platterhof and Bormann's house, was a very beautiful area of meadows, forests, and mountain streams. Only a few paths, well-tended, and a little road pierced the landscape of this section of the Obersalzberg, which was known as "Hitler's run." Hidden by trees from view of the Berghof was a little teahouse, which Hitler visited daily when he was on the Obersalzberg.

A complaint of most visitors to the Berghof was that they could not take their ease there. Only those persons who did not have to take part in Hitler's daily routine enjoyed the Berghof to the fullest. The others were restricted by the strenuous schedule that Hitler followed rigorously every day. Most of the morning the Berghof was very still and quiet; only the adjutants and the domestics were active then. About noon Hitler's "home" awakened. Automobiles began delivering generals and diplomats at the Berghof in preparation for conferences with the Führer. The beautiful terrace became crowded with men waiting to see Hitler, men who couldn't get along without their cigars or cigarettes and who knew they were not permitted to smoke inside. Sometimes the winter-garden room was jammed with orderlies carrying maps and briefcases, looking out of place among the flowers. As soon as Hitler appeared from upstairs, the generals, diplomats, and orderlies immediately entered the main part of the Berghof to await his pleasure. Before long the large, beautiful conference hall with the massive window became a place of violent arguments, serious deliberations, and life-or-death decisions.

Meanwhile more and more people showed up at the Berghof, people who had nothing to do with the military or political matters being discussed. They came in hopes of getting lunch sometime. Otto Dietrich, the Nazi press chief, and Heinz Lorenz, press secretary, came down from the guest house; physicians Morell, Brandt and Hasselbach arrived; and sometimes Hoffmann, the photographer, or the Braun parents would come. Also among the regular guests were Frau Anni Brandt; Herta Schneider, Eva Braun's friend; Frau von Below, the Luftwaffe adjutant's wife; and Gretl Braun, Eva's sister.

These guests were at the mercy of Hitler as far as lunch was concerned. They had to stay outside, or in one of the rooms other than the conference hall, while the deliberations proceeded. Often Hitler became so engrossed in discussion that he forgot completely about his guests and it was three or four o'clock in the afternoon before the last general or diplomat departed the Berghof. At that moment Hitler would walk the few steps from the conference hall to the living room, where by now the guests were assembled, still patiently awaiting lunch. Eva Braun would appear at about the same time, having been notified by an adjutant that the conferences were over. Hitler then kissed her hand and greeted everyone in the room whom he had not had a chance to speak to earlier in the day. While they awaited the summons to the table, there was always light conversation. Hitler often teased Eva Braun about her two small terriers, calling them "hand lickers."

Junge was amazed at Hitler's attitude: "It was fascinating the way Hitler could change character. A few minutes earlier he was in serious discussion about matters that often affected the entire world but when he entered the living room where the guests were assembled, he promptly forgot those matters and became a typical good-natured host who was entertaining guests in his house."

When it was time to eat, Heinz Linge, Hitler's manservant, would approach and notify the woman Hitler had selected to accompany him to the table that day. Orderlies would arrange the other guests in the proper order, and Hitler would then lead the way to the dining room, his honored guest on his arm. The Führer always sat at table facing the window, with Eva Braun on his left and Martin Bormann on his right. Directly across the table from Hitler was the honored guest of the day. This seating arrangement was constant. In the middle of the table there was always a beautiful flower arrangement. Strangely enough, Hitler never had flowers on the table at the Reich Chancellery or the Brown House. At the Berghof, however, where Eva Braun reigned, there were always flowers on the table. The table was set with Rosenthal porcelain that had a flower motif at the upper left. At every place setting the napkin was placed in a holder marked with the name of the person supposed to sit at that position. Hitler was very particular about such matters and often checked the table setting before a meal.

As soon as everyone was seated, the doors opened and two orderlies, carrying piles of warm plates, entered the dining room. Other orderlies removed the Rosenthal plates and replaced them with the warm ones, and the food was brought in. Linge brought a tray with the Führer's food, while other servants brought large bowls of salad for each side of the table. Two servants circled the table, asking each guest what he or she wanted to drink. After the salad and drinks were consumed, the next course was brought to the dining room. Most new guests were relieved when they saw the sauerbraten, or whatever else the main course might be. They knew then that they would not be restricted to the Führer's diet of oatmeal gruel, linseed gruel, and vegetable juices. Hitler had a passion for linseed oil. One of his favorite dishes, for example, was baked potatoes covered with cottage cheese that had been saturated with raw linseed oil. Eva Braun disdained Hitler's foods, although she too was careful about what she ate. She was very proud of her slim figure. Hitler often teased her about it. "When I first met you you were so nice and plump. Frankly, now you are too lean. A woman always says she wants to be beautiful for a man and then does everything to work against his taste."

The conversation at the table was casual. Often Hitler took the opportunity to tease his associates. One favorite target was good-looking, popular Walther Hewel, the young bachelor liai-

Hitler's birthday cake, in the foreground. His gifts cover the background tables. *(National Archives)*

son officer from the Foreign Office. For many years he had lived in India, and his anecdotes about his life there amused Hitler and the guests. Hitler once asked Hewel when he was going to write his book *From Bush Knife to Diplomat's Dagger.* The Führer also thought that Hewel should be married and constantly tried to pick a mate for him.

"Would you like a tree monkey from India for a mate?" he asked. Hewel just laughed.

Hitler wanted Hewel to marry Gretl Braun, Eva's sister, but Hewel wan't interested. Later Hitler pushed him discreetly toward Isabel Troost, the daughter of the famous architect Paul Troost, but Hewel didn't take this hint either.

Lunch usually lasted about an hour. The Führer then took his walk to the little teahouse behind the Berghof. If the weather was bad, he would go in a small Volkswagen. All guests were invited to join in the walk, but Hitler was not insulted if one did not want to go. The only requirement was that the same number of men went on the walk as women. Bormann almost always begged off; he believed that this was wasted time, because it didn't afford him the chance to talk business privately with Hitler. Eva Braun, however, loved to walk and always accompanied Hitler. The Führer would put on his soft, peaked hat, the only hat he did not put on straight like a lid, pull on a long, black rain cape or a trench coat, take his walking stick in one hand and Blondi's leash in the other, and start for the little teahouse. Hitler kept his dog on a leash because the area was a paradise for game and he didn't want Blondi harming the nearly tame animals. Eva Braun's two terriers often went racing through the high grass, barking loudly, but the grazing deer would merely look at them without fear or move a few steps to get out of their way.

The little teahouse lay on a flat area that fell away sharply to the north. It was a natural observation post. The scenery was beautiful, and Eva Braun almost always brought her camera along and tried to get Hitler to pose for her. She was the only person permitted to photograph him without prearrangement, but even she had problems. It was very difficult to get good candid shots of Hitler. His refusal to remove his hat left his face in shadow. Often he would wear sunglasses. After this picture-taking game between Eva and Hitler, the Führer and his guests would enter the teahouse. It was a round, stone building, very ugly on the outside, more like a silo or a small powerhouse. Inside there were a kitchen and several small rooms for the SS guard, servants, and other necessary personnel. The predominant feature, however, was the large, round tearoom, which could be entered both from the outside and from a beautiful hall that connected it to the servant's section of the teahouse. In the hall were several colorful upholstered chairs and little tables. There was also a telephone. The round room was very attractive. It had a domed ceiling, and its walls were of marble decorated with gold. Six large windows were on one side, and a huge, open fireplace was on the opposite side. In the center of the room was a round table surrounded by 20 upholstered chairs of beige and terra cotta, placed alternately by color. On the fireplace side were four soft, high-backed chairs for the Führer and his honored guests. Coffee or tea was served. Hitler himself usually had apple peel tea or caraway seed tea and fresh apple cake or biscuits. There was pastry from Berchtesgaden for the others.

It was very difficult to hold a conversation in the teahouse because of the breadth of the table. One either raised one's voice or gathered with others in smaller groups to chat more intimately. Eva Braun tried many times to get Hitler to permit films to be shown, in the teahouse, but he refused. Even when she told him she would select serious film, not light entertainment, he was adamant. He allowed records to be played in his presence, but he would not change his mind about viewing films.

"I can't see films during the war when the people have to sacrifice so much," Hitler repeatedly told Eva. "Besides I have to spare my eyes for looking at maps and reports from the front."

Usually, as soon as Hitler had finished eating and drinking, he fell asleep. The guests ignored him. Most of the men would rush outside for a smoke, often accompanied by Eva Braun, who smoked too. Eventually Hitler would awaken, listen to the conversation for a moment, and then take part in it just as though he had not been asleep. It was a ruse that fooled no one, but the guests refrained from commenting. A few minutes later Hitler would tell one of the adjutants to get the car, in which he would ride back to the Berghof. On the Obersalzerg he used a special-edition Volkswagen, a black convertible with black leather seats. It was, of course, driven by a chauffeur. Hitler never drove. There were other cars for guests who might want to ride back to the Berghof, but most preferred to walk.

On returning home Hitler would go to his upstairs rooms and take a nap before the evening session. The guests were free to do what they wanted during this period. Eva Braun often invited some of them to her room to show them films she had taken personally; or, ignoring Hitler's ban on showing theatrical releases, at his residences, she would show such movies in the basement rooms of the Berghof. Sometimes she and the guests would enjoy bowling in the same underground area.

About seven o'clock in the evening the official automobiles again began arriving at the Berghof, and the business of the Third Reich prevailed once more. Again Hitler forgot time and hunger as he conferred about military and political matters. It was seldom earlier than nine o'clock that the guests were summoned for dinner. The same general routine was followed for the evening meal as for lunch. Most of the men wore civilian clothes for dinner, and the women were better dressed than they had been for lunch. Eva Braun never wore the same dress twice for dinner and was always elegantly attired. This perturbed Hitler, who thought that she should wear his favorite dress every day. Nevertheless Eva continued her personal fashion show. She did listen to him about her hairstyle though. Once she changed the color to a much darker shade, and he was so disappointed and angry that she quickly restored the lighter color and never altered the style or color again. Hitler had definite tastes and opinions and didn't hesitate to make them known. He closely observed all the women of the inner circle and expressed either admiration or criticism of their grooming and attire.

The main dish of the evening meal, served with a salad, was usually a cold platter; a favorite was "Hoppelpoppel," which was baked potatoes with eggs and meat. Or the guests might be served noodles with tomato sauce and cheese. Hitler often took

The children of the Berghof also celebrated Hitler's birthday, and with fine china, too. *(National Archives)*

two fried eggs with mashed potatoes and tomato salad. Fresh vegetables and fruits were available the year around from Bormann's model garden and greenhouses on the Obersalzberg. Bormann also furnished this produce by airplane for Hitler's meals at his military headquarters, at the Reich Chancellery, or at the Brown House. Hitler believed he could digest only Bormann's vegetables and fruits and wouldn't accept them from any other source. Hitler ate quickly but plentifully. At the same time he observed his guests' eating habits and would immediately tell them if he thought they were eating insufficiently or an improper balance of foods.

As dinner drew to a close the adjutants would once again assemble the official visitors who had arrived at the Berghof to confer with Hitler. When all was ready, they would notify the Führer. He would get to his feet: "Remain sitting everyone, this will not take long."

Hitler did not want the women of the Berghof to mix with the military officers and diplomats who came to confer with him. So after the evening meal, the guests were again left to themselves for an indefinite time while Hitler took care of business. If neither Göring nor Goebbels nor any other high-ranking NSDAP official was present for a conference, Hitler often told his visitors to wait in the dining room for him. If such luminaries were present, the guests knew they were in for a long wait.

It was usually near midnight when Hitler rejoined his guests and ushered them into the conference hall for the nightly conversation session. The orderlies would have a fire roaring in the large fireplace and chairs drawn up near the flames. On the opposite side of the huge room a single floor lamp was lighted, and candles flickered on the tables. Hitler always sat on the right side of the fireplace, while on his right Eva Braun snuggled into a deep chair, her legs drawn up under her. The other guests took chairs at random. Also permitted into the room were Eva's dogs. Hitler's dog, Blondi, was excluded. Sometimes, however, Hitler would ask, quite modestly, "May I let Blondi come in for a moment?" The two terriers would then be taken out and the Alsatian allowed into the room for a few minutes.

Hitler always drank tea. The others had their choice of beverages—champagne, wine, brandy, cognac—since there was no restriction of alcohol just because the Führer did not partake. Pastries and Hitler's favorite apple cake were always provided. Sometimes Eva Braun was able to convince Hitler that sandwiches were better than sweets at this time of night, but she didn't prevail often. After eating and drinking and listening to the crackle of the fireplace while sitting in the subdued light of the room, most guests became sleepy, but Hitler kept talking. He didn't want to be lost in his own thoughts, didn't want to be left alone, despite the late hour. Quite often Hitler would start a conversation with Blaschke, the dentist, because he was aware Blaschke's definite views would cause discussion regardless of the subject. Blaschke, in his 60s, was a scholar, reserved and quiet until engaged in discussion of matters he considered important. Then he would express his viewpoint very firmly, regardless of whether it corresponded with Hitler's. Hitler would smile as he looked at the graying dentist, whose walrus-like mustache would bobble up and down as he talked. He liked Blaschke and seldom criticized him. Others of the inner circle said the two got along so well because the dentist was also a vegetarian and believed that the teeth and the human body were made for the consumption of vegetables, not meat. There was one obstacle to their association, however. Blaschke was a constant smoker and would never agree with Hitler that smoking was injurious to the teeth and body. The dentist insisted that it disinfected the mouth cavity and killed germs. The Führer and the dentist had many arguments about this matter. Naturally all the smokers agreed with Blaschke. Their opinons never fazed Hitler. He ordered that candy, not cigarettes, be in the Christmas packages distributed to the soldiers, even when he was informed that the soldiers would exchange the candy for smokes as soon as possible. Himmler sent out his own Christmas packages to his SS in order to get around Hitler's ban and keep morale high.

Hitler always looked forward to his nightly tea party. He once told Junge, "I never have a vacation where I can go somewhere and relax so I divide my vacation into hours which I spend with my guests here before the fireplace." During these private get-togethers he enjoyed jokes and teasing—often at others' expense and never at his own. He often mimicked Neville Chamberlain, Sir Eric Phipps, and others. One of his pet jokes dealt with Göring and Goebbels. Asking nearby guests if they knew the difference between a volt and an ampere, he would quickly answer himself.

"Goebbels and Göring. Goebbels represents the amount of nonsense a man can speak in an hour and Göring represents the amount of metal that can be pinned on a man's chest." He told the joke whether the two men were present or not.

One night he was whistling a tune when Eva Braun told him he was whistling it wrong. She whistled the correction, but Hitler argued that he was right.

"I'll bet you I'm right," she insisted.

"You know I don't bet with you," Hitler replied. "I fail in any case. If I win I have to be gracious and renounce my winnings. If I lose I have to pay."

"Well, let's play the record and see who is right," suggested Eva.

Bormann put the record on; Eva was correct. She was elated.

Hitler, however, had an answer. "You are right but if the composer was as musical as I am he would have written it the way I whistled the music."

Everyone laughed, but they were not certain whether he was serious or not.

As the evening and early morning hours passed, the guests, bored or in need of a smoke, would slip quietly from the room. When Hitler finally discovered that he was left with Morell, the loyal Eva, and a few others, he would have his orderlies tell the others he wanted them to come back into the conference hall with him.

Around four or five o'clock in the morning Hitler would ring for his adjutant and ask if there were any urgent reports that had just arrived. During the war years he also checked to see if there were any air raid alerts for the Berghof area ... and would not go to bed until he was certain the Obersalzberg had the "all clear." Finally he got up, shook hands with everyone in the room, and retired to his upstairs quarters. The smokers immediately got out their cigarettes or cigars, the drinks flowed, and the conversation became more animated. There was now little or no boredom evident among the guests; there was a sense of good humor, a levity that Hitler probably would have enjoyed had it predominated while he was still in the room. Within a few minutes, after a smoke and a mint to hide the traces of it, Eva Braun joined Hitler upstairs. One by one the other guests drifted off to their own quarters.

The Berghof would be quiet until the next day at noon, when the Führer's routine would start all over again.

13

Nazi Gays and Addicts

Hitler did not believe it was necessary for him to dictate the private individual's code of morality as long as the individual actively supported the NSDAP code and Hitler himself.

One who himself partook of a mind-boggling spectrum of mind-altering substances, Hitler said little or nothing to his associates who quaffed alcohol or popped pills, sniffed cocaine, smoked marijuana, or used heroin, opium, or hashish ... as long as they performed their duties as he ordered. He vehemently denounced *Bettschnüffelei* (bed-sniffing), the behavior of moral snoopers and chastity committees trying to determine the sexual practices of others. But Hitler was very clever: he never really committed himself to any one set of moral principles. In this manner he accomplished three tactical goals: he reassured those who believed in more morality and less hypocrisy; he convinced them that he supported those who demanded that Nazi regimentation extend to private life; and at the same time he reassured others that their easygoing attitude toward pleasure was the sensible one to follow.

"You can't revert back to the Stone Age," he often told his inner circle when discussing private morality.

Hitler's attitude on homosexuality points up his cleverness. Publicly he supported the precepts of Professor Max von Gruber of Munich University. A famous hygienist, Gruber insisted that homosexuality should be banned by the state or there would be an astronomical increase of its practitioners. In the early 1930s a survey indicated that the number of homosexually inclined in Berlin was approximately 55,000; and Hitler, who campaigned against the moral corruption of the Weimar Republic, felt compelled to publicly denounce the practice. Yet one of his closest associates at the time was Ernst Röhm, a practicing gay. Hitler's attitude towards the homosexuality of Röhm and the charges of homosexuality against Werner Frei-herr von Fritsch, the commander-in-chief of the German Army, clearly illustrates his amorality.

Ernst Röhm, a fanatic swashbuckler who enjoyed fighting, in 1919 joined the *Freikorps* (Free Corps), the quasi-military force that replaced the banned German Army after World War I. Seeing Hitler's climb to power as an adventure, Röhm joined the NSDAP early and was at Hitler's side during the 1923 putsch. Hitler went to prison. Röhm was paroled. While Hitler was imprisoned at Landsberg Röhm wanted to use a secret cache of weapons he had hidden near Munich to seize power for the Nazi party by force. Hitler talked him out of it, favoring a legal takeover of the government. Disappointed and bored by inactivity, Röhm departed for Bolivia.

Röhm had problems in Bolivia, however. As he stated to a friend: "My favorite form of activity seems to be unknown." His favorite form of activity was homosexuality. Hitler had known for years that Röhm was a homosexual, but this knowl-edge did nothing to impair their friendship. He also knew that Röhm's assistant, Edmund Heines, was gay; but instead of avoiding the pair, he recalled them both when he organized the Nazi storm troopers. Erich Ludendorff, the famed general who had joined Hitler in the 1923 putsch but had later parted company with him and the NSDAP, thought he had Hitler just where he wanted him when he heard about the recall of Röhm and Heines. He wrote an associate: "I have in my possession documentary evidence that Herr Hitler was acquainted, as early as 1927, with grave abuses inside the organization stem-ming from the homosexual proclivities of his subordinates Röhm and Heines and, in particular, with the corruption of the Hitler Youth by Heines."

Hitler just laughed at the charges and ignored Ludendorff. The charges were certainly not new. Röhm had never tried to keep his homosexuality a secret. In fact he even filed charges of theft against a 17-year-old male prostitute in Berlin's Central District Court. At the public hearing the youth, Hermann

Siegesmund, stated that Röhm had asked him to engage in a form of sexual intercourse that he found abhorrent and to which he wouldn't agree. He left in a hurry, according to his testimony, but not so fast that he didn't take a baggage claim check, which he promptly exchanged for Röhm's suitcase. The suitcase contained some compromising letters. Siegesmund planned to use them to blackmail Röhm, but Röhm called the police and filed charges. He couldn't have cared less if the public knew he was a homosexual. He saw nothing wrong with acting in accordance with his preferences.

Nor did Hitler. He appointed Röhm his SA chief shortly after he had appointed himself *Oberster SA-Führer* (OSAF), or SA supreme commander. On February 3, 1931, Hitler made clear his views on Röhm when he issued the following public statement:

The Supreme Command of the SA has considered a number of reports and charges leveled at SA officers and men, most of them embodying accusation in respect of their personal conduct. It emerges from an examination of these matters that most of them fall entirely outside the scope of SA service. In many cases, attacks by political or personal opponents have been taken on trust. Some people expect SA commanders of high and senior rank to take decisions on these matters, which belong purely to the private domain. I reject this presumption categorically and with all the force at my command.

Quite apart from the waste of time which could better be employed in the fight for freedom, I am bound to state that the SA is a body of men formed for a specific political purpose. It is not an institute for the moral education of genteel young ladies but a formation of seasoned fighters. The sole purpose of any inquiry must be to ascertain whether or not the SA officer or other rank is performing his official duties within the SA. His private life cannot be an object of scrutiny unless it conflicts with the basic principles of National Socialist ideology.

In other words, Hitler believed that if a person did his or her job homosexuality was his own private affair.

Even Martin Bormann, Hitler's trusted aide, wasn't as liberal in his thinking as his leader. Referring to Röhm in a letter to Rudolf Hess, Bormann said: "I have nothing against Röhm as a person. As far as I'm concerned a man can fancy elephants in Indo-China and kangaroos in Australia—I couldn't care less. But if the Führer hangs on to this man after this business, I can't fathom him any longer." Bormann was referring to the publicity and controversy Röhm had created by his admitted homosexuality. Hitler "hung on" to Röhm, however, and in later years Bormann learned to "fathom" the Führer better.

Hitler was wholly indifferent to the orgies Röhm held at his headquarters and of his bizarre sexual activity at the *Kleist-Kasino*, the *Silhouette*, and the Turkish baths in Berlin. When Röhm began using his influence over the 500,000-strong SA to oppose Hitler's policies, however, the Führer took notice. He didn't care if Röhm bedded down with young men, but he did care when Röhm threatened to bed down, figuratively, with Hitler's opposition. When Röhm ignored Hitler's orders once too often, friendship was forgotten. On June 30, 1934, Hitler arrived at the Munich-Oberwiesenfeld airfield shortly after 4:00 A.M., stepped into his armored car, and with an escort of six trucks filled with soldiers headed for Wiesee, where Röhm was vacationing. Röhm was sound asleep in the Pension Hanslbauer when Hitler arrived to confront him. For once he was alone in bed. Hitler screamed accusations at him, accusing the half-asleep Röhm of plotting to overthrow the NSDAP regime, then ordered him taken to Stadelheim Prison in Munich. In what he considered a heroic gesture, Hitler ordered that Röhm be given a gun so he could die as a "good soldier." Röhm spat on the gun.

"If Adolf wants me dead, let him do it."

Sepp Dietrich, leader of the SS *Obergruppe Ost*, did it.

Edmund Hienes, Röhm's deputy and homosexual associate, was yanked from his bed, where he was sleeping with a young boy, and was shot, too, as were many other Röhm sympathizers. Hitler had no qualms about Röhm's homosexuality and, as we have seen, publicly stated that Röhm's private actions were his own business. But when Röhm interfered with Hitler's plans, he died.

The Werner Freiherr von Fritsch affair, described in an earlier chapter, was handled entirely differently by Hitler. In

Fritsch's case, Hitler saw that he could use an accusation of homosexuality as a weapon to remove an obstacle to his ambition. By falsely accusing Fritsch, a Wehrmacht general, of having a homosexual relationship with a known homosexual, he kept the general from being appointed commander-in-chief of the army, a post Fritsch deserved; and he did so without affronting the Wehrmacht high command. The morality of homosexuality had nothing to do with Hitler's decisions in either case. It was a matter of ambition.

Was Hitler a homosexual? Albert Speer says absolutely not, that Hitler was "normal" in his sexual activity. "Such accusations have no truth in them. Hitler's worries and long hours often made his sex drive taper off and he would request drugs from Morell to help, but as to being a homosexual—no!"

Otto Skorzeny agreed with Speer. "He was much too interested in women, their appearance, and their bodies to have been a homosexual. Nor was he bisexual."

Others, however, are not so positive. Kurt Krüger, a doctor who treated Hitler in Germany during the early days of the Third Reich, vows that he was forced to flee Germany in 1934 shortly after Röhm was killed because he knew a secret: that Hitler was a homosexual. During a discussion about sex with Hitler, Krüger says he brought up the subject of homosexuality.

"Suppose you tell me how you have fared with your own sex?" he asked.

Hitler was stunned. "My own sex?" His face turned very red and he stammered, "I don't know what you mean, Doctor."

"You know exactly what I mean, Adolf, or you would not be blushing. But perhaps I should point my question a little more sharply. How do you get on with your friend, Captain Röhm?"

"That is an outrageous question!" Hitler cried, rising from where he was sitting and striding to the window, where he remained with his back toward the doctor.

Finally Krüger calmed him by explaining that such questioning was merely routine. "If a doctor analyzed a man who had lived in an army barracks and did not ask him such a question, he would be a fool."

Hitler stared at him. "Are you sure you did not ask the question because of little bits of gossip that you picked up?"

Krüger shook his head. It was a lie. He *had* heard the gossip.

After he became
chancellor. Hitler rarely
was seen at church.
(National Archives)

Luftwaffe Technical Department chief Ernst Udet. front center with dishev-
eled tie. was a womanizer. alcoholic. and drug addict. Hitler put up with the
behavior until it became clear that it was interfering with Udet's official
duties. Then Udet committed suicide or was murdered on Hitler's orders.
(National Archives)

"You did not know as a matter of fact that anything had transpired between me and Captain Röhm?"

Krüger was convinced that something *had* happened between Röhm and Hitler. He was also convinced that when Hitler had Röhm killed in the 1934 purge, it was not only to solve his political-military problems with the captain but to also eliminate the erotic domination of the man.

Yet Dr. Jacob Dressler, who survived the Third Reich, vehemently denies this theory presented by Krüger. "I was called to the Berghof on several occasions to assist Brandt, 'usually in the treatment of the children staying on the Obersalzberg, and I talked with Hitler quite often. I can tell you unequivocally he was not a homosexual. Not one of us." Now nearly 80 years old, Dr. Dressler does not hesitate to admit that he was a homosexual.

If Hitler was not a homosexual, he certainly had no hesitation about associating with them. One of the men closest to Hitler until 1941, Rudolf Hess, was a homosexual, known to many as "Fräulein Anna." Sometimes, because of his adulation of Hitler, he was called "Fräulein Hess" behind his back. Hess served at first as Hitler's secretary. During their imprisonment in Landsberg after the 1923 putsch, he helped with *Mein Kampf*, not only writing down Hitler's words but also instilling into the Führer's mind many of the thoughts contained in the book. After this time, until 1941, Hess was never far from Hitler.

"Hess's real name should have been Yes," according to Pauline Kohler, the maid at Berghof. "He had never been known to contradict Hitler."

It can be stated that Hess would certainly not have said no if Hitler had made advances, but all known facts indicate Hitler did not make such advances, that he was not a homosexual. On May 10, 1941, Hess astonished the world by flying alone from Germany to Scotland and parachuting to earth near the estate of the Duke of Hamilton. There have been many theories regarding the reason for this flight. Skorzeny believed that Hitler knew about the flight, in fact had ordered it, thinking Hess, with his contacts in England, could bring about an alliance between Germany and England to oppose Soviet Russia.

Skorzeny said, not long before his death: "That is the real reason the Soviet Union will not agree to the release of Rudolf Hess from Spandau after all these years."

Others think Hess acted on his own, although for the same reason Skorzeny had advanced. But many are convinced that Hess made his dramatic flight because he was losing the affection of the Führer and hoped that by bringing about an alliance between England and Germany he once again would become Hitler's "favorite."

Despite the fact that Hitler's hero, Frederick the Great, was a homosexual, evidence uncovered by long years of study of Hitler's secret life indicates that he himself was not. The testimony of the women he slept with, and many are still alive, proves that he appreciated female flesh. They laugh at the accusation that he was a homosexual, and their evidence is convincing.

In addition, a once-secret document indicates that the women who should know and who vow that he was not a homosexual are correct. On November 15, 1941, the Führer's Decree Relating to the Maintenance of Purity in the SS and Police was issued by Heinrich Himmler. It stated:

1. In order to keep the SS and police free from homosexually-inclined weaklings, the Führer has ruled that any member of the SS or police who engages in indecent behavior with another man or permits himself to be abused by him for indecent purposes will, regardless of age, be condemned to death and executed. In less grave cases, a term of not less than six years' penal servitude or imprisonment may be imposed.
2. The Führer's decree will not be published because it might give rise to misinterpretation.

Hitler's liberal, if inconsistently applied, attitude on homosexuality carried over to his outlook toward the use of drugs. There was probably no official of the NSDAP who took more drugs than Hitler himself, although some, including Göring, were much less disciplined in the habit. As we have already noted, it was determined that by the end of the war the Führer used as many as 28 different drugs every day. When the Führer felt tired, Dr. Morell was ready with an injection that banished the exhaustion; before a long speech Morell fortified him with a drug and afterward revived him with another; if Hitler was depressed by a military defeat, the doctor was quick to cheer him with a shot; and when Hitler awakened after going to bed at four or five o'clock in the morning, a Morell drug provided the energy that the brief, restless sleep had failed to restore. Headaches, backaches, sore throat, nervous tension, fever, stomach aches, and chilblains all disappeared when Morell came with his hypodermic needle. Eventually Hitler reached a stage where even without these symptoms he demanded the drugs.

Once, when Morell was ill, Dr. Giesing painted the inside of Hitler's nose with cocaine. The Führer's head cleared, and he asked for more and more applications. The cocaine soon was added to the already long list of drugs he required.

It was shortly after the July 1944 attempt on his life that Hitler could not get out of bed one morning at the headquarters. That's when the four doctors decided that the Führer should be told that Morell's drugs were killing him.

The change in Hitler had been dramatic. First he became very quiet, very depressed, and it was impossible to arouse his interest. Morell himself was ill, unable to run to Hitler's side with his needle, and the other physicians, knowing that Morell's injections were the cause of the problem, refused to give Hitler the drugs. Suddenly Hitler, who always enjoyed eating with members of his staff, decided he would eat alone. Nor would he join his associates in the afternoon ritual of the tea party. Then one day he didn't get out of bed. No one, not even his servants, had ever seen Hitler in bed, except, of course, his women friends. In the morning it was standard practice for the servants to place his newspaper outside the closed bedroom door and awaken him by calling from the hall.

No one was permitted into his bedroom at that time except the servants, doctors, selected adjutants, and, later, his secretaries. The doctors couldn't help him; the adjutants couldn't get through to him with their reports.

"The Führer is completely indifferent," Otto Günsche told Traudl Junge. "We don't know what we should do. Even the situation in the east doesn't bother him, although we are doing rather badly there."

Those who got into Hitler's bedroom to see him were shocked. The room was very small, very shabbily furnished. It looked like a room that would normally be used by a lower-ranking officer. A huge wooden box in the room where his dog, Blondi, slept made the room appear even smaller. Hitler wore a gray flannel robe, black socks, and mottled pajamas. His skin was very white, his legs spindly. Visitors understood after seeing him in bed why he never wanted to be seen in a swimming suit. The secretaries were allowed in the room only when he began to improve and when he felt it was imperative to dictate a report or letter. He always tried to keep himself covered with the blankets, as though it would be obscene if they saw his bare legs. With his hair mussed, his nondescript night clothes and black socks, and the covers pulled up to his chin, he looked less like a dictator—or lover—than he did a sick and confused old man. After Morell's health improved and he could resume the injections, Hitler too recovered and finally got out of bed. It was a bizarre episode in his life and one that he never mentioned later.

Hitler was very lenient about the use of drugs by others and, as in the case of a man's sex practices, as long as drugs didn't affect an associate's performance at work, he ignored the factor completely. Ernst Udet, the boisterous, likable combat and stunt pilot who was appointed chief of the Luftwaffe Technical Department, was a drug addict and an alcoholic. Hitler was aware of his habits, but he didn't criticize Udet for them. When it became obvious, however, that Udet's trips to the hospital for "cures" were interfering with his official duties, the Führer came down hard on him. Very hard. Udet committed suicide.

One of the projects dearest to Hitler's heart was the collection of paintings, sculptures, books, and *objets d'art* for the museum he planned to establish in his hometown of Linz, Austria, after the war. As the German military forces overran Europe, Hitler's aides overran the conquered countries' museums and confiscated the best for the Linz museum. The man Hitler personally appointed to collect armor for the museum was Dr. Leopold Ruprecht, a morphine addict. Hitler didn't care how much morphine Ruprecht used as long as the armor collection grew in size and value.

Without question, the best indication of Hitler's attitude toward drugs (other than his own well-documented use of Morell's assortment) was his association with Göring. Göring was in and out of hospitals and institutions for many years because of narcotics. During the early years his habit was kept secret. Hitler helped perpetuate the story that after the 1923 putsch during which Göring was seriously wounded, he took refuge in Italy until 1927. Actually Göring spent most of that time in Sweden fighting his drug addiction and his wife's legal suits against him. He had married Carin Fock, of Stockholm, and his new in-laws tried desperately but unsuccessfully to cure him of the addiction. Hitler was aware of this effort but continued to cover up for his companion.

On April 22, 1926, however, a legal case at the Magistrate's Court of Stockholm before Magistrate Carl Lindhagen revealed the facts about Göring. His wife had been married previously, and when she obtained a divorce to marry Göring, her son, Thomas, had been awarded to her ex-husband. On April 22 she sued to regain custody. The ex-husband decided that his best tactic was to prove to the court that the Görings would not be fit parents. He concentrated on Hermann Göring's problems, and his first move was to obtain a statement from Göring's personal physician, Dr. Karl A. R. Lundberg.

It is hereby certified that Captain Göring is a victim of morphine, and that his wife Carin Göring, nee Baroness Fock, suffers from epilepsy for which reason their home must be considered inappropriate for her son Thomas Kantzow.

Stockholm, April 16, 1926
Karl A. R. Lundberg

The case was postponed twice. During the third attempt another statement was read, a statement procured from a famous Swedish psychiatrist, Professor Olaf Kinberg. He had

Hitler was constantly searching for art treasures for the museum he planned for Linz. his hometown. *(National Archives)*

Frau Gerdy Troost and Hitler examine Arno Becker's "Ammut" ("Grace") in the House of German Art. Munich. *(National Archives)*

kept Göring under close observation and treatment at the Langbro Psychopathic Hospital. Kinberg provided the following testimony on May 8, 1926.

Captain Hermann Göring, who is to begin a cure from the consequences of narcotics, is expected to be discharged within six or eight weeks . . . .

A year later Göring was still in need of help. The records of the Stockholm Police Department show that he was taken to the Konradsberg Lunatic Asylum on September 6, 1927, and later transferred back to Langbro. Meanwhile the Görings lost the court case, and the son of Carin Göring remained with her ex-husband. Hitler was aware of Göring's addiction but obviously didn't feel that it mattered. He helped Göring every way he could. Göring served early as Hitler's agent in Berlin; became one of the first Nazis to serve in the Reichstag; became President of the Reichstag in 1932; and was with Hitler during the delicate negotiations that culminated in Hitler's being named chancellor. After Hitler became Führer, Göring's rise in the Nazi hierarchy was fast. In quick succession and sometimes holding down more than one position at a time, he became Reich minister without portfolio; Reich commissioner for air; Prussian minister president; and Prussian minister of the interior. In 1936 Hitler made him a full general and gave him even more power, making him the economic dictator of Nazi Germany. On June 19, 1940, he reached the peak of his power when he became *Reichsmarschall* and commanded the Luftwaffe to victories over Poland and France.

Hitler was often as silent about his personal affairs as was this bust, his favorite. *(National Archives)*

Meanwhile he ate pills by the handful, and his judgment began to show it. It was all downhill for Göring after the Battle of Britain. When he lost that great air battle in 1940, his standing with Hitler faded; and during the last hours of the Third Reich, Hitler condemned him to death when Göring tried to seize power. The Führer had finally realized, much too late that the addicted *Reichsmarschall*'s impaired mental capacity had cost Nazi Germany victory in the air.

On the night of December 28, 1941, Hitler observed to his guests: "Probably none of us is entirely 'normal.' Otherwise we should spend all our days in the café at the corner. It is not fair to demand more of a man than he can give. Who escapes from criticism?"

He had summed up his attitude toward all manner of behavior that deviated from the conventional.

14

Hitler's "Jewish Princess"

On May 23, 1939 J. Edgar Hoover, Director of the Federal Bureau of Investigation, wrote a letter to George S. Messersmith, Assistant Secretary of State. In the first paragraph he stated:

"It has come to the attention of the San Francisco Office of this Bureau that Princess Stefanie von Hohenlohe Waldenburg, the Nazi adventuress, is reported to be en route to San Francisco, California from the Orient. It is our understanding that Princess Waldenburg will be immediately attached to the staff of the German Consul, Captain Fritz Wiedemann, upon her arrival in San Francisco."

Who was the "Nazi adventuress," as Hoover called her? That question has puzzled and frustrated historians for well over a quarter of a century. It is only now, since her death and due to the recent declassification of secret documents of the Federal Bureau of Investigation and the Department of State, that the facts about this amazing woman have emerged.

In 1939 Hoover didn't even know her full name, which was Princess Stephanie Hohenlohe von Waldenburg-Schillingsfürst. She was known to her friends by the much less imposing names of "Steffi" and "Toffi." Nor had she started life with a high-sounding name. She was born in Vienna's Second District, often called the ghetto of the Austrian capital, in December 1897. Her father was Dr. Rudolf Richter, a struggling and obscure Jewish lawyer; her mother, Ludmilla Kuranda, a devout Catholic. Their third-floor apartment at 27 Augartenstrasse was definitely middle class, and that, to some extent, was an exaggeration. But Steffi Richter had no intention of remaining in that environment. By the time she was 16 years old she was making the best of her striking beauty. A chorus girl at the famous Theater an der Wien, cradle of the Viennese operetta, she had many admirers.

According to one story, an early conquest of the red-haired adventuress was a Czech industrialist, whom she demanded marry her. When the wealthy tycoon objected, Steffi walked out of his life, vowing that one day she would be a princess and get her revenge. Whether she got her revenge against the reluctant industrialist is not known, but within a short time after leaving him she was being pursued ardently by two aristocrats. One was the Polish Count Gimczynski. The other was Prince Frederick Franz Augustin Hohenlohe von Waldenburg-Schillingsfürst, a name that definitely impressed the young Steffi. So impressive did she find it that On May 12, 1914, in Westminister Cathedral, London, the prince with the long name and ex-chorus girl with the red hair were married. Their honeymoon was spent in England. Hitler during this period was involved in trench warfare in Flanders as a volunteer in Company 1, Sixteenth Bavarian Reserve Infantry Regiment; and the NSDAP was not yet even a gleam in his eye.

Steffi had a problem: She was half-Jewish, and the relatives of Prince Hohenlohe refused to associate with her or accept her as a member of the stiff-backed family. So Steffi, against the will of her father, was baptized a Christian. There was a family reunion at the Hohenlohe castle, and the former dancer, who swore to obey all rules and regulations of the House of Hohenlohe, was accepted. Her vow was a farce; Steffi had not obeyed any rules and regulations up to that time, nor would she after her marriage. The marriage was not a happy one, even though the union had produced a son, Franz. On July 21, 1921, the princess was granted a divorce from the prince. She was also granted a sizable alimony.

The same month that Steffi obtained her divorce, Hitler rejoined the NSDAP. He had resigned earlier in order to pressure the party into electing him its president and to force it to follow his guidelines, which he assured them would lead to power in postwar Germany. While he promoted the party, acquired a newspaper, the *Völkischer Beobachter,* to further spread his views, gave the NSDAP the swastika symbol and the "Heil" greeting, and organized the SA, Hitler's brown-shirted storm troopers, under the command of Rohm, Steffi was doing her own self-promoting in Paris, where she had gone after her divorce. She used her marriage to Prince Hohenlohe to penetrate the circles of high society. Count Ferdinand Wurmbrand, Count Coloredo Mansfeld, and the Archduke Franz Salvador all recognized the sensual qualities the prince had noted earlier and aided her in return for her favors. She was invited to many fashionable affairs. In 1924, when Hitler was residing in prison at Landsberg am Lech, Steffi was living in an elegant apartment on the fashionable Avenue Georges V near the Champs Elysées. The chances that the obscure imprisoned German politician and the playgirl of Paris would ever meet and form a close, if secret, association were practically nonexistent. Two factors led to their meeting. One was Steffi's passion for adventure, for involvement in intrigue. The second was Hitler's often unrecognized talent for using beautiful or wealthy women to further his own aims.

The catalyst of the association was the wealthy and influential Lord Rothermere, owner of the *Daily Mail* of London. Steffi met the English publisher in Paris, and he was attracted to her, as were so many other men in the French capital. They were seen together in many chic nightclubs and restaurants. But Rothermere had more on his mind that just wining and dining beautiful women and publishing newspapers, although some of his strange ideas were developed in order to fill the pages of his newspaper with sensational news. One day Rothermere asked Steffi if she had any suggestions for news items, and to his surprise she did. She came up with a real journalistic windfall by convincing him to take up the cause of Hungary.

At the time Hungary, divided from Austria by the 1920 Treaty of Trianon, was in turmoil. Large parts of the country had been given to Yugoslavia and Rumania, and no one besides the Hungarians seemed to care. Steffi suggested that if Rothermere, through the *Daily Mail,* took up the fight to reunite the country, he would gain a great deal of prestige and sell a lot of papers. He took up the challenge . . . and Steffi was proved correct. The campaign stirred up interest across all of Europe, and Rothermere became known as "the uncrowned king of Hungary." Steffi outlined many of the articles about Hungary and even wrote some of the pieces. It was then she decided she should share in Rothermere's success. She suggested firmly that he should pay her for her efforts. The very wealthy Rothermere, infatuated by the brilliant beauty, quickly agreed to give her the equivalent of $20,000 a year as a retainer and additional sums for special assignments. It was an oral agreement that cost Rothermere a lawsuit and a quarter of a million dollars in later years.

Steffi went to Belgium and offered the widow of the last Austrian emperor a generous annual allowance, paid by Rothermere, for her support of Rothermere's efforts to reestablish the monarchy in Hungary. She also traveled to Budapest and there sounded out government leaders on their thoughts about restoration of the monarchy. More important, she met with Prince Wilhelm III of Germany to learn his views on the current political trends in Europe. Although Prince Wilhelm was not an active member of the Nazi Party, he had announced his unconditional allegiance to Hitler and ostentatiously wore the swastika badge. He was fascinated by Steffi and delighted with Rothermere's decision to work for the restoration of the Hohenzollern and Hapsburg dynasties [in the role of a modern Warwick-the-King-Maker using a continental rather than an English field.] Prince Wilhelm was the Hohenzollern heir to the throne of the German Reich, and under the Weimar Republic he had let it be known that he would be available for such a restoration or would be pleased to be elected president of the republic. When it became evident, after Hitler took control of the government, that the Führer had no intention of recalling the Hohenzollern dynasty, Prince Wilhelm decided to call both sides of the coin at the same time in a royal gamble. He supported Hitler; and he encouraged Rothermere.

Rothermere had introduced Steffi to English society. She had a long acquaintance with French society. She had been married to a prince of Austria. And now Prince Wilhelm introduced her to certain segments of German society and leadership. Among those whom she met at this time was Fritz Wiedemann, a close friend of Adolf Hitler's. Wiedemann had been Hitler's battalion adjutant during World War I. After the war Wiedemann retired from the army with the rank of captain and became a farmer in southern Bavaria. When Hitler and the NSDAP came into prominence in the early 1930s, Wiedemann promptly left the farm to rejoin his former comrade. Hitler appointed him his personal adjutant.

During these early years of the Third Reich, Wiedemann was already convinced that an alliance between Germany and England would be best for both countries. After meeting Steffi and learning that not only was Lord Rothermere interested in the restoration of the Hohenzollern and Hapsburg dynasties but he also was convinced that England and Germany should be allied, Wiedemann immediately recognized the worth Steffi could be to Hitler and the Third Reich. It is not known exactly when he introduced her to Hitler, but it is known that she was asked to leave France in 1933 because of her activities in behalf of the Nazis. Certainly it did not take her long to convince Rothermere that he should back Hitler rather than the Hohenzollern heir.

On June 20, 1934, Prince Wilhelm wrote a letter to Lord Rothermere, stating, in part:

Princess Hohenlohe's visit gives me the opportunity to send you a letter safely, a letter which might possibly interest you. It is hardly necessary to accentuate that the contents of the letter are meant only for you personally.

... Then came the day at Potsdam, the 21st of March 1933, when Adolf Hitler delivered a speech at the old Garrison Church at Potsdam, a speech deeper and more moving than any I had ever heard from a German statesman. Only one who has been present on that occasion can realize the sublime mood of the Germans in those hours. Large parts of the nation expected already then that Adolf Hitler would express on that day the reunion with the monarchy in some form.

... In my personal view the Führer would strengthen and fortify his own position in the German nation to a quite extraordinary extent if he could bring about a reunion with the monarchy in some form or another. How this is to be done is a question of staging. But for the time being it does not seem as if the Führer has already arrived at the recognition of such a necessity. In view of your great experience and of the respect which you enjoy in Germany, it might be of great profit to our fatherland and to the whole world if you, dear Lord Rother- mere, would acquaint our Führer with some of these observations and thoughts, provided that you also consider them true and that an opportunity for doing so should arise. Only quite independent men like you, Lord Rothermere, who are also elements of power in them- selves, can afford to tell the Führer the truth frankly.

Rothermere took Steffi's advice and decided to back the winner. Meanwhile Steffi became acquainted with Göring; Goebbels; Otto Abetz, the German ambassador to France; and Ribbentrop, then the German ambassador to England. She often gave expensive parties at her fashionable apartment on London's Brook Street, and her residence became a popular rendezvous for diplomats, politicians, and journalists of France, Germany, England, and other countries. And through her newly made Nazi friends it was easy for her to arrange for Rothermere to meet with Hitler. It was a mystery to most persons where Steffi obtained the money to entertain so lavishly and travel so extensively; her intimate association with Rother- mere was kept secret.

Her activities were no secret to Hitler. Many of her travels and meetings were undertaken in his behalf, and he was grate- ful. In appreciation he presented her with a golden swatiska, the Order of the German Red Cross, and a personally auto- graphed photograph inscribed "In memory of a visit to Ber- chtesgaden." He also wrote her a note to say:

... I have been informed how sincerely and warmheartedly you also championed New Germany in the past year and her necessity for living. I know very well that many embarrassments resulted from this. Therefore I should like to express to you, highly esteemed Princess, my sincere thanks for the great understanding you have always shown for our people generally and for my work especially. ...

Rothermere, after meeting personally with Hitler in Germany, became obsessed with the idea of an alliance between the Third Reich and England. After presenting his views on appeasement and compromise, Rothermere received a seven-page letter from Hitler. The letter, dated December 7, 1933, began, "You have been good enough to communicate to me through Princess Hohenlohe ..." and expressed Hitler's personal viewpoint on many subjects threatening world peace at the time. He was convinced, he stated, that an Anglo-French friendship for the maintenance of a real peace could be very useful. He emphasized that Germany herself had no aggressive intentions.

"However fanatically the way be resolved to defend ourselves against an attack we are against any idea of provoking war ourselves," Hitler declared. "Germany has no more ardent desire than to achieve with the other European nations a situation excluding the future use of force in Europe, possibly by a system of nonaggression pacts."

With Rothermere paying the bills and Hitler calling the shots, Steffi's efforts to promote Hitler and the NSDAP were often successful in a number of countries during the next few years. Most of her time was spent on improving Anglo-German relations, however, and while Rothermere thought she was working exclusively for him, she was really working for Hitler. Both Rothermere and Hitler wanted better relations between their respective nations at that time, however, so the Englishman didn't realize Steffi had already switched houses. In fact on July 15, 1936, Rothermere was so satisfied with Steffi's liaison work between him and Hitler that he renewed her oral contract. By this time the publisher and the Führer were very friendly. On December 6, 1935, Rothermere wrote Hitler on *Daily Mail* stationery emphasizing his support.

I believe in timing things well. I think the moment has come to give more publicity again to Germany. Certain happenings arising out of the present situation provide an advantageous opportunity to stress again the cause of Germany....

Any information you might give me, my dear Reichskansler, will be dealt with, as you know, only in the way you may desire. As heretofore nothing will be published except by your special wish. . . .

Steffi kept the dialogue active between Rothermere and Hitler, with Hitler's guidance, and the Englishman showered gifts and compliments on the Führer. After German troops marched into the Rhineland, in 1936, and Great Britain denounced the Locarno Pact, Rothermere remained devoted. He had Steffi deliver a magnificent Gobelin tapestry to Hitler. In turn Hitler, in a letter dated December 19, 1936, invited Rothermere to the Berghof between the fifth and eighth January. Later, after a secret consultation with Hitler, the publisher sent the Führer a jade bowl and other gifts, many selected by Steffi.

As 1938 started and Hitler ordered his troops across the Austrian border, the European situation heated up. It was then that Steffi did her best work for Hitler. Her fruitful efforts began with the meeting between Lord Runciman, a Liberal

After a diplomatic reception Hitler reviews the honor guard in the courtyard of the presidential palace. *(National Archives)*

English peer, and Konrad Henlein, the leader of the Nazi Sudetenland party. Sudetenland, an area in Bohemia adjoining Germany, had been awarded to Czechoslovakia by the 1919 Treaty of Saint-Germain-en-Laye between Austria and the Allies. Hitler wanted the area back in the German fold and threatened war if he did not get it. Secretly he coveted all of Czechoslovakia, not only the Sudetenland. He ordered Henlein to foment unrest in the disputed area and then publicly denounced the atrocities allegedly commited against Germans in the Sudetenland. When several Germans were killed in a frontier incident, Hitler sent troops to the border. The Czechs did likewise, and France and the Soviet Union vowed that they would support the Czechs if the Germans crossed the border. War seemed imminent, but suddenly Hitler withdrew his troops.

At first the backdown of the Führer was a mystery, but many years later it was discovered that Steffi had convinced Hitler that if he was patient he could conquer Czechoslovakia without fighting. Her plan was to have England convince the leaders of Czechoslovakia to make concessions that would enable Hitler to gain the foothold he wanted—the Sudentenland—and later take the entire country. It wasn't until Steffi, with the assistance of her influential English contacts, convinced British Prime Minister Neville Chamberlain to send Runciman to Prague as an unofficial arbiter that the Führer postponed his military action. Runciman did a fine job pressuring Eduard Beneš and Emil Hácha of Czechoslovakia into accepting Henlein's and Hitler's eight proposals. Hitler, who really coveted all of Czechoslovakia, was nevertheless impressed with Steffi's influence with the British statemen. He even permitted her to reorganize the famous Salzburg music festival in an effort to persuade international celebrities to return to the city so that the event would regain the prestige and popularity it had enjoyed before the Nazi takeover of Austria. She was only partially successful in this venture, but Hitler didn't discourage Steffi from even greater undertakings in his behalf.

In June 1938 she met with Göring at Karinhall to discuss a meeting between a representative of Germany and British Foreign Secretary Lord Halifax. Göring told her that he thought he could bring about a better understanding between Germany and England and avert war. Steffi went to the Berghof and obtained Hitler's consent to send Wiedemann to London to arrange for a Göring visit. Once that was accomplished, she too hurried to London, where she set up the meeting with Lord Halifax for Wiedemann. The meeting was very successful. However, Ribbentrop then discovered that he had been by-passed, and he complained so forcefully to Hitler that the Führer changed his mind about the Göring visit. He forbade Göring to travel to England to meet with Lord Halifax. He informed Steffi that the conference between leaders of Germany and England must be held in Germany.

That didn't deter Steffi. She was able to convince Prime Minister Neville Chamberlain, through her influential intermediaries, to go to Germany and meet with Hitler. The Führer was amazed. Chamberlain was aged and in poor health, and he had never flown before. Yet on September 15, 1938, Chamberlain made a trip to Berchtesgaden to confer with Hitler; a second trip on September 22, when they discussed the Czechoslovakian situation at Bad Godesberg; and a third trip on September 29, to Munich, where the infamous Munich Pact was signed the following day. During these 15 days the princess was at her German home, Schloss Leopoldskron, just across the valley from Berchtesgaden. She could sit in her retreat and see the lights of Hitler's Berghof on the next mountain.

Three months later she was instrumental in arranging the meeting between Ribbentrop and French Foreign Minister George Bonnet, during which the Franco-German nonagression pact was signed. It was another coup for Hitler ... and Steffi. Following ratification of the pact she held a reception for German and French leaders in her Paris apartment. She had helped dupe the French in Hitler's behalf.

Trouble was brewing for the lively Steffi, however, trouble of which she was aware even before her outstanding accomplishments for Hitler and the Nazis were realized in the last quarter of 1938. By January of that year Rothermere had become suspicious of both Hitler and Steffi. He lost confidence that the Führer would not go to war to achieve his aims, and he began to suspect that Steffi was actually working for Hitler. When she asked for her yearly stipened, which he had always advanced her during the first month of the year, on January 19, 1938, Rothermere wrote her from London, enclosing a check and telling her that it was his final payment. "My mission to create a better feeling between Britain and Germany has largely succeeded," Rothermere wrote. "You have helped much to achieve this better understanding. I think any further activity on my part would be misunderstood."

Just to make certain she grasped the message, he added: "I do not wish any steps to be taken to maintain any liaison with the ruling authorities of Germany."

Steffi ignored his order, of course, and helped arrange Runciman's visit to Prague and Chamberlain's visit to Munich.

She did not ignore Rothermere's statement that he did not intend to make any additional payments to her after 1938. She filed suit in London, seeking damages from Rothermere and accusing him of breach of contract. She covered every angle. Her suit was divided into two separate claims. The first demanded damages for wrongful dismissal or repudiation of a contract of employment. The second maintained that she had intended to take legal action against certain French newspapers which had allegedly defamed her, but that she was restrained from doing so by Rothermere, who didn't want the publicity and who had said he would take proper steps to clear her name. He had promised, moreover, to look after her financially, Steffi said. She stated that Rothermere had entered a verbal agreement with her to pay her $20,000 a year for life and to give her $100,000 for not publishing her memoirs in the United States. When asked why her memoirs would be worth such an enormous sum, she intimated that Rothermere did not want the public to know about his correspondence with Hitler and was willing to pay that amount to keep it from being printed. It was then that Rothermere learned Steffi had photographic copies of every piece of correspondence between him and Hitler over the years! Rothermere was furious and accused her of copying private material.

After a trial of several days before Justice Tucker of the King's Bench Division in London, during which it became evident that she was an intimate friend of Adolf Hitler, the suit was dismissed. Steffi was disappointed but not exactly brokenhearted. After all, a letter from Wiedemann, Hitler's adjutant, introduced during the trial as evidence of her closeness to Hitler, assured her that she would not be destitute.

There is no doubt in my mind that Hitler will grant her any help he can in her fight to reestablish her personal honor and financial status."

Steffi had been to United States earlier, but when she decided to visit again after the Rothermere trial, she created a furor. One reason was that Wiedemann had been sent to San Francisco by Hitler as German consul general but it was suspected that he was actually a spy. On March 7, 1939, after Hoover had received two anonymous letters accusing Wiedemann of being engaged in espionage activities for the German and Japanese government, George S. Messersmith, assistant secretary of state, wrote a letter to J. Edgar Hoover explaining the situation from the viewpoint of the Department of State.

I have to acknowledge the receipt of your letter of February 27 addressed to the Secretary of State with which you transmit two copies of anonymous letters which set out information to the effect that Captain Fritz Wiedemann, who allegedly has been appointed German Consul General in San Francisco and a Princess Stephanie Hohenlohe are engaged in espionage activities for the German and Japanese Governments. You state that no investigation is being conducted in connection with this matter by your Bureau in the absence of a specific request from this Department.

In this connection I may inform you that Captain Wiedemann has been appointed Consul General for Germany in San Francisco and has arrived in this country. We understand that he is proceeding to his post in the immediate future. The Princess Stephanie Hohenlohe referred to in your letter has not yet arrived in this country but it is understood that she is planning to come here. The activities of Princess Hohenlohe have been under a good deal of suspicion in several countries and should she arrive in this country it will undoubtedly be found desirable to follow her activities.

In August more information on Steffi was forwarded to the office of the secretary of state by Bert Fish an American official at Lisbon. He reported that in a Cairo newspaper article on July 27, 1939, there was a news item that seemed to confirm Steffi was the Nazi agent cooperating in January and February in Syria with Baron von Flügge, Nazi agent for the Near and Middle East.

"The Baron's prestige among German Foreign Service circles appeared to be such that even the Beirut Consul General Seiler clicked heels first when meeting him," Fish reported.

The newspaper article referred to Steffi as a "high-flying Hitlerian agent" who had set London agog the previous year by arranging for Wiedemann to meet with Chamberlain and Runciman. Now, according to the article, she was establishing relations with certain personalities of high British society who up to that time had shown no sympathy for the Third Reich and "will extend to them a personal invitation from the Führer to visit him either on the Obersalzberg or in Berlin."

Hitler did receive many visitors in 1939 before the start of the war in September. After Great Britain and France declared war on Germany on September 3, however, it became obvious to both Hitler and Steffi that her usefulness in those countries was ended. On October 3 she applied at the American Consulate General in London for a nonimmigrant visa to visit United States. Declaring herself to be a citizen of Hungary and carrying Hungarian passport No. 1-1657, she gave her London address as 95 Park Street. She stated that her purpose in going to the United States was to visit her son, who was ill. Her mother intended to accompany her. The Consulate General, lacking any valid reason to deny the visa, issued her and her mother the necessary papers.

The Department of State, aware of her reputation in Europe, kept track of her and informed Hoover and the FBI that "Princess Stephanie Hohenlohe arrived at New York on December 22, 1939, on the steamship *Veendam* with her mother, the Baroness Szcpessy. She was traveling under the name of Maria Waldenburg." When the secretary of state discovered that the visa had been issued, the Consulate General was criticized for not having checked first with Washington. A confidential letter to London stated, in part:

... I am extremely sorry that this matter was not brought to the attention of the Department at the time of the issuing of the visa. In the light of the contemporaneous press accounts of her suit against Lord Rothermere and the sensational nature of the testimony, some of which seems to border on blackmail, it appears that the Department might well have been apprised of the departure of this woman for the United States.

The letter was signed by James Clement Dunn, who also wrote that if Steffi's son had been sick—recalling that the serious condition of his health was the ostensible purpose of her visit—he had made a miraculous recovery and was now in very good physical condition. He also stated that although Steffi had been kept under constant surveillance since her arrival, so far she had not done anything that could be perceived as espionage. However the FBI, aware that Wiedemann and Steffi comprised the Nazi team that had worked so successfully to bring about the preliminaries to the Munich Pact, was vigilant. Agents were close by when Steffi arrived in Fresno, California, on May 29, 1940, and joined Wiedemann at a restaurant. The agents followed the pair to the Sequoia National Forest and then to Wiedemann's home in Hillsborough, a suburb of San Francisco. It was a long summer for the FBI agents, who trailed her and Wiedemann daily, but by fall it became evident that the pair had set up a meeting with an influential Englishman to discuss either peace or an alliance between Germany and England. Arrangements were made to secretly monitor the meeting.

The three met on the evening of November 26, 1940, in Room 1026 of the Mark Hopkins Hotel in San Francisco. After a two-hour discussion they met again the following afternoon and evening. The FBI report of the discussions was detailed, stating in part that the Englishman told Steffi he represented a group of his countrymen who believed satisfactory peace terms could be arranged between the two countries before the United States was drawn into the war. This was exactly what Hitler desired, too, but the two Nazi agents were aware that the proposal would have to be further beneficial to the Third Reich, or the Führer, flushed with victories over Poland and France, wouldn't be interested. On the other hand, the Luftwaffe's recent defeat in the Battle of Britain might make him amenable to a peace feeler or alliance proposal at this time. Obviously Wiedemann and Steffi were under orders from Berlin to try to arrange a meeting between London and Berlin to discuss the matter, but an air of showmanship the pair conveyed at the Mark Hopkins Hotel lent the Englishman doubt that such a meeting could be arranged. Finally Steffi said she was willing to go to Berlin to place the proposals before Hitler and Ribbentrop, and the Briton quickly said he would recommend to his prime minister that Steffi's visit to Berlin be given unofficial approval.

The charming and wily Steffi, however, was suddenly to come up against the rock-hard, ice-cold attitude of the FBI and the U. S. Department of State. Three weeks after the San Francisco meeting she learned that her application to extend her stay in the United States had been refused. Through her lawyers she made several appeals, all of which were turned down by Maj. Lemuel B. Schofield, head of the U. S. Immigration and Naturalization Service. More than 40 other countries (excluding Nazi Germany) were asked to give her a visa, and all refused. By this time Hitler had concluded that Steffi's notoriety had ended her usefulness to him, and so his followers in the United States were ordered to ignore her plight. But Steffi wasn't a quitter. By March 1941 she had raised trouble by filing various appeals, taking an overdose of sedatives, and exhibiting hysteria. Finally she was admitted to the hospital room of the Immigration Service headquarters in San Francisco. Schofield then decided that he should interview the princess himself and explain the facts of the case to her. A blunt, efficient man who ran his bureau in a no-nonsense manner, Schofield stormed into her room a tiger full of fire, and walked out a pussycat full of admiration. Her tearful story, enhanced by her beauty, sensuality, and winning ways, completely overwhelmed the major, and he ordered her release. His reason: She had given him some "interesting information." It was the beginning of a friendship that lasted until Schofield's death in July 1954.

Still, Steffi couldn't leave the United States to visit Hitler in Berlin, as had been proposed at the Mark Hopkins Hotel; nor did Hitler want anything to do with her now. Yet her ordeal seemed to be over as far as her stay in the United States was concerned, and she traveled extensively within the country, always under the watchful eye of the FBI. She was in Philadelphia, using the name "Mary Reihert," on December 7, 1941, when Japanese planes attacked Pearl Harbor. The following day she was arrested as an enemy alien. Schofield arranged that she be interned at Gloucester City, New Jersey, but when reports reached President Franklin D. Roosevelt that she was receiving special treatment, the president was furious. He notified the attorney general: "Honestly, this is getting to be the kind of scandal that calls for very drastic and immediate action."

Steffi was sent to the internment camp at Seagoville, Texas, on February 13, 1942, where she stayed until the end of World War II despite her many protests. She was the last person released from the camp.

Steffi was the same appealing and intriguing woman that she had been before and during the war. For several years she helped Major Schofield restore his "Anderson Place" estate a large farm in eastern Pennsylvania. When he died she moved to Red Bank, New Jersey. She was sued by the Internal Revenue Service for $250,000 back income taxes for 1951–53, evidence that she certainly was not destitute. She won the case. Later she became a correspondent for the Washington *Diplomat,* an international society review, and then for *Quick* and *Stern,* the German magazines. She interviewed President John F. Kennedy, President Lyndon B. Johnson (whose inaugural she had attended, by invitation), Princess Grace of Monaco, Queen Frederika of Greece, Farah Diba of Iran, and many other notables. In June 1972 she entered the hospital for a routine ulcer operation, but as usual Steffi did the unexpected. She died.

So ended the career of Hitler's most fascinating and beautiful secret agent. Steffi outlasted her Führer by 27 years.

15

How Hitler Duped J. Edgar Hoover

The reputation of J. Edgar Hoover, director of the Federal Bureau of Investigation, frightened bank robbers and presidents of the United States alike. After his appointment by Calvin Coolidge as the nation's number-one policeman, Hoover began to build himself a kingdom inside the government; he succeeded beyond his expectations. He became unassailable. The reputation of his organization as one of the most efficient police forces in the world was rarely challenged even by those who disliked him. He had many solid accomplishments to celebrate. He eliminated political influence in appointments in the FBI, promoted scientific standards in detective work, and founded the National Police Academy, which trains selected officers throughout the country in the latest scientific procedures. Yet, Hoover met his match when Adolf Hitler became the Führer of Germany. The recent release of classified documents, obtained through a Freedom of Information request by the National Commission on Law Enforcement and Social Justice, indicates that Hitler completely outwitted J. Edgar Hoover until the week before Pearl Harbor. While the world moved toward war, Hoover sent an autographed photo of himself to Berlin. As the Nazis overwhelmed France, Hoover exchanged information with Third Reich officials on passports and wanted criminals. It was not until Germany had overrun all of Europe and invaded Russia and North Africa that Hoover finally decided to correspond no longer with Berlin. Even then the decision was taken only upon the recommendation of his top lieutenants and was primarily a device to protect the public image of Hoover and his FBI.

Hitler recognized early in his career that he needed a secret police force dedicated to tracking down and eliminating dissidents, complainers, and outright opponents. In those early days he was personally protected by a personal bodyguard, the *Stabswache,* (Headquarters Guard) which later became the SS, or *Schutzstaffel,* under the direction of Himmler. In April 1933 Göring, who at the time headed the police of Prussia, incorporated his force into the Gestapo (an acronym for Secret State Police) to form the Central Secretary Office of the Third Reich. Meanwhile a struggle for power in the party took place between Himmler and Göring, since each wanted to head a national police force. Himmler finally won the internal battle; in April 1934 he took command of the entire unified police force, and on June 17, 1936, Hitler designated him Reichsführer of the SS and leader of the Gestapo. Heydrich, who had been kicked out of the navy because of a sexual escapade, was his assistant.

Another member of the organization was Arthur Nebe, head of *Einsatzgruppe B,* a special mobile unit that was ultimately designated to carry out liquidations in occupied countries and supervise the *Endlösung* or Final Solution of the "Jewish problem" by extermination.

Hitler, however, kept the duties of his police force secret from the outside world and even did his best to project a favorable image with it. One of his moves was to make certain that his police force was a member of Interpol, the International Criminal Police Commission, and that his people dominated that organization. The commission dated from 1914, but during World War I it was inactive. In 1923 it was reorganized, and its first character was drawn up that year. Files on international criminals were built up gradually, until, by 1933, they were of great value to all member countries. The commission was a respected organization and Hitler knew that if his police force were a member its reputation would be enhanced. Besides, the headquarters was in Vienna, the capital of a country he had decided to annex. The FBI director was unconcerned when Hitler did just that, on March 12, 1938. The following year Hoover also ignored the occupation of Czechoslovakia just a few days before he received a telephone call from the Department of State inquiring whether the director had heard whether

Germany planned to foster Interpol, or whether it had taken over control of the organization. His reply, dated March 28, 1939, stated:

Tolson: Please explain to her [Miss Macdonald at the State Department] that the meeting is being held in Germany this year; that the organization is an independent entity which holds its meetings in different countries at different times.

By then the Führer had complete control of Interpol and had no intention of holding any of its meetings anyplace but in Berlin.

As late as July 20, 1939, Hoover was completely unaware of the atrocities being committed by the Gestapo and the German Criminal Police. The tentacles of the autonomous Gestapo extended throughout Germany. It even had its own legal system to achieve the annihilation of those Hitler had declared enemies of the Reich. The Gestapo controlled the lives, freedom, and property of all Germans; it hunted down Jews and Communists; and anyone brash enough to be overheard telling an anti-Nazi joke was imprisoned. It reported persons who celebrated Emperor William II's birthday, for they were considered dangerous monarchists opposed to Hitler. The average citizen dreaded the brutal Gestapo. An individual suspected of opposition to Hitler was often warned once; if he then persisted, he disappeared. Most of these "offenders" ended up in concentration camps, but those considered really dangerous would be interrogated, and many were beaten to death. Even if he received a legal hearing it was a farce because the Gestapo had its own court. As reported at the International Military Tribunal at Nürnberg after the war:

The Gestapo was used for purposes which were criminal involving the persecution and extermination of the Jews, brutalities and killings in concentration camps, excesses in the administration of occupied territories, the administration of the slave labor program and the mistreatment and murder of prisoners-of-war.

On July 20, 1939 Hoover answered a letter that had been
written to him by Reich Criminal Director Arthur Nebe. Nebe
wrote him about the 1939 annual Interpol meeting, scheduled
for August 30 to September 7, 1939, in Berlin. Datelined Wor-
dorachar Markt, Berlin, it stated:

Most Esteemed Mr. Hoover:

As I have learned from the Secretary-General of the International
Criminal Police Commission, Dr. Dressler of Vienna, you expressed
your intention of participating in the 15th regular session of the
International Criminal Police Commission taking place in Berlin from
August 30th to September 7th of this year. I should like to express my
delight at this and hope to be able to greet you personally at the
meeting in Berlin.

As you may know, the purpose of this convention will be to further
the cooperation of Criminal Bureaus in the international fighting of
criminals and to help make it even more successful. During the course
of the 1939 Berlin Convention there will take place for the first time a
"Day of Practitioners" in which not only members of the commission
will participate but other workers in various important fields of crimi-
nology as well. These will be from different states. In addition, the
International Police Radio Technical Committee will present its opinions and findings on the further development of an international
police radio network.

I may assume that the convention will be of particular interest for
the criminal police of the United States as well and above all I should
be highly pleased if the commission may look forward particularly to
a valuable contribution on your part.

> With highest esteem, I am
> Respectfully yours,
> A Nebe, Reich Criminal
> Director

Included in the letter was a program of the meeting. On
Wednesday, August 30, at 12:00 noon there was scheduled a
lunch hosted by the chief of the SS and the German Police,
Heinrich Himmler. Ladies were also invited. This was six years

after Himmler had set up the first concentration camp, the infamous Dachau, twelve miles northwest of Munich.

One of the most brutal and notorious camps, Dachau was the scene of medical experiments carried out on hundreds of inmates. When the Luftwaffe developed two processes for making sea water potable and wanted to test the method that left the salt in the water but removed the unpleasant taste, Himmler was contacted. In a formal request, Himmler was asked to approve a plan to provide 40 men from Dachau for four weeks to conduct human experiments with the water obtained by this process. As the letter indicated, "from a medical viewpoint and from our present knowledge this process must be regarded doubtful since the intake of concentrated salt solutions may give rise to serious symptoms of poisoning."

The man who was asked his opinion on the proposal experiment was Arthur Nebe, the same man who invited Hoover to the Interpol meeting in Berlin on the pretext of developing new ways to combat criminals. Nebe's criminal reply was brief and to the point. He wrote, "I agree to the proposal to test a process for making sea water potable on prisoners in concentration camps. I suggest that the antisocial gypsy half-breeds in the Auschwitz concentration camp be used for this purpose."

Himmler and Nebe were to be hosts at the Interpol meeting Hoover planned to attend, and a tea party was scheduled to be held on Friday, September 1, by Chief of the Uniformed Police Kurt Daluege. The tea party host Daluege ultimately ended up at the end of a rope, on October 24, 1946, sentenced to death by the Czechs for crimes against humanity.

For the evening of September 2 a party was arranged at Wannsee, where less than two years later, on January 20, 1942, Reinhard Heydrich would submit a comprehensive plan for "the final solution of the Jewish question." Nor was Heydrich among the missing at the Interpol meeting. On Thursday, September 7, Gruppenführer Heydrich was scheduled to give a lunch for the delegates. Hitler made certain that all his police officials were involved in the Interpol meeting.

Because of the pressure of business in Washington, Hoover did not go to the meeting. Not a word in his papers indicates that the presence of Himmler, Daluege, Heydrich, or Nebe deterred him from attending. In fact later correspondence verifies that he kept in close contact with the Germans. In another letter from the Criminal Police Bureau of the Reich in Berlin, Hoover was thanked for sending a copy of the FBI annual report. In return he was sent information and photographs of a new criminal laboratory in Berlin. The last paragraph of the letter written by the German officials says that he would be "very happy" if he could have a photograph of Hoover. Hoover sent it.

The year 1940 made it obvious to the entire world what sort of plans Hitler had for mankind. That year saw the deportation of Jews from Germany, the Nazi invasions of Denmark and Norway, the capitulation of the Dutch Army, the tragedy of Dunkirk, the surrender of Belgium, the German occupation of Paris, and the Battle of Britain. All these occurred before September 16, 1940, when Hoover sent a letter to a Nazi Interpol official. Dr. Bruno Schultz had inquired about certain passports, and Hoover replied promptly, giving him all the information he wanted. By this time the Gestapo was arresting German citizens in large numbers, especially those who protested against Hitler's police state policies. Some of these Germans obtained forged passports and tried to leave the country, but the information from the FBI and various other nations helped trap them. Many were Jews.

This cooperation between Hoover and the Nazi police officials continued until *three days* before Pearl Harbor, and not once is there any indication in the director's declassified papers that he felt guilty about the association or that he denounced the tactics German officials carried out in their own country. In fact an FBI "wanted" notice published in the Nazi Interpol magazine of June 17, 1940, lists the suspect as being of the "Jewish race," the sort of statement that Himmler's police force would use. Eventually, however, a letter to Hoover from Interpol, dated September 23, 1941, regarding information Hoover had requested from the Germans, exasperated other FBI officials. They questioned corresponding with Interpol at the Berlin address since by so doing the FBI might be said to tacitly recognize Germany's takeover of the International Criminal

Police Commission. Hoover was angered by their remarks but became concerned about the image of the FBI and himself. He decided that no further communications should be sent to Berlin and in a three line memo, gave the order to cease cooperating with Interpol. The memo was dated December 4, 1941, a year and a half after France fell to the Nazis and three days before Pearl Harbor.

How much valuable information did Hitler obtain from Hoover and the FBI during the period the Nazis controlled Interpol? It is a difficult matter to assess, but obviously Hitler's police had access to the huge file of fingerprints kept by the FBI and could easily check on persons in the United States. Hitler took pleasure in blackmailing German citizens to get them to halt the actions of their relatives in other countries who opposed the Third Reich. The aid of the FBI made this task easier in the United States. It is known that Hitler had an amazing amount of information about American citizens. Shortly before the United States entered the war, for example, it was discovered by U. S. intelligence that the Führer had a file on the Universal Motor Company of Oshkosh, Wisconsin, a firm that manufactured marine engines. Hitler's card index had the employees listed by name, country of origin, religion, social contacts, and political preferences in state, national, and international affairs. Other reports on Hitler's desk named prominent pro-Nazis in the United States as well as anti-Nazis and those United States citizens who opposed the American national interests, the police and military forces of the country. It is not known how much of this information was obtained by the Nazi police through inquiries to Hoover using the Interpol cover, but much of this information was in fact available in FBI files.

How the FBI and Hoover were unaware of the domination of Interpol by the Nazi police and how the names Himmler, Heydrich, Nebe, and Daluege meant nothing to the director as late as 1941, eight years after the beginning of Hitler's regime, is a mystery. To his dying day Hoover would never explain the strange circumstances of his cooperation with the Nazis.

16

The Führer and the Cowboys

Hitler had a secret passion that abetted his devotion to the Obersalzberg area, a passion that not many persons were aware of at the time. He was fascinated by cowboys and Indians! The mountainous, rugged area where his Berghof was located fit in very nicely with his fantasies about the "Wild West." He was particularly fond of the stories written by Karl May, a German who wrote about the American frontier. Of course Hitler wasn't that author's only fan, May's works sold more than 70 million copies, assuring him a spot among the top ten of the all-time fiction best-seller list. Einstein read May when he was tense; Albert Schweitzer praised his courageous stand for peace; and Hermann Hesse called his fiction "indispensable and eternal." Hitler patterned many of his actions on those of May's protagonist Old Shatterhand.

Karl Friedrich May was born in a small town in Saxony in 1842 and studied to become a teacher. At 17 he was expelled from school for stealing candy, and he spent the next 15 years in and out of prison. The official files state that he was a dangerous criminal, but actually his thefts, frauds, and impostures were always small-time. He was 32 years old when he finally got out of prison for the last time and he decided to try writing instead of stealing for a living. He went to work with incredible diligence and wrote more than 25 novels, none very good. But in 1880 he started writing about faraway locales, and his novels began to sell very well. The most remarkable thing about these travelogues, full of local color and detail, is that the author never left Germany. His American novels made him most of his money and brought him fame. In these novels his hero is always a very strong, daring man with self-proclaimed wisdom and judgment far beyond his years, a crack shot, a powerful swimmer, and a fine horseman, a man concerned with leading and protecting others. In real life May was a pathological liar, maintaining that he had visited the American West, fought all the battles he wrote about, and undergone all the hardships and adventures in his books. He spoke no language but German yet vowed he could speak 40 languages. But, as Hitler once told Skorzeny, "Dante was never in Hell, either."

In some ways he was an ideal hero for Hitler. They shared many fantasies, many faults. After he became chancellor, Hitler had a special shelf built in his study at the Berghof just to hold his collection of Karl May novels. He read and reread the books and often recommended them to others among his inner circle. In fact he was obsessed with the idea that May's tactics against the Indians were ideal for use by the German troops against the Russians.

"I have ordered every officer to carry with him Karl May's books about fighting the Indians," he told his valet. "That's the way the Russians fight—hidden like Indians behind trees and bridges, they jump out for the kill." It was not the first time he invoked the novelist as a tactician. When his generals were reluctant to follow his plan for the invasion of France, the Führer insisted on having his way. "They should have read more Karl May," he said.

Luis Trenker was one of Hitler's favorite actors during the early years of the Third Reich because of Hitler's fascination with cowboys-and-Indians themes. *(Luis Trenker)*

The mountains of the Obersalzberg did, of course, give Hitler the opportunity, by way of his fantasies, to "play cowboy" to his heart's content. One takes no serious liberties in saying this. More than one of Hitler's intimates and biographers has seen evidence that supports this reading of the man's psyche. He could and did roam the area, following the wooded paths, looking for "Indians" behind each tree while leading his men— and women—to the isolated teahouse. Blondi, of course, was protection against the imaginary "Indians," and seldom did Hitler take a stroll on the Obersalzberg that his dog did not accompany him. Few were aware that inside his pants near the right pocket he'd had sewn a leather holster in which he carried a Walther 6.35-mm pistol, so that in his own mind during these walks on the mountains he was "the Gunman," the crack shot of May's novels. Hitler could look down from the Berghof and see the beautiful Königsee, where cattle grazed on the shores.

Even years before he assumed power, Hitler gave those who met him the firm impression that he was trying to live in Karl May's fantasy world. Karl Alexander von Müller, a guest who watched Hitler's arrival at a small, private social gathering, saw him "laying aside [his] riding whip, velour hat and trench coat, finally unbuckling his cartridge belt with revolver attached and likewise hanging it on the clothes hook. It all looked very odd, reminiscent of Karl May's American Indian novels."

But Hitler also acted out the May "cowboys and Indians" fantasies in ways that affected millions.

May's protagonist loved to slaughter the members of a particular tribe of "Redskins." Perceived as deceitful and grasping, these venal outcasts were characterized as an inferior species. And Hitler's hero, while wallowing in self-glorification, could quote Scripture to legitimize the trail of blood he left.

The "misfit" was another example. In the Wild West of May's books, the misfit usually led a tortured existence because of the harassment and brutality of the stronger, "quick-on-the-trigger" bully. Hitler played the latter role well. "Misfits" were an extreme irritant to him: His brutality was never equaled in the mountains and plains of the American West. Hitler considered Gypsies to be misfits, racially inferior, a burden to his Third Reich. Three years after he became chancellor he set up a special research department to "investigate" the Gypsies, and he amended the anti-Jewish Nürnberg laws to include the Romany as well. In September 1939, after the start of the war, Hitler decreed that all Gypsies living inside the Reich were to be evacuated to Poland. There were approximately 30,000 Gypsies; two thirds of them in pre-Anschluss Germany, the remainder in Austria's Burgenland province and in Bohemia-Moravia. The man in charge of getting them out of Germany was none other than Arthur Nebe, the same Nazi who had corresponded with J. Edgar Hoover in such a friendly manner. The following telegram was sent from Gestapo headquarters in Berlin on October 13, 1939. Addressed to the Gestapo office in Bohemia-Moravia for delivery to SS Captain Adolf Eichmann, it stated:

SS Colonel Nebe called on [October 12, 1939] and asked for information when he can send the Berlin Gypsies. I asked him to be patient for a couple of days until I can find out where SS Captain Eichmann is and ask him to get in touch with SS Colonel Nebe. If the transport of the Berlin Gypsies is to take much longer, the city of Berlin will have to build a special camp for Gypsies at great cost and still greater difficulties. SS Nebe asks that you phone him.

Nebe didn't really have to worry. Hitler ordered the Gypsy transports to start moving out on October 20, 1939. Many Gypsies were sent into the Jewish ghettos, especially into those in Warsaw, Lublin, and Kielce. Often they were killed on the spot by SS gunmen. After Hitler invaded the Soviet Union, Eichmann's *Einsatzgruppe D* had orders to annihilate all Gypsies in the Ukraine and in the Crimea. No one will ever know how many Gypsy "misfits" were murdered on orders from the Obersalzberg "cowboy."

Neither had Hitler sympathy for the congenitally weak, sick, and deformed. His euthanasia program was designed to get rid of the misfits who couldn't keep up the pace on the trail, those who didn't fit into the "gang." Hitler supported the program as a stimulus to national health and the racial integrity of the German people. To insure secrecy, only tried and trusted Nazis were involved, men such as Philip Bouhler, police president of

Munich, and Dr. Karl Brandt, one of Hitler's personal physicians. Hitler wrote to these two men on September 1, 1939:

Reichsleiter Bouhler and Dr. Brandt M.D. are charged with the responsibility of enlarging the authority of certain physicians to be designated by name in such a manner that persons who, according to human judgement, are incurable can, upon a most careful diagnosis of their condition of sickness, be accorded a mercy death.

The "mercy deaths" ordered by the Karl May-influenced "cowboy" were often the result of experiments involving high altitude, low temperature and high temperature, typhus, infectious jaundice, bone grafting, and mustard gas. Like the wolf of the Wild West, with whom Hitler often liked to compare himself, he gave his victims no mercy, despite his use of the term "mercy death" in the order to Bouhler and Brandt. One physician at Dachau concentration camp wanted to test a remedy for malaria. He imported mosquitoes from southern countries, had 300 prisoners assigned to him, and let the insects bite them. Unfortunately he made no effort to heal those "misfits" who contracted malaria. Another physician wanted to test a remedy for ulceration. Instead of choosing inmates who were already suffering from the disease, he selected healthy "misfits" and induced the disease in them. Purulent sores as big as the palm of a hand covered the feet, legs, and arms of the victims. Some died; some survived temporarily, after having arms or legs amputated, only to be gassed later.

Hitler dubbed some of the punishment at Dachau with what he thought were western terms. Punishment "at the stake" was carried out in 1940–41 on a spot near the bunker where special posts had been set up. The hands of the condemned man were put behind his back and fastened with an iron chain around the wrists. Then he was hung up on a hook by the chain at such a height that the heels did not touch the ground. According to the regulations this punishment lasted one hour. Usually it lasted much longer, and often the man was beaten to death by the supervising SS officer. A victim "stretched on the trestle" was tied on the device in such a way that the upper part of the body lay horizontal and the legs dangled over the sides. The SS men who were in charge of the punishment used specially finished leather whips, which they soaked in water before using. They would then beat the prisoners about the buttocks without paying any attention whatever to where the strokes fell, so that frequently the kidneys and other parts of the body suffered serious injury. The prisoner usually received 100 strokes, and each stroke had to be counted by the screaming victim. If he missed count, the strokes started all over again.

A famous "misfit," Lia Graf, wasn't able to avoid the SS roundup. Graf, in June 1933, was a plump, well-proportioned dwarf 27 inches tall. She gained international fame when she was placed on the lap of J. P. Morgan, the financier, while he was testifying before the Senate Banking and Currency Committee in Washington, D. C. It was quite a change from the Ringling Brothers Barnum and Bailey Circus, in which she was then appearing. The photograph appeared in newspapers around the world. Lia Graf returned to Germany, her homeland, in 1935, and two years later Hitler had her arrested as a "useless person." She and her mother, who was also a dwarf, and her father, who was not, were taken by the Gestapo to a concentration camp. Among the charges against her were the fact that she was a dwarf and the allegation that she had been a tool of Wall Street, which had turned down Hitler's request for a loan. In 1944 she was shipped to Auschwitz and gassed. During his "euthanasia" program Hitler ordered approximately 10,000 dwarfs gassed.

The story of the Holocaust has been told and retold many times. Hitler considered Jews less than human, and much as Old Shatterhand exterminated Ogellallah Indians, Hitler herded the Jews to ghettos and death camps. He was the "range boss" of this tragic roundup but such a clever leader that as yet no document signed by Hitler ordering the extermination of the Jews has ever been found. Yet it is obvious he knew every key move being made by Heydrich, Eichmann, and Himmler toward the Final Solution of the Jewish "problem." Nothing, from the love affairs of his associates to the military plans at the front to the death of the Jews, was a secret from the Führer.

There is no question that he read a copy of the speech Himmler made to the SS gruppenführers in Poznan on October 4, 1943, when SS chief said, in part:

I also want to talk to you quite frankly on a very grave matter. Among ourselves it should be mentioned quite frankly and yet we will never speak of it publicly. Just as we did not hesitate on June 30, 1934 to do the duty we were bidden [Blood Purge of Ernst Röhm, SA chief] and stand comrades who had lapsed up against the wall and shoot them, so we have never spoken about it and will never speak of it. It was that tact which is a matter of course and which I am glad to say, is inherent in us, that made us never discuss it among ourselves, never speak of it. It appalled everyone and yet everyone was certain that he would do it the next time if such orders are issued and if it is necessary.

I mean the clearing out of the Jews, the extermination of the Jewish race. It's one of those things it is easy to talk about. . . . Most of you must know what it means when 100 corpses are lying side by side, or 500 or 1000. To have stuck it out and at the same time to have remained decent fellows, that is what has made us hard. This is a page of glory in our history which has never been written and is never to be written."

The extermination of the Jews was not a subject discussed at the Berghof or Eagle's Nest. At least that is the testimony of Junge, Linge, Kempka, and many other Nazis who survived the Third Reich and who swear that they were completely unaware of the death camps. Just as the ranch owner didn't talk about his range problems while at the family dinner table, neither did the Karl May-inspired "cowboy" talk about the death of the Jews while on the Obersalzberg. In fact few persons did talk about the matter publicly or in print, but secret documents uncovered by the Office of U. S. Chief of Counsel for Prosecution of Axis Criminality are gruesome evidence that Hitler was more heartless than any "hanging judge" of the Wild West. When it appeared that the extermination of the Jews was progressing too slowly, Göring, using his multiple titles of "the Reich marshal of the Greater German Reich," "commissioner for the four year plan," and "chairman of the Ministerial Council for National Defense" tried to speed up the process. In a letter to Heydrich he urged completion of the assignment "given you which dealt with arriving at a thorough furtherance of emigration and evacuation, a solution of the Jewish problem as advantageous as possible. Wherever other governmental agencies are involved, these are to cooperate with you for the accomplishment of the desired solution of the Jewish question."

Hitler's "range hands" in this speeded-up operation used trucks converted to mobile gas chambers. Secret documents indicate that the men involved were not upset by what they were doing to the Jews as much as they were by the mechanical failures of the trucks, the shortage of trucks, and the method used to gas Jews inside the trucks. One illustrative document is in the form of a letter from a SS untersturmführer, or second lieutenant, who headed one of the teams giving a detailed report on executions by gas.

The taking over of vehicles by Group D and C is finished. While the vans of the first group can be utilized in not too bad weather, the cars belonging to the second group are absolutely immobilized in rainy weather. For instance, often it has rained for half an hour, these vehicles cannot be used because of skidding. They can only be used in absolutely dry weather. The only question is whether these vehicles can be put into action only on the execution spot.

First, a vehicle must be brought to this place. That is only possible in good weather. The execution spot is generally stationed 10 to 15 kms from main roads and due to such location already of difficult access, but in wet weather absolutely impossible to reach. If those to be executed are driven or conducted to this place they notice at once what is wrong and become frantic which is most of all to be avoided. There is only one solution: to gather them on the same spot and then to drive off.

As for the vehicles of Group D, I had them camouflaged as cabin trailers by putting in them one window on each side of the small vans and two on each side of the big ones, like windows which are seen in peasant houses. But the vehicles were so well known that not only the authorities but also the civilian population called them 'Death Vans'. My opinion is that we shall not be able to keep this camouflage secret very long.

The untersturmführer went on to complain that the clutches on the trucks, some built by Westinghouse, were not reliable and there were few replacements available. He thought that the rough terrain was responsible for the problem. He then discussed another problem that was bothering him and his team of executioners.

Furthermore, I ordered, during the gassing, to keep all the SS men as far away as possible in order that they could not eventually be injured by gas fumes. On this occasion I wish to draw your attention to the fact that after the gassing several commanders let their own men unload the truck. I have drawn attention to the commanders of the atrocious and spiritual effect that this kind of work may have on the men, if not now then in the future. The men complained to me that they got headaches after every van unloading. Anyhow, this order is not observed as it is feared that the prisoners chosen for this work will use the opportunity to try and escape. In order to prevent the men from being injured, I should be obliged if orders are given accordingly.

After showing this concern for the men doing the gassing, the untersturmführer turned his comments to those he was gassing.

The gassing is not done in the right manner. In order to get the work over with as quickly as possible, the driver gives full gas. Through this measure the people to be executed die from suffocation and not by being put to sleep as planned. My method has proved that by releasing the pressure on the lever at the right time death comes more quickly and the prisoners slip peacefully away. Distorted faces and excretions, which have been previously seen, are no more to be observed.

The influence of Karl May over Hitler is reflected in many facets of the Führer's life. For instance one of Hitler's favorite films made during the years of the Third Reich was *Heimkehr*.

Always a fan of Karl May. the German author of cowboys-and-Indians tales. Hitler established the Karl May Museum near Dresden after becoming chancellor. *(National Archives)*

This movie had its premiere in Vienna on October 10, 1941, and was awarded the coveted "Film of the Nation" designation after Hitler expressed his approval. In fact some critics believe that Hitler himself suggested the ending for the film to Goebbels, who was in charge of the Nazi film industry, and that Goebbels ordered Gustav Ucicky, the director, to use it. The story is set in Poland in the spring of 1939, when the Poles were still suspicious of the German-speaking minority in their midst. In the movie the heroine and her friends go to the local cinema to see Jeanette MacDonald in *Maytime,* arrive too early, and are forced to watch a newsreel that praises the Polish army. The Poles are shown harassing and brutalizing the German community in a later scene that summarized much of Nazi ideology. The Poles are shown ransacking and burning a German farmstead, running around like crazed animals, tearing swastikas from the bosoms of terrified German women and terrorizing them in a multitude of ways. The film, of course, reversed reality and projected the crimes of the Nazis onto the Poles, their actual victims. When the Polish national anthem is played in the movie, the heroine and the other Germans refuse to stand, and the heroine's husband is murdered by angry Poles. Finally the entire German colony is thrown into jail, where the Poles plan to kill them all by firing a machine gun at a blank wall so that the ricocheting bullets would hit them. Naturally German planes arrive in the nick of time, and the prisoners escape. In this "the-Germans-are-coming" ending, the Luftwaffe and the German army troops are analogous to the Wild West cavalry riding to the rescue at the last minute. The Germans, like the beseiged white settlers of the American West, are desperately trying to hold off the Poles, or, as they probably were in Hitler's mind, the Indians.

At dinner on February 17, 1942, Hitler talked about Karl May. "I've just been reading a very fine article on Karl May. I found it delightful. It would be nice if his work were republished. I owe him my first notions of geography and the fact that he opened my eyes on the world. I used to read him by candle light or by moonlight with the help of a huge glass. The first thing I read of that kind was *The Last of the Mohicans.* But Fritz Seidl told me that Fenimore Cooper was nothing, that I must read Karl May. The first book of his I read was *The Ride through the Desert.* I was carried away by it. I went on to devour at once the other books by the same author." During his first months in power Hitler reread every one of May's novels.

The swastika was, of course, the paramount symbol of Nazism. The hooked, or crooked, cross was adopted by Hitler as the official emblem of the NSDAP before its rise to political power and was popularized by the propaganda machine of Goebbels. Hitler selected the symbol personally, and he often mentioned that the American Indians used the swastika in their handicraft work, usually to denote the movement of the sun. Whether his reading of Karl May influenced his selection of the swastika as the official Nazi emblem cannot be proved, although the coincidence is striking. In any case, Hitler ultimately acknowledged his debt to May's influence by establishing the Karl May Museum, near Dresden.

17

Eagle's Nest or Berlin?

At 3:15 P.M. on November 20, 1944, Hitler's private train silently pulled away from the Wolf's Lair, near Rastenburg, in East Prussia, for the last time. He was dejected, distant. He kept his eyes riveted on a spot on the white tablecloth and didn't speak. It was obvious that he knew he would never return to East Prussia, that Stalin's troops would soon overrun the area. Not only was Hitler depressed about the progress of the war, but now his throat was bothering him. He could barely whisper, and it hurt to eat. As fearful as he was of operations, Hitler had finally agreed to permit the throat surgeon Eicken to remove a polyp from his throat as soon as they reached Berlin.

The Führer was worried about the war and the medical operation, but he had an additional concern. Even in November 1944, Hitler was considering his alternatives if and when it appeared the Third Reich would collapse. Should he make his last stand at Berlin? The capital was the objective of the Americans and British, moving towards it from the west, and the Soviets, racing from the east. One alternative was the Obersalzberg, where, if defeat was certain, escape from Germany would be possible at the last minute. Hitler publicly projected the image of a confident leader with no thoughts of defeat but privately he admitted to Bormann and Goebbels he was preparing for the worst.

Hitler's private train pulled into Grunewald station in Berlin at 5:30 the next morning, just after an Allied air raid. If he noticed the serious damage to the capital as Kampka, his driver, weaved among the rubble, he said nothing. In fact, he didn't speak a word all the way to the Chancellery. He seemed to fear someone would ask him a question he didn't want to answer, or couldn't. Also his throat was very sore, and he feared that he had cancer, despite the reassurances of his doctors that he did not. At the Chancellery, which, surprisingly, had suffered only minor damage to one wing, Hitler studied the reports from the front, updated his situation map, and reviewed the defense of Berlin with Fegelein, Himmler's liaison officer. After a light meal in the evening he went to bed early, shocking his associates, who were accustomed to having the Führer deliver long-winded monologues until the early hours of the morning. They were happy enough to miss the monologue but concerned over his health and attitude.

Eicken operated on Hitler the next morning, November 22, and the inner circle suffered a scare. In calculating the amount of morphine his patient needed, the surgeon neglected to take into consideration that Hitler neither smoked nor drank alcohol. He gave Hitler an overdose, and it was nearly eight hours before the doctor could bring the Führer back to consciousness. Everyone, including Eicken, thought it was the end for Hitler, in which case, the surgeon knew, it would be the end for him too. Fortunately for the doctor, Hitler recovered with no after-effects.

Hitler's secretaries didn't see him for three days, but on the fourth day he unexpectedly appeared at the breakfast table. He could only whisper, since Eicken had forbidden him to speak aloud for a week. Within a short time everyone was whispering. Finally, through sign language Hitler made it clear that his hearing was all right and did not have to be saved, that it was his voice that couldn't be used. Everyone laughed, including Hitler. He seemed much happier than he had been before the operation, and even an air-raid alarm didn't upset him. In fact rather than discuss the Allied planes that were obviously in the area, he preferred to explain about his dog, Blondi, whom he thought was going to have pups.

"She is not going to have any little ones," he wrote. "She got fatter and I thought sure she was going to have little ones but I believe she only got fatter because she had more to eat. Nor was she exercised much." He was sorely disappointed.

Hitler admitted to his secretaries that Eva Braun wanted him to come "home" to the Berghof for Christmas.

"She thinks I need a rest after the assassination attempt," he scribbled, "but actually I think Gretl is behind it. She wants Fegelein her husband home for the holiday."

The secretaries were aware that Gretl was expecting her first child in the spring and understood why she wanted her husband with her, but Hitler had no intention of going to the Berghof for Christmas. He had other plans, secret plans, which he hoped would stop the Allied forces in the west. On December 10 he left Berlin shortly after five o'clock in the afternoon, and at two o'clock the next morning he was at his Alderhorst headquarters near Ziegenberg. He was ready to launch the Ardennes offensive; the Allies would come to call it the Battle of the Bulge. Hitler knew that if he lost the Ardennes battle, he could still make his last stand either at the Eagle's Nest or Berlin. He also knew that this would mean only a slight postponement of the inevitable.

Hitler was aware that the British and the Americans were both experiencing supply problems. He concluded that the weak spot in the enemy line was held by the U. S. First Army, which was using only four or five divisions to hold a 100-mile Ardennes front. If his forces could penetrate the American lines in a surprise attack, Hitler felt, the U. S. First Army could be routed and a gaping hole would be opened in the Allied front. He foresaw Gen. Sepp Dietrich's SS Sixth Panzer Army going all the way to Antwerp. In conjunction with this surprise counterattack against the Americans, Hitler also emptied his bag of military tricks in an effort to completely confuse the Allies and, he hoped, make them settle for a negotiated peace. He still believed that he could convince the Allied powers to join with Germany in the battle against the Soviet Union. His secret weapon, the V-1, was now operational. The V-1 was a flying bomb, a cheaply built pilotless plane with a one-ton warhead of high explosive. It was powered by a simple jet engine that made such a peculiar sound that the V-1 was dubbed the "buzz bomb." More than 8000 V-1s were launched against England before the Ardennes attack. British officials estimated that the weapon killed nearly 6000 persons, injured 40,000 more, and destroyed almost 100,000 public buildings and homes in London.

Hitler also had a more formidable "wonder weapon" that

was so secret most of his generals didn't know about it. Called the V-2, it was a supersonic rocket nearly 50 feet long. It too could carry a ton of explosive. While many of the V-1s had been shot down by RAF fighters, the V-2, which traveled 3500 mph, was untouchable. Because of its speed and because it could climb as high as 116 miles, the rocket could not be seen or heard until it hit the target. Just before launching to the Ardennes attack Hitler began firing the V-2s from sites in the Netherlands.

But even then his bag of secret weapons wasn't empty. He had the Me-262, his new jet plane. Work on this plane had begun in 1938, and an experimental model was flown in 1941. Powered by two 1980-pound thrust turbojet engines, it was counted on by Hitler to offset the Allied bombings that were destroying so many German cities. But on May 23, 1944, he made a shocking discovery. His generals, most notably Erhard Milch of the Luftwaffe, had ignored his orders to manufacture the jet plane as a bomber. They had developed it as a fighter. He was furious.

"How many of the Me-262's already manufactured can carry bombs?" he demanded.

"None, mein Führer," answered Milch during the conference at the Berghof. Milch explained that in order for the jet plane to carry a thousand-kilo bomb, it would have to be extensively redesigned.

Hitler had been depending on the Me-262 to retaliate against England for the disastrous Allied bombing raids. He was convinced that the high-speed bomber could not be stopped by the conventional RAF and American fighter planes. He now ordered the cannon, armor, and ammunition removed from the plane and replaced by bombs. Milch and Göring promised to do so, not telling the angry Führer that such a modification was impossible because the armor and cannon were all forward of the plane's center of gravity and that structural reasons made it impossible to hang a bomb from that location on the fuselage. To do what Hitler ordered would make the Me-262 unflyable. The Me-262 was introduced into combat during the final weeks of 1944, but it operated only as fighter. By this time Hitler was beginning to realize that his generals were not obeying his orders as they had done in earlier years. His authority was diminishing as the Allied troops closed in on him.

Hitler's fantasy of bombing New York was another idea that was now ignored. Never plausible, it would nonetheless have been seriously attempted had Hitler so insisted early in the war. Now, when he discussed the plan, which had been devised by General Werner Baumbach of the bombers force, Göring, Milch, and Speer nodded in apparent agreement but did nothing to support the effort.

In support of the Ardennes attack the desperate Führer had accumulated nearly four million litres of gasoline, 50 trainloads of ammunition, nearly 2000 aircraft, and 28 army divisions. On December 16, 1944, he gave the order for the Ardennes attack to begin. Rain and fog were his allies, grounding American and British aircraft that otherwise would have opposed the German attack. Neither Gen. Dwight Eisenhower, Supreme Allied Commander, nor Gen. Omar Bradley, Commander of the Twelfth Army Group, seemed to understand the extent of Hitler's offensive until the following day, and by this time the Fifth Panzer Army was pushing towards Stavelot, where the Americans had most of their supplies stored. The U. S. First Army, commanded by Gen. Courtney Hodges, was forced back on a 50-mile front. Hitler was elated during these initial days of the attack, able once again to contemplate a retreating enemy and a possible victory for his troops. Within five days 25,000 American prisoners were taken, 375 U. S. tanks were destroyed or seriously damaged, and Eisenhower had called off his attacks in other areas of the western front to cope with the Ardennes offensive.

It was a relatively happy Christmas eve for Hitler at his Adlerhorst headquarters. His surprise attack was progressing well; the V-1 and V-2 had shocked the British; the Me-262 was in action; and Göring's Luftwaffe was planning a 1000-plane attack on Allied airfields. On December 24 Hitler lunched with his secretaries as usual, took a short nap, and then invited his close associates at the headquarters, Keitel, Fegelein, Bormann, Jodl, and others, to tea. There was a small Christmas tree in the bunker; the secretaries had placed candles on it. Eva Braun, of course, was missing. Hitler never permitted her to travel to the

war fronts for fear she might be injured. He admitted to Junge
that he missed the Obersalzberg and Eva but stated that it was
much more important for him to be on the western front directing the war than at the Berghof enjoying himself. After sitting
by the candle-lit Christmas tree for a few minutes after dinner,
Hitler called his generals together for another conference and
worked until morning.

On January 1, 1945, Göring, in extremely bad weather,
launched his all-out air attack on the Allied fields, hoping to do
enough damage that American and British planes would not be
able to come to the aid of the besieged U. S. troops in the
Ardennes. The mission was only a partial success. Göring lost
277 of the 1040 planes he launched, more than half of those to
German flak because he neglected to notify the German gun-
ners of the raid. Despite his claim that the Luftwaffe destroyed
500 Allied aircraft, when the weather cleared more than 5000
were still available to strafe and bomb the German forces and
supply the trapped Americans. On January 3 the Americans
started a counteroffensive, aided by their air support, and
within 13 days the bulge was eliminated and the German forces
were in full retreat. Hitler knew he had lost the Ardennes
gamble. Three days later Stalin began a new offensive in the
east.

Hitler returned to Berlin on January 16, although his
thoughts were on the Obersalzberg, the Berghof, and the Eagle's Nest, all of which he longed to see again. He had last been
at the Berghof on July 14, 1944, the day he left for East Prussia.
He had bid his final farewell to the Wolf's Lair and to the
headquarters near Ziegenberg. Now he wondered if he would
ever see the mountains of Bavaria again. If he was going to go
to the Obersalzberg once more, time was running out. He
would have to make his choice soon.

Hitler had long planned to live and die on the Obersalzberg
and to be buried there near his friend, Dietrich Eckart, who
had introduced him to the area. He had expected to die of old
age, but during the war years Hitler became convinced that
when his time came his probably would be a violent death.
Consequently he had given a great deal of thought to his end.
Where? How?

Hitler walking beside his private train with Col. Nicolaus von Below, his Luftwaffe adjutant. *(National Archives)*

After all, hadn't the Eagle's Nest actually been a self-sponsored mausoleum? It was logical he should go there to die. Most of his important decisions had been made in the area of the Obersalzberg, and now that the greatest decision of all had to be made, the urge to return to the mountains was almost overwhelming. But there was another reason also: If at the end he decided he wanted to escape the Allied dragnet and leave Europe, there would be an opportunity to do so from the Obersalzberg. The little-known roads and paths between and over the Hoher Goll, Jenner, Kehlstein, and other mountain peaks in the area afforded excellent opportunities for him to slip from Germany undetected and board a plane for another part of the world. He was well aware that some of his inner circle and their staffs already were making such plans. Hitler also knew that there was still time to follow through on an idea that had been given him first by Gauleiter Franz Hofer of the Tyrol. Hofer had suggested that the region of Aussee, extending roughly from Lake Constance in the west to Bad Aussee and including the Obersalzberg, be developed as a mountain fortress. He argued that the Allied troops would be months, if not years, searching out well-armed German military units in this

Alpenfestung (Alpine redoubt). Meanwhile Hitler could have a safe headquarters on the Obersalzberg, at the Eagle's Nest or the Berghof. Hitler had liked the plan for several reasons. He preferred to make his final stand at his home. He also knew that the longer he could keep his forces engaged in guerrilla-type warfare and thus hold off the Allies, the more chance there was that a disagreement would develop among the Western Allies and the Soviets, allowing him to secure better peace terms. The temptation to go to the Obersalzberg was great, but Hitler hesitated.

The day after he arrived in Berlin from his western head-quarters at Bad Nauheim, Warsaw was liberated by the Russians and approximately 80,000 Jews were freed by Soviet troops in Budapest. On January 30 Hitler made his last radio broadcast. He spoke from the Reich Chancellery, and despite the worsening situation it was an optimistic speech. His adjutant Alwin-Broder Albrecht wrote the following day in his diary: "From all sides the response to the Führer's speech has been indescribably positive." As if to rebut him, four days later the U. S. Eighth Air Force sent nearly a thousand bombers over Berlin and destroyed a great deal more of the Reich Chancellery while Hitler huddled in the bunker.

While in the bunker, listening to the bombs exploding on the city, Hitler remarked to Junge that the Berghof had never been bombed. "Bombers fly over it all the time but they never bomb my home," he remarked. "It is much safer there."

It was true. One of the most puzzling questions of the entire war was why the Obersalzberg was not bombed. As early as 1939 it had been established by Allied authorities that Hitler had a mountain retreat there, and reconnaissance photographs of the Berghof had been taken and analyzed. Intelligence sources also received information throughout the war from anti-Nazi informants when Hitler was in residence at the Berghof or the Eagle's Nest. Yet not once was an attempt made to destroy the Berghof complex or any other installations on the Obersalzberg, although Munich, 100 miles to the north, was often bombed. Finally, on April 25, 1945, when for all practical purposes the fighting was over, the RAF dropped high explosives on the Berghof.

Luftwaffe General Adolf Galland, who commanded the

fighter aircraft, thinks he knows the reason. "Hitler's mountain retreat, the Berghof, was a relatively small house on the Obersalzberg which wasn't easily detected from the air. Attached to the Berghof were the bomb shelters which guaranteed full safety for Hitler even against direct hits by armor-piercing bombs. The same held true for Göring's house in the area which was not bombed either. Furthermore there was an artificial fog system which guaranteed one hundred percent camouflage. When the bombers reached Munich the fog was used to conceal the Berghof."

Others believe there was a more altruistic motive behind the failure to bomb the Obersalzberg area and Hitler's home. Allied intelligence sources had determined that Hitler's confiscated art treasures were being stored in the area. The treasures included paintings, sculptures, and jewels from the Rothschild collections, the Perugia collection, the Neufforge collection, the Mason-Perkins collection, and other collections that had been the property of museums and galleries throughout Europe. Wealthy and influential persons with an interest in the treasure prevailed upon Allied military authorities and civilian leaders not to take a chance of destroying these irreplaceable objects by bombing the Berghof and the surrounding area. If this theory is true, Hitler's death was deemed less important than the security of the art treasures. Obviously such a decision could only have been taken quietly, behind the scenes. After the war most of the art treasure was discovered in the salt mines of the proposed Alpine redoubt area, as had been suspected. At the Heilbronn salt mine there were 830 paintings, 147 pieces of sculpture, 295 antiquities, and 4610 cases of books—the partial contents of museums at Karlsruhe, Mannheim, and Stuttgart. At the Kochendorf salt mines the total was 534 paintings, 52 pieces of sculpture, and 3600 cases of books, besides numerous tapestries. Included among the paintings were Rembrandts, Titians, Brueghels, and Dürers. These valuable items were returned to their owners after the war, as were others located in the same area.

So there was good reason for Hitler to believe he would be much safer on the Obersalzberg than in Berlin. As the days wore on the Allied air raids on Berlin became increasingly frequent and more severe. Hitler insisted that Eva Braun leave Berlin and go to the Berghof. At first she was reluctant to leave him, but Hitler finally convinced her it was for the best and they would be parted only a short time. Gretl Braun Fegelein, pregnant, accompanied her.

On March 7, 1945, the American troops crossed the Rhine at Remagen. The following day Heinz Guderian of the German General Staff told Hitler that Stalin's main attack on Berlin would begin within one week. On March 13 RAF Mosquitoes made a low-level night attack on Berlin, and although other Allied bombing raids had been more devastating, the Mosquito mission affected Hitler and Goebbels personally. Goebbels's ministry building was destroyed. The Führer, who rarely expressed concern over the deaths of German men, women, and children in Berlin during the bombings, seemed as heartbroken as Goebbels over the loss of the building. Ironically, the edifice was destroyed 12 years, to the day, after Goebbels became minister of propaganda and moved in. By the end of March Germany's position was militarily hopeless, and Hitler knew it. So did his inner circle and those military experts who were with him constantly. His followers who were with him in the Berlin bunker began to seek their own salvation.

Otto Dietrich, who received six weeks' leave on displeasing Goebbels, hurriedly left Berlin for safer quarters. That was the last time Hitler saw the Reich press chief. Robert Ley, Labor Front leader, decided this was an excellent time to organize an "Adolf Hitler Free Corps" in Austria and bid Hitler and Berlin farewell. Hans Lammers, chief of the Chancellery, suddenly developed extremely high blood pressure; he asked for and received permission from Hitler to go to Berchtesgaden. Guderian, one of Hitler's favorite generals, began to suffer from poor health, and Hitler dismissed him. Himmler, knowing that Hitler was furious with him because of the defeat of the SS troops in Hungary, avoided Berlin completely and began seeking Allied contacts. Göring and Speer shuttled back and forth between the bunker and their quarters outside the underground death trap.

Watching his "loyal" followers desperately seek excuses to get away from him and the bunker, Hitler realized that his hypnotic power was waning. No longer did Nazi officials fight each other to stay close to their Führer. They were now struggling to get as far away from him as possible, knowing that he was the prize the Allies were seeking. Hitler, however, was determined that he would never be captured. He was still toying with the idea of going to Bavaria and then putting into operation the escape plans he had formulated years earlier. In the triumphant early years the escape plans had seemed more a joke than a real contingency. He planned to fly or go by submarine to South America, where he would be welcomed and given refuge. Given the time and the money—months earlier he had ordered the Nazi treasure hidden in the mountains or placed in secret accounts in banks around the world—he could reestablish his Reich and take power again someday.

The alternative was to stage-manage his own death so that it would go down in history as the tragic end of a great leader who had tried to "save the world from the Soviets and the Jews." Berlin was the spot for the elaborate fight-to-the-death drama to be enacted, since a leader should die in his own capital. Hitler's sense of showmanship tempted him to take this way out; his love of the Obersalzberg lured him to the mountains.

He was still hedging when, during the first week of April, Hitler ordered the completion of the plans for Operation Seraglio. This was the planned evacuation of the Reich Chancellery group from Berlin to Berchtesgaden. Hans Baur, Hitler's personal pilot, was ordered to oversee the construction of an emergency airstrip near the Brandenburg Gate. Altogether Baur had ten aircraft available for the aerial evacuation, some of which were stored in an underground hangar at Templehof and some at Gatow, both airports that were still usable then. The planes were ordered packed with files, documents, valuables, and personal possessions of those to be airlifted out of the beseiged city when Hitler gave the order. No one knew whether Hitler would be one of the passengers. Johanna Wolf and Christa Schröder, his two eldest secretaries, Admiral Karl-Jesco von Puttkamer, his naval aide; Albert Bormann, Martin Bormann's brother; and Theodor Morell, Hitler's physician, were scheduled for the first flight and were waiting frantically for Hitler to give the word. Others, not certain that they would be permitted on one of the planes unless Hitler himself went along, waited just as frantically for Hitler's decision.

Each day in the new month of April brought the outer rim of the Nazi-controlled area closer and closer to the Hitler bunker. On April 17 Hitler ordered the autobahn bridges blown up and every Luftwaffe aircraft, jets included, into the air to defend the capital. But it was useless. The Russians raced at full speed from the Oder toward Berlin. On the opposite side of the city the Americans and British, already across the Rhine and deep into Germany, were also within striking distance of the city, but for a reason unknown to Hitler, their military forces were halted. They were ordered to hold their positions due to supply problems and political considerations. By the eve of his birthday, April 20, the Russians were on the outskirts of the city. Sick at his stomach and suffering a severe headache, Hitler summoned Morell as usual, and the physician gave him an extra portion of his drugs. Hitler then ordered him out.

There had been only one bright moment during the previous week: On April 15 Eva Braun had suddenly walked into the bunker. Hitler was both amazed and delighted. He tried to sound angry as he reminded her that he had ordered her to go to the Berghof, but it was obvious to everyone who witnessed the reunion—the secretaries, Schaub, Magda Goebbels—that he was happy she had returned.

"Who else would come back to Berlin when they had the opportunity to go to the Berghof?" he asked those in the room several times.

The joy of having Eva with him didn't completely outweigh the fact that on his fifty-sixth birthday Berlin came under a heavy bombing attack by the Allies and long-range Russian artillery guns were zeroing in on the city. Even as his inner-circle members and generals paid their final courtesy call on his birthday, Hitler was thinking about the next few days, the last days left for the Third Reich, and what he should do. Keitel and Jodl, his two faithful military advisers, suggested he should leave for Berchtesgaden immediately, while it was still possible to get out of the city. When Hitler didn't respond to this suggestion, Keitel had another. He advised Hitler to move his headquarters to Zossen, 15 miles due south of Berlin. Zossen was headquarters of the German General Staff and the location of Amt 500—the largest long-distance central communications layout in Germany. Hitler grunted. What did he need telephone communications for at this late date? More important, he had no intention of dying in an unknown hamlet. He wanted a superlative stage when the final curtain came down, and there was no better stage than a flaming Berlin.

On his birthday Hitler divided the command of the military forces. Karl Dönitz, grand admiral and builder of the German U-boat arm, was named to command all forces in northern Germany. Hitler left open the name of the commander of all German military forces in the south, giving the impression that he would soon go south to the Obersalzberg and take charge himself.

After the war conference on his birthday, Göring approached Hitler and asked, "Mein Führer, do you have any objection if I leave for Berchtesgaden now?"

Hitler gave his old comrade permission and turned away without bidding him farewell. He felt betrayed.

Himmler, after staying away from Berlin and Hitler for weeks, did return to the capital and the bunker for the Führer's birthday. He was not invited to talk with Hitler in private, despite his 15-year intimate association with the Führer, but was told to wait with the rest to offer his congratulations. Bormann, who watched Himmler closely every minute, noted that Hitler greeted him coldly when they finally met face-to-face and, after a short conversation during which Himmler received the impression the Führer would be leaving for the Eagle's Nest area soon, Himmler bid his leader farewell. He was in a hurry to get out of the bunker to meet with Norbert Masur, a representative of the World Jewish Conference, and Count Folke Bernadotte, son of the brother of Swedish King Gustavus V, who had volunteered to act as the go-between for armistice negotiations with the Allies, which Himmler was instigating without Hitler's knowledge.

Bormann, the most important man next to the Führer, the heavy-set, hated court intriguer who had wormed his way into the number-one spot in Hitler's confidence, now found his power and influence were for naught as the Russians closed in on the bunker. His loyalty didn't waver, however, and he gave no evidence that he would consider leaving Hitler and Berlin. He did keep trying to get Hitler to go to the Obersalzberg. The day after Hitler's subdued birthday celebration, he telephoned his wife at Berchtesgaden and instructed her to take the children to the Tyrol and there pose as a director of refugee youngsters. He didn't tell Hitler about the call.

The same day, with the German-held territory in the Berlin area reduced to a mere 18 square miles, Hitler finally gave the order to put Operation Seraglio into immediate effect. He called Christa Schröder and Johanna Wolf to him and told them it was time to leave.

"You can take two suitcases. You'll fly at dawn."

Hitler also met with his two remaining secretaries, Traudl Junge and Gerda Christian (née Daranowski; she had married General Eckhardt Christian a few months earlier); Konstanze Manzialy, his faithful cook; and Eva Braun.

"It is best that you go to the Obersalzberg immediately," he told them. "There will be aircraft leaving at dawn."

He turned to leave the room, but Eva quickly walked to his side and took both his hands in hers. As though speaking to a sad child, she said, "But you know that I'll stay with you. I won't let myself be sent away."

At that moment Hitler leaned over and kissed Eva on the lips, the first time any of those present had ever seen him do such a thing in all the years they had known him. Just before Eva and Hitler left the room together, the two secretaries and the cook told him that they too intended to stay with him. His powerful attraction for women was still intact, even in his hour of defeat.

As dawn was breaking over rubble-strewn Berlin, Hans Baur's planes took off from the emergency airstrip near the Brandenburg Gate, carrying his passengers to the already loaded larger aircraft at Gatow. Hitler had finally decided where he would make his final stand . . . or had he?

18

The Bunker Mystery

For more than three decades the events in the Führer's bunker during the last days of April 1945 have been depicted according to the immediate postwar investigations and interrogations. Recently, however, new information has been uncovered that gives fresh insight into many of the incidents in the bunker during those final days. The new revelations help explain the motives behind many of Hitler's strange actions.

Hitler and his mistress weren't altogether "roughing it" in the bunker, which by April had become their home. Their apartment, 50 feet underground, was air conditioned and carpeted and had a private bath. To the left of Hitler's small waiting room was the *Lagebesprechungszimmer* (situation conference room), where Hitler met daily with Keitel, Jodl, and other military leaders. A few steps away from their apartment and across the corridor were three rooms assigned to Hitler's physicians for living quarters, medical supplies, and examinations. Near by was the diesel engine used to ventilate the bunker, emergency telephone equipment, and rooms for the guards and secretaries. The corridor running through the bunker was 9 feet wide and 21 feet long, and on its walls hung many famous paintings. At the end of the corridor opposite Hitler and Eva's apartment was a circular staircase of 13 steps, which led to another part of the bunker. This section had 12 rooms: 4 for the kitchen and pantries, 4 for guests, 2 for servants, and 2 for storage. The corridor in this part of the bunker was furnished with tables and chairs and was used as a general-purpose dining room. There were SS guards at each door, and no one could get near the Führer's apartment without the proper identification.

Outside the bunker the territory still held by the German Army was so small that, as one dejected citizen muttered, "It's possible to go from the eastern front to the western front by subway!" The city suffered periodic bombing by Allied planes and constant hammering by Russian artillery. Unter den Linden, the boulevard that had been made famous in song and poem, was the outer rim of the German defense line. It was barricaded by tree trunks and sandbags, behind which were the German soldiers who had vowed to defend their Führer to their dying breath. In the rubble-strewn city, the confused, hungry, and homeless citizens were not even aware that Hitler was in Berlin; they didn't know of the drama that was being enacted below their feet. And that was exactly what Hitler was doing—enacting the final scenes of a historic drama.

Shortly after the Operation Seraglio planes left Berlin for Berchtesgaden on April 21, Hitler collected all his documents and written materials from the cabinets and the desk in his study and ordered Julius Schaub to burn them. Schaub took the material up the stairs to the Reich Chancellery garden and, as instructed, burned it. Hitler then gave him orders to perform the same duty in Munich and Berchtesgaden. With the departure of Schaub, the only members of the Berghof "gang" left were Hewel, Bormann, Fegelein, Below, Günsche, Eva, and the two secretaries.

On April 22 Hitler amazed all his Berghof associates as well as his generals and the others in the bunker. Until recently there was never an adequate possible explanation for the events of that day. At about 3:00 P.M. Hitler routinely began his daily war conference. Although he followed various aspects of the fighting, he was particularly interested in the attack supposedly being made by SS General Felix Steiner 25 miles north of Berlin. He had earlier ordered Steiner to drop back toward the city and attack the Soviet troops already encircling the bunker area. It was an impossible assignment, and it is now believed that Hitler knew that, but on April 22, when he was informed that Steiner had not yet attacked as ordered, Hitler enacted a scene that scared and enthralled everyone who witnessed it. He began to breathe very heavily, his head jerked as though he were having a fit, and he stalked back and forth in the conference room, raving and screaming and swinging his right arm wildly. This scene lasted several minutes. Suddenly he stopped, his jaw dropped, his mouth hung open, and he stared straight ahead into space. It was several minutes before he moved again, and when he did move, he walked out of the room without another word to the stunned visitors.

"The Führer's had a nervous breakdown!" Walther Hewel muttered.

The word was immediately flashed from the bunker to Munich, to OKW headquarters at Zossen, to Munich, and to Berchtesgaden. Yet while this message was being radioed and telephoned throughout Germany to Nazi officials and military officers, Hitler was calmly talking with Goebbels about a final radio broadcast that Goebbels was to make. He was coherent, calm, in complete control of himself. Junge, the secretary, spoke with him after the meeting with Goebbels and found nothing different about him, no indication of a "mental collapse." Neither did Gerda Christian. It appears possible, based on facts now available, that Hitler had wanted to know whom he could trust and whom he couldn't—that he wanted to know this because of a secret plan he had formulated and expected to put into effect shortly.

It didn't take him long to discover that Göring was willing, ready and able—or so Göring thought—to take advantage of Hitler's "collapse." Within hours Hitler received a telegram from Göring stating that unless he heard from Hitler by 10:00 P.M. that night, he was going to take control of the Reich in accordance with a decree of June 29, 1941. Similar telegrams were sent by Göring to Ribbentrop, Keitel, and others, adding the request that they join him in Berchtesgaden, where he was establishing his new headquarters. Hitler ordered the SS commandant at the Obersalzberg complex to place Göring under arrest immediately.

Speer was at Bad Wilsnack when Below telephoned him from the Berlin bunker to inform him that Hitler had had a "mental collapse." Speer reacted differently from Göring. He decided to go to Berlin and personally check on Hitler's condition. This was a very dangerous decision. Hitler was aware that Speer had been traveling throughout Germany in an attempt to convince the German generals not to carry out the Führer's scorched-earth policy. Speer knew he would be walking directly into Hitler's hands, and if the Führer was demented ... Besides, a trip to Berlin was very hazardous then because of enemy action. Speer, despite these odds against him, went anyway. He started from Bad Wilsnack by automobile but discovered that due to clogged and damaged roads, such a trip was impossible. He changed his plans and headed for the Luftwaffe base at Rechlin, where he boarded a transport plane that took him to Gatow airport, near Berlin. From there, instead of commandeering an armored car to take him to the bunker, Speer convinced a daring pilot to fly him to the emergency airstrip near the Brandenburg Gate in a Fieseler Stork observation plane.

When Speer walked into the bunker on April 23, Eva Braun ran to him with outstretched arms.

"I knew you would come," Eva told Speer. "You wouldn't leave the Führer alone."

Speer took her hands in his and smiled. After a few seconds he said, "I'm leaving again tonight." Then he went to find Hitler.

He was shocked to see the change in the bunker. The floor was littered with empty bottles, mess kits, pieces of sandwiches, and other debris. Several of the military officers were drunk, some were sleeping. There appeared to be no discipline, no optimism. He walked alone through the upper bunker and down the 13 steps to the lower section, heading toward Hitler's apartment. The first person he saw on the lower level was Bormann, whom he detested. Now, however, Bormann was all smiles and put out his hand. Speer soon learned the reason for his friendliness.

"When you see the Führer," Bormann said, "try to induce him to leave Berlin and fly to Berchtesgaden."

Speer just shrugged and walked on.

Hitler was in his study when Speer located him. The Führer looked up as he walked in, but there was no smile on his face, no greeting for the man who had been so close to him during the glory years of the Third Reich. Hitler showed no emotion. He didn't even indicate that he appreciated the dangerous trip Speer had made to visit him again. Speer was disappointed, realizing that Hitler hadn't cared whether he saw him again or not. Finally Hitler asked him his opinion about the leadership qualities of Dönitz, the naval officer Hitler had appointed to command all German troops in the north and was now considering as his successor. Speer commented that he thought the admiral was an excellent leader, and Hitler dropped the subject.

"What do you think, Speer? Should I stay here in Berlin or fly to the Berghof?"

Speer didn't hesitate to give Hitler his candid opinion. "Mein Führer, I think it is much better that you meet the end in the capital rather than in your mountain chalet."

Hitler nodded. "I agree."

At that moment Hitler was called to his daily war conference, so Speer went out of the study to Eva's room. He wanted to bid her goodbye, expecting the farewell to be a tearful scene, but much to his surprise she was the calmest person in the bunker. Her hair was newly set, her makeup was perfect, and she was wearing one of her Munich dresses that he had admired. She greeted him with a smile and immediately got him a snack and a bottle of champagne. He was later to remember her cheerful attitude with sadness.

He talked with Eva until 3:00 A.M. and then went to say his final farewell to Hitler. He wanted to get out of Berlin before daylight. The last meeting between Speer and Hitler was very brief. There were no words of praise for past performances, no good wishes, no handshake for the architect who had planned to build a new Berlin for Hitler. The Führer merely nodded and muttered, "So, you're going? Fine."

As he climbed the stairs of the bunker, Speer was convinced that Hitler had not had a "mental collapse" as reported. The Führer was tired and depressed, but far from not knowing what he was doing. He didn't know why Hitler had acted as he had the day before, but from past experiences with the Führer, Speer decided he'd had a reason.

Between April 23 and 26 the bunker drama was confusing to everyone. The hours were filled with terror and uncertainty. No one could sleep.

"We slipped around the bunker like shadows, not knowing

what to do, where to go," Junge explained. "Now and then we slipped up the stairs and looked out at the desolation. Then we would go back down the stairs, glad to be out of the path of the bombs and artillery shells."

Outside the bunker the perimeter held by the German forces became smaller by the hour. Hitler had ordered his generals in the south, southwest, northwest, and north to attack the Soviets immediately and relieve the bunker personnel, but only two of the commanders even tried, and their efforts were ineffective. Dönitz sent some naval troops from his northern sector to help defend Berlin, but it was merely a delaying action. The Russians constantly moved forward toward the small group in the bunker.

On April 26 Hitler gave an order that at the time was very confusing and controversial but now is better understood. He ordered Robert Ritter von Greim, a Luftwaffe general, to report to him in Berlin. At the time Greim commanded Luftflotte VI, in Munich, but Hitler wanted to appoint him commander-in-chief of the entire Luftwaffe to replace Göring. It was an appointment he could have made by telephone or telegram and saved Greim the very hazardous trip into the capital. But Hitler insisted that Greim come to the bunker personally. Why? Probably because Hitler wanted to know if an aircraft—specifically, an autogyro—could still get in and out of Berlin despite the critical military situation. The plan was for Greim to prevail upon Hanna Reitsch, the famous German aviatrix, who was the general's close friend, to fly him by autogyro from the airfield at Rechlin to the street by the bunker. In the early morning of April 26 Greim and Reitsch flew to Rechlin but, once there, discovered that the only autogyro on the field had been damaged by strafing American fighter planes earlier that day. A Luftwaffe pilot offered to fly Greim to Gatow in a Focke-Wulf 190, the fast German fighter plane. Reitsch was to stay behind, since the plane was only a two-seater, but, unseen by Greim, the diminutive lady flier squeezed into an open space behind the back seat and went along.

At Gatow Greim and Reitsch got into a Fiesler Stork observation plane and, with Greim at the controls, hedgehopped toward the center of Berlin. They made it across the Havel

River, flying so low the wheels nearly touched the water. But as Greim cut south of the Olympic Stadium, an artillery burst penetrated the floor of the aircraft and wounded him in the right foot. He lost consciousness almost immediately. Reitsch grabbed the controls and maneuvered the small, crippled plane to a safe landing near the Brandenburg Gate, an exhibition of skill and courage notable even for a woman who'd once suggested to Hitler that she be allowed to pilot a V-1!

A passing vehicle took the pair to the bunker. It was nearly 7:00 P.M. by the time they reached the first level, where they were met by Frau Goebbels. She embraced Reitsch and, between tears and kisses, expressed her astonishment that anyone still possessed the courage and loyalty to come to the Führer; so many had deserted him. Greim was immediately taken to one of the medical rooms across the corridor from Hitler's apartment, where a physician treated his wound. A few minutes later Hitler walked into the room and greeted Reitsch and Greim, remarking that they had been very brave to obey his order when everything indicated that to carry it out would be futile and hopeless.

"Do you know why I have summoned you?" Hitler asked.

Greim shook his head. "No, mein Führer."

"Because Göring has betrayed and deserted both me and his Fatherland," Hitler replied. "Behind my back he has established against my orders connections with the enemy. His action is a mark of cowardice. I hereby declare you Göring's successor. In the name of the German people I give you my hand."

Reitsch was wearing her Iron Cross on her black turtleneck sweater. As Junge said later, "she was so small and delicate-looking one would not have expected manly bravery from her." Hitler, however, knew differently. He was aware that if anyone could get an airplane in and out of Berlin during these final days of the siege, it was Reitsch. After he had bestowed the command of the Luftwaffe on Greim, Hitler and Reitsch went into his study alone and had a long, secret talk. She states that she tried to convince Hitler to leave Berlin, that he should save himself for the good of Germany. She insisted that she could fly him out of the city, take him wherever he wanted to go, but, according to her, he refused. The American interrogators accused her of planning and carrying out Hitler's escape from the city when they questioned her after the end of the war in 1945. When they confronted her with the rumor that Hitler might still be alive in the Tyrol and that her own flight to that area after she left the bunker might have been more than just coincidental, she was upset and kept repeating, "Hitler is dead. Hitler is dead."

Two nights later, after, she vowed, Hitler refused to leave the city, Reitsch and the wounded Greim left the bunker. Outside in the Reich Chancellery garden they saw that the whole city was aflame. Heavy small-arms fire was plainly audible a short distance away. SS troops assigned to guard Hitler until the end were moving about in the garden. They brought up a small armored vehicle in which they took Greim and Reitsch to an Arado 96, a training plane, hidden near the Brandenburg Gate. The sky was filled with the noise of bursting shells, and several hundred yards short of where the aircraft was hidden, their vehicle was badly damaged. They had to walk the remainder of the distance with Reitsch half-carrying the wounded Greim. She helped him into the small plane and leaped in behind him, and they took off in a hail of Russian fire. Searchlights intermittently lit up their aircraft, and exploding shells knocked the Arado 96 about like a feather in a windstorm. They weathered the enemy attacks, however, and flew north to see Dönitz. Why? Reitsch has said they were seeking Himmler, but her answer is unconvincing.

Himmler didn't figure in Hitler's final plans, but when the Führer learned through a Reuters news report on April 28 that Himmler had made a peace-feeler to the Allies in the west, he felt the sting of one more betrayal. Press Secretary Heinz Lorenz intercepted the message and quickly relayed it to Bormann, who was determined to destroy Himmler's remaining standing with the Führer just as he had helped destroy that of Göring, Speer, and other inner-circle members whom he thought might have more influence with Hitler than himself. The Führer quickly agreed that Dönitz, at his command post approximately 300 miles to the north on the Plöner See, should be notified to move quickly and decisively against all traitors, including Himmler. Reitsch says she was supposed to take this message to Dönitz, but it is known that the order was dispatched in a telegram several hours before she and Greim left Berlin by air. Renewed investigations during the 1970s into the bunker events indicate Dönitz figured prominently in Hitler's final plan, but in a different manner.

Intertwined with the Himmler betrayal of the Führer is the strange case of Hermann Fegelein, Eva Braun's brother-in-law. Fegelein was the liaison officer between Himmler and Hitler and was one of the Berghof circle. After he married Gretl Braun he was even closer to Hitler and rose in the Nazi hierarchy. On Friday, April 27, one day before Hitler learned of Himmler's secret attempt to contact the Allies, Fegelein was missing from the bunker. Hitler suddenly recalled he hadn't seen him for a couple of days, and he became curious. He gave Johann Rattenhuber of the SS orders to find Fegelein at once. With the help of Otto Günsche, the SS located him in bed with his mistress in an apartment on Bleibtreustrasse and took him back to the bunker. By the time Fegelein returned to face Hitler, however, the news of Himmler's treason had reached the bunker. Fegelein was doomed. Despite Eva Braun's plea that her sister was pregnant and that the father of the child should be allowed to live, Hitler was adamant. He bellowed that Fegelein undoubtedly was a part of the Himmler plot, that he was a traitor who had been caught trying to escape. Hitler never explained how Fegelein was trying to make his getaway while in bed with a blonde. Shortly before midnight on April 29, Fegelein was executed. But subsequent information indicates there was an entirely different reason why Hitler wanted him dead before another day had passed.

With Göring, Speer, and Himmler gone from the bunker, the only intimate Nazi associates of rank left with Hitler were Bormann and Goebbels. The minister of propaganda played out his role to the end in a manner which might have made his children proud—except that none of his children survived the bunker either. All six died with Goebbels and his wife, Magda, leaving only a stepson alive. Hitler himself approved the murder of these children.

On April 22 Goebbels, after holding a conference with Hitler, walked into the room where Junge was working, looked around to make certain no one else was in the room, and then stepped to her side.

"In a short while my family will be coming to the bunker," Goebbels told her. "Please be so kind as to receive my family."

The Goebbels family arrived from their residence near the Brandenburg Gate later that same day. Magda Goebbels was immediately received in private by Hitler, while Junge took charge of the children. The five little girls and the boy were unaffected by the turn of events. They were happy to be with their "Uncle Adolf." They knew nothing of the fate that awaited them. Junge, cheered somewhat by their laughter and playing, took them to the room where Hitler's birthday presents were stored, because she knew there were also toys packed away in that same room. The children selected the playthings they wanted and were soon busily occupied with the new items, completely oblivious of the artillery shells bursting outside the bunker. Meanwhile Hitler and Goebbels were discussing the

Joseph and Magda Goebbels and three of their six children, all of whom they murdered before committing suicide themselves on April 29, 1945. *(National Archives)*

final propaganda move the Führer should make. It was decided, at Hitler's insistence, that Goebbels would announce
over the Berlin radio that Hitler was in Berlin and would die
with his troops, defending the capital. This would be the first
time that the Berliners were made aware the Führer was in
their midst. The citizens of Germany had not heard from Hitler
since his radio address on January 30, and he had not told them
where he was then. Now, however he wanted everyone to think
he was prepared to die in the besieged bunker.

The six children continued to play contentedly in the corridor of the bunker. They often sat at the round table in the
corridor and read fairy tales. In the afternoon "Uncle Adolf"
drank chocolate with them and listened while they chatted
about their various school experiences, this routine suggesting
that Hitler was far from being a depressed, raving madman
during the final days in the bunker. On one occasion Helmut,
the only boy, read an essay he had written especially for Hitler's birthday, and "Uncle Adolf" was extremely proud. Sometimes during these sessions they were joined by their mother,
Magda, who already had in her purse the poison destined to be
used on the six children—Helga, 12; Hilde, 11; Helmut, 10;
Holde, 8; Hedde, 6; and Heidi, 4.

During the short visit to the bunker by Hanna Reitsch, she
and Eva Braun put the children to bed at night. Magda Goebbels was unable to act calmly with her own children as the time
approached to put them to death, so others aided her.

"One evening when Hanna and Eva were putting the children to bed I passed their room and heard all six children
singing," Junge said. "I entered. They were sitting in their little
bunk beds, each holding his own ears so he wouldn't hear the
voices of the others. Hanna was singing with them and directing the Goebbels choir. They then wished each other goodnight
and went to sleep peacefully, the only ones in the bunker who
could do so. Helga, the oldest, however, often had a sad, knowing expression in her large brown eyes. I think she was aware
that the adults were play-acting, that death was near."

Junge couldn't understand how parents could allow such
innocent and beautiful children to die. Magda Goebbels tried
to explain.

"Our children would rather die than live in shame and misery," she told Junge. "They will have no place in the Germany that will exist after the war." Of course no one had asked the children their opinion.

In a way, Junge felt sorry for Magda Goebbels, who faced a many-fold task; others had only themselves to be concerned about at the end. Yet Junge felt that the deaths of the Goebbels children were a tragedy that could have been avoided.

On April 29, a critical day for Hitler and for the others still in the bunker, Goebbels attached his own final remarks to the private testament Hitler had dictated to Junge. The following day Hitler put his plan into effect, and Joseph Goebbels and his wife Magda knew it was time for them to do the same. The mother, in the end, was the stronger and performed the deed. She gathered her children around her and gently told them that Uncle Adolf had gone away for a while and they would join him shortly. As a treat she gave them each a chocolate ... containing a sedative. Within minutes they were asleep. Sometime during the next few hours Magda Goebbels administered the cyanide poison to each child. Evidently she had trouble giving the oldest girl, Helga, the lethal dose, because the Soviet autopsy report of a week later reported that there were several black-and-blue bruises on the girl's body. It was deduced that the sedative had not been strong enough for the 12-year-old.

Magda reappeared from the bedroom after the murders, went to a table in the corridor of the bunker, drank a small bottle of champagne, and left the immediate area. A short time later she and her husband walked up the stairs from the bunker to the Reich Chancellery garden, where Magda crushed a cyanide capsule between her teeth. Her husband leaned over her fallen body and put a bullet into her blond head. A few seconds later he took poison and simultaneously shot himself.

The events that had convinced them of that really began during the night of April 28–29. Early on the evening of April 28 Eva Braun received a note of appreciation from a young Waffen SS orderly, Hermann Grossman. Two days earlier she had interceded with Hitler on Grossman's behalf and obtained permission for him to marry his longtime girl friend. She had even convinced Hitler to attend the wedding with her. When she received a note of appreciation from the orderly on April

28, she went to Hitler and read it to him: "If I am killed in battle now I will die happy because I was permitted to marry my sweetheart and the Führer congratulated me personally."

Hitler didn't say a word; he just stared at Eva as she held the note to her breast and murmured, "I am so happy for them."

Eva returned to her chair at the other side of the room, but Junge saw Hitler suddenly get to his feet and walk over to her. He leaned down and whispered into her ear, and Eva appeared shocked at his words. Hitler smiled, nodded to reassure her, and walked from the room. Eva, now smiling broadly, walked over to Junge and said, "Tonight you will cry."

Junge and the others, who had been waiting for Hitler to end his life so they could try to escape from the bunker, were now certain that Hitler and Eva intended to commit suicide together, possibly that very night. Junge, however, couldn't understand why Eva seemed so happy.

The secretary soon found out. Hitler summoned her and told her he wanted to write his private testament and will. As soon as he started dictating, Junge knew the reason Eva was so happy.

Although during my years of struggle I believed I could not take the responsibility of marriage, I have now decided at the end of my life's journey to marry the young woman who, after many years of true friendship, came of her own free will to this city when it was already almost completely under siege in order to share my fate. At her own desire she will go to her death with me as my wife. This will compensate us for what we both lost through my work in the service of my people.

Eva was not going to die that night. She was going to be married. Goebbels dispatched several soldiers from the bunker to get Walter Wagner, a justice of the peace who had been drafted to fight in the front lines during the final defense of Berlin. After Wagner arrived, Eva and Hitler appeared for the ceremony. Eva was wearing Hitler's favorite dress, a black silk with pink shoulder straps. Her accessories were black suede shoes, a pearl necklace, and a platinum watch with diamonds for numbers. It was a short ceremony punctuated by artillery bursts overhead. Wagner was more nervous than Eva and Hitler and even asked for Eva's identity card, although he had the presence of mind to write "personally known" in the blank requiring verification of Hitler's identity.

After the wedding Eva and Adolf and their bunker friends went to Hitler's study for the *Hochzeitsmahl* (wedding breakfast). It was now about 2:00 A.M., and after a few toasts and idle conversation Hitler once again joined Junge to complete the draft of his will and testament. The next morning Below, the Luftwaffe adjutant, left the bunker to try to get a copy out of Berlin so it would be preserved for history. Just when Hitler joined Eva for their first night as man and wife is not known, but it was very close to dawn on April 29.

April 29 was the pivotal day for the Führer and his new wife. Eva, radiant, appeared at the breakfast table at 11:00 A.M., and when the others didn't know how to address her because she was now married, she solved the problem easily. "You may call me Frau Hitler." She joined Hitler at the table and was pouring herself a cup of coffee when an adjutant handed a note to the Führer. Hitler was so engrossed in the message that he spilled his tea on his pants. Eva, using a towel, began to wipe the tea from his clothing, but he just shook his head and handed her the note.

Benito Mussolini is dead. Captured by Italian partisans as he attempted to escape into Switzerland from northern Italy, he was taken before a tribunal and sentenced to death. In the village of Dongo the sentence was executed by partisans who machine-gunned him in the back. His mistress, Clara Petacci, who was with him at the time of his attempted escape, was also captured and killed with the ex-Duce. Their bodies were taken to Milan and subjected to public degradation. After being dragged through the streets they were hung head downward in the public square where thousands spat at and reviled the corpses.

It was a Reuters despatch, and Hitler didn't doubt its authenticity.

Hitler motioned for Dr. Ludwig Stumpfegger, the quiet, unassuming doctor who had replaced Brandt and Morell, to join him. "Would my dog Blondi respond to the cyanide the same as a human?"

"Yes, mein Führer."

Hitler gave the doctor a cyanide capsule and motioned towards the small anteroom where the dog was kept. A minute later there was the bitter-sweet odor of the poison and Stumpfegger returned.

"The dog is dead."

Eva kept fingering her capsule and staring at the table. She didn't say a word. Hitler, however, wanted to know if he would still have the strength to pull the trigger of his pistol once he took the poison. Stumpfegger assured him he would. It was obvious to everyone in the room that the stage was set for the final act. When? That was the question.

On April 30 Hitler didn't appear until nearly noon. Eva, however, was up early and took care of several personal matters. While walking past the adjutants' room, she heard Otto Günsche ordering jerricans full of gasoline to be placed near the bunker exit so they would be available to "burn the bodies of the Führer and his frau." She hurried to her bedroom and called Junge. Opening her closet door, she pointed to the beautiful silver fox coat that she adored.

"I want you to have this coat as a farewell gift."

Junge nodded, knowing that her own chances of ever getting out of Berlin alive were not good and she certainly couldn't take a silver fox coat under her arm or wear it during the attempt. She began to cry and hurried from the room.

At 2:30 P.M. Eva and Hitler had lunch with Junge, Christian, and Manzialy. Hitler had a small dish of spaghetti; Eva had only a cup of tea. After eating, Eva went to her bedroom. Hitler went to his study and spoke with Baur, his personal pilot. Baur once again suggested Hitler try to escape to Argentina or Japan, but Hitler only smiled.

At 3:30 P.M. Günsche announced throughout the bunker that the Führer wished to bid farewell. Hitler and Eva appeared in the corridor outside his study. Eva's hair was freshly washed and set. She wore Hitler's favorite dress and the watch he had given her several years earlier. Incredibly, she was smiling. Hitler, however, was very somber as those still remaining in the bunker bid the pair farewell. Goebbels, contemplating his own end, shook hands with the Führer. Some were obviously relieved that the end of the Führer was near, releasing them from their loyalty to him; others were near panic in the realization that they would be alone. Junge kissed Eva and quietly said, "Farewell."

Eva embraced her and whispered, "Tell everyone in Munich farewell. Tell my parents I love them."

Then it was time. Hitler motioned for Eva to go into the study, and he followed her. Just before the door closed, Eva turned and looked back at Junge and smiled. There was complete silence in the bunker. Suddenly a shot rang out. No one moved for several seconds. All were stunned by the knowledge that the Third Reich was no more. Then the door was opened. Hitler was slumped on one end of the blue-and-white couch, blood running down his face from the single bullet he had fired from his Walther 7.65 pistol after he had swallowed the poison. On the other end of the couch Eva was reclining as though asleep, her feet pulled up underneath her. Her little pistol was beside her, unfired.

Hitler was dead . . . or was he?

19

Hitler's Final Secret

On May 2, 1945, the headline of *The New York Times* proclaimed the news that shook the world: HITLER DEAD IN CHANCELLERY, NAZIS SAY. This headline was based on a radio announcement made by Admiral Karl Dönitz, Hitler's appointed successor, on the evening of May 1. Dönitz eulogized Hitler as "one of the greatest heroes of German history," who died "fighting at the head of his troops in Berlin." On the basis of this single announcement by an admiral nearly 200 miles from the bunker, a man who had not been in Berlin since April 21, Hitler's death was accepted as fact—especially after a telegram was discovered at Dönitz's headquarters upon the arrest of the admiral by the Allied Control Commission on May 23.

Grand Admiral Dönitz
Most secret—urgent—officer only
The Führer died yesterday at 1530 hours. Testament of 29 April appoints you Reich president, Reich Minister Dr. Goebbels as Reich chancellor, Reichsleiter Bormann as party minister, Reich Minister Seyss-Inquart as foreign minister. By order of the Führer, the testament has been sent out of Berlin to you, to Field Marshal Schörner and for preservation and publication. Reichsleiter Bormann intends to go to you today and to inform you of the situation. Time and form of announcement to the press and to the troops is left to you. Confirm receipt. Goebbels.

Dönitz based his statements about Hitler's death on the information from Goebbels, who, during his career as minister of propaganda, had often made false announcements for self-gain or for the benefit of Hitler. The British and Americans demanded that the Germans deliver Hitler's body to them so that the proper indentification could be made by medical experts. The Germans were willing, or so they professed, but unable to do so because the Soviet Union had authority over the area containing the bunker where Hitler had supposedly died. American and British authorities then made the same request of the Russians and were completely ignored—for good reason, we now know. The Russians couldn't find the body of Hitler or the body of his mistress, Eva Braun, and didn't want to lose face by admitting this fact. There was considerable controversy between the Soviet authorities in Berlin and Stalin in Moscow over the location of Hitler's burial, or whether he was even dead. Stalin believed that his search teams were trying to appease him by declaring that a body they had found in the Reich Chancellery was Hitler's. Marshal Georgi Zhukov, the Soviet commander in Berlin, was convinced that the corpse was Hitler's, and he told that to several western military officers and diplomats. However on June 9 Zhukov retracted his statement and later told Gen. Dwight D. Eisenhower that there was no solid evidence of Hitler's death. Eisenhower made a similar announcement to the press while in Paris a few days later, basing his opinion on the information given him by Zhukov.

By autumn 1945 rumors were heard every day about sightings of Hitler and Eva Braun. Argentina, Spain, Bavaria, Italy, the Panama Canal—supposedly the Führer had been seen and identified in each of these spots and in many others. The British and the Americans, stymied in investigating further because of the Soviet Union's refusal to permit them into the Russian zone on such a mission, launched another type of investigation, an indirect sleuthing effort by Hugh Trevor-Roper, for the British, and Michael A. Musmanno, for the United States. Hampered by their inability to do any on-the-scene detective work and the refusal of the Russians to permit them to talk with any of the Germans taken prisoner in Berlin, Trevor-Roper and Musmanno had to rely on circumstantial evidence. Their task was to interview witnesses who had not been captured and imprisoned by the Russians: Erich Kempka; Artur Axmann Hitler Youth Leader; Traudl Junge; Gerda Christian; Göring;

Speer; Else Krüger, Bormann's secretary; and the Braun parents. Some had been in the area at the end of the Third Reich, but only Kempka, Junge, Axmann, Krüger and Christian were in the bunker, and their stories varied considerably. Kempka said he had heard a shot as he stood outside the Führer's study, but Axmann, in the same location, said he hadn't. Junge was on the upper level of the bunker with the Goebbels children after saying her final farewell, and she heard the shot. In fact she stated that one of the Goebbels children yelled "Bulls-eye!" when the shot rang out. Later, when Heinz Linge was found, he too said he was standing beside the door of the study and heard the shot. Yet evidence produced later proved that Linge was nowhere near the study but had been so panic-stricken that he was running up and down the stairs leading to the Reich Chancellery garden. Kempka, it was learned later, also was not in the bunker at the time but was still above ground, hurrying towards the underground headquarters. Those not in the bunker told the two investigators what they knew about Hitler's plans, but obviously they couldn't give any hard evidence. The most valuable find during the investigations was Hitler's last will and testament, in triplicate. This document was interesting but certainly was not proof that Hitler had died in the bunker. The conclusions of both Trevor-Roper and Musmanno, however, were the same: Hitler *had* died there. They came to this conclusion then primarily because in their opinion there was no obvious way Hitler could have escaped from the bunker on April 30. There was no substantial proof of his death, no body, no verification by the Russians that they had found Hitler's body.

Missing during these investigations immediately after the war were the witnesses who had been in the bunker but who were taken prisoner by the Russians. They were Günsche, Rattenhuber, Baur, and Harry Mengershausen, an SS officer who supposedly had helped bury Hitler's body. These men were not released until 1956 from the Lubianka Prison, in Moscow; Vorkuta Prison, in the Arctic; and the prison at Sverdlovsk. Immediately thereafter, those who were convinced Hitler was dead and those who were convinced Hitler was still alive converged on these men and interrogated them. Trevor-Roper was among the investigators. Unfortunately the newly released prisoners could not actually verify Hitler's death. Trevor-Roper stated that their revelations did not conflict with his 1945 conclusions; but his 1945 conclusions were based on circumstantial evidence, and the new information was not intrinsically more valuable. Mengershausen said he had given the Russians a statement that he had helped bury the body of Hitler, but he admitted later that he had done so after another German had told his captors that Mengershausen had participated in the incident, and Mengershausen wanted to please the Russians. The second German, whose testimony allegedly coerced Mengershausen into confessing his part in the affair, was never identified by the Russians, nor was it ever proved that Mengershausen actually did aid with the burial. In addition, later reports indicate that the corpse that was dug up was so badly burned it was not recognizable. Even if Mengershausen had helped bury a body, he would have had no way of knowing it was Hitler's body except through hearsay.

Until 1968, 23 years after the end of the Third Reich, Hitler's death was predicated on hearsay, circumstantial evidence, the doubtful testimony of Henry Mengershausen that he had helped bury a burned body, and the statement of Käte Heusemann, an assistant to Hitler's former dentist, Hugo Blaschke, that she recognized a number of dental fittings the Russians had shown her in a cigar box. No court in the world would normally accept such evidence as proof of death. In 1968 the long-awaited "official" Russian report on Hitler's death was published. If before the report there was confusion and speculation about what happened to the Führer, there was rampant disbelief of the evidence afterwards.

The first and greatest discrepancy, if previous testimony by eyewitnesses considered the most reliable is to be believed, was the autopsy report headed Mortuary CAFS No. 496, Forensic Medical Commission of the Red Army, and dated May 8, 1945. As cause of death this report stated, in part:

On the body, considerably damaged by fire, no visible signs of severe lethal injuries or illnesses could be detected. The presence in the oral cavity of the remnants of a crushed glass ampule and of similar ampules in the oral cavity of other bodies and the marked smell of bitter almonds emanating from the bodies and the forensic chemical test of internal organs which established the presence of cyanide compounds permit the Commission to arrive at the conclusion that death in this instance was caused by poisoning with cyanide compounds.

No bullet hole! Yet most of the eyewitnesses in the bunker on April 30 said they had heard a shot. Mengershausen testified that [there was a hole in Hitler's head from a pistol shot.] Linge vowed there was a bullet hole in Hitler's right temple and blood was streaming down his face. Kempka told interrogators that he believed Hitler shot himself in the mouth. Yet the Russian report stated there was no bullet hole in the corpse their experts identified as the body of Hitler.

When it came to the identification of the teeth and dentures, the report strained the credulity of even the most devoted "Hitler-is-dead" believer. Trevor-Roper learned during his 1945 investigation that two Russian officers had gone to the office of Hitler's former dentist, Hugo Blaschke, on May 9 of that year. When Blaschke could not be located—he had gone to Bavaria—his assistant, Käte Heusemann, was questioned by the Russians about Hitler's dental records. When she told them that Hitler never went to Blaschke's office but that the dentist was always summoned to the Reich Chancellery, they took her with them to the building. No records could be found, so she was taken to Russian headquarters and shown a number of dental fillings in a cigar box. One look and this assistant did what she knew the Russians wanted her to do—she identified the fillings as belonging to Hitler. For her cooperation she was arrested and sent to a Russian prison camp. To strengthen this "evidence" the Russians vowed that Heusemann had described every detail of Hitler's teeth—bridges, crowns, and fillings— from memory and these details matched "exactly" with X ray pictures the Russians already had in their possession. Of course we have to take the word of the Russians, because no one in the west has heard of Heusemann since. And if Hitler shot himself in the mouth, as Kempka stated, where did the undamaged fillings, crowns, and bridges come from?

In 1972 Dr. Reidar Soggnaes, a dental forensic expert from

UCLA looked at pictures of the dentures supposedly taken from Hitler's corpse and stated that they exactly matched the X ray head plates of Hitler taken in 1943. However, it is not unthinkable that the Soviets could have obtained a copy of OI Final Interrogation Report (OI-FIR) No. 31, which is titled *Hitler's Teeth.* Bearing until 1974 the relatively low U. S. Army security classification "Confidential," it is a report by Dr. Hugo Blaschke, Hitler's personal dentist. The report gives details about the Führer's natural teeth, replacements, cavities untreated, and color of teeth, and has many drawings. Any dentist or dental technician could easily make dentures to match the drawings, and many think this is exactly what the Russians did sometime between 1945 and 1968. If they did, obviously Dr. Soggnaes would conclude the photograph and the X rays matched.

Another discrepancy pertaining to the dental identification is minor but throws still more suspicion on the Soviet report. Käte Heusemann, Blaschke's assistant, was questioned by the Russians one day *after* the date of their report. It appears that in an effort to convince the world that they had identified Hitler's corpse within a few days after the end of the Third Reich, the Russians backdated their report and then held it secret for 23 years.

The one section of the report that has caused more controversy and gained more publicity than any other is the "missing testicle" statement. The Soviet document, under item (c) of the conclusion, states: The left testicle could not be found either in the scrotum or on the spermatic cord inside the inguinal canal, nor in the small pelvis." This claim has been disputed by many persons who certainly should know, including several women still alive today, who for obvious reasons shall remain nameless. As one former intimate female friend of Hitler's told me, "I just want to emphasize that his organs were entirely normal. Do normal men only have one?"

But even more damning to the Russians' delayed report is the evidence given in *Hitler's Medical Report,* on file at the National Archives, in Washington, D.C. Listed as OI Consolidated Interrogation Report No. 4, it includes testimony by six physicians who examined Hitler at various times: Dr. Morell and Dr. Giesing, mentioned earlier; Dr. Walter Loehlein, director of the clinic in Berlin; Dr. Karl Weber, of Bad Nauheim; Dr. A. Nissle, of Freiburg; and Dr. E. Brinkmann, of the Medical Diagnostic Institute, Berlin. Not one stated there was any thing abnormal about Hitler's genital region.

Why, then, is it generally accepted that Hitler is dead? No one in the west ever saw Hitler's corpse. The photographs distributed 23 years later by the Russians certainly prove nothing except that there was a burned corpse in a wooden box, and in 1945 there were literally thousands of such corpses in the Berlin area. The Russians admit they cremated the body and scattered the ashes, on or about May 15, 1945. Those Nazis who escaped the bunker and the Russians after Hitler's supposed suicide agree on few details, and during the past 30 years many of them have changed their stories repeatedly to fit the occasion. Those who were imprisoned by the Soviets and returned many years later offered no more reliable verification of Hitler's death. In prison, hundreds of miles from Germany and at the mercy of the Russians, these Nazis were in no position to antagonize their captors. They told the interrogators what they wanted to hear, and the Russians incorporated it into their "official" report released nearly a quarter of a century after Hitler's supposed death. Hitler is believed to be dead because most people want to believe it, not because hard evidence confirms his death.

Anyone who spends much time studying the reports and the errors contained in them, errors discovered after cross-checking with information that has surfaced during the past three decades, realizes there is a good possibility that Hitler did *not* die in the bunker on April 30, 1945. I first realized the existence of this possibility eight years ago, many years after I had accepted at face value the conclusions of Trevor-Roper, Musmanno, U. S. and British authorities, and even most present-day German leaders.

On March 21, 1970, I was staying at the Palace Hotel in Bari, Italy, while doing research about one of the most successful Luftwaffe missions of World War II. Göring's planes had pulled a sneak attack on Allied ships in the old harbor at Bari on a December night in 1943, sinking a large number of ships that were bringing supplies into Foggia for the newly formed USAAF Fifteenth Air Force. One of the ships had contained mustard bombs, and when it sank the escaping poison caused havoc. I was interviewing several Italian citizens about their experiences during the German air raid. One of the citizens suggested I contact a Hans Abert, a former Luftwaffe pilot who had taken part in the 1943 mission to Bari and was now living nearby. I called Abert, and that afternoon, as I sat in his apartment, he gave me many details about the raid on the city. When I told him I thought it was the most daring and successful air mission of World War II, however, he shook his head.

"Not as far as I am concerned," he said. "The mission I flew to Berlin the night of April 30, 1945, was the most dangerous."

I was well aware that the emergency airstrip Hans Baur had maintained near the Brandenburg Gate was not usable on April 30. My research indicated that Hanna Reitsch, on April 28, had been the last one to use the airstrip. Shortly afterward Russian artillery bursts had ripped it apart. I told Abert this.

"Perhaps," he said, "but I did not land there. I landed on the Havel river."

I immediately decided that he had the wrong date, because it had been determined by various investigators in 1945 that on the night of April 29 a lumbering, metal-skinned Ju-52 equipped with floats had indeed landed on the Havel to pick up Willi Johannmeier, Hitler's army adjutant, Heinz Lorenz, and Wilhelm Zander, deputy to Bormann, each of whom were carrying a copy of Hitler's last will and testament. The copies were to be delivered to Dönitz, Field Marshal Albert Kesselring, and Field Marshal Ferdinand Schörner. Through a mix-up in identification, the plane had taken off without the three couriers. I told Abert that he must mean he made the flight to Berlin on the night of April 29.

"No. April 30," he insisted. "I was after a more precious cargo than the Führer's last will and testament."

"Such as?"

Abert just smiled. "It wasn't Bormann."

No matter how many additional questions I asked, he would not elaborate. I knew he had mentioned Bormann's name because of the publicity that the search for Hitler's deputy had garnered in the media over the years. After leaving Bari I completely forgot about Abert's remarks, convinced that either he was in error on his dates or he was trying to impress me about a flight that never took place. I didn't think of him again until three years later, when I was in West Germany, talking with a former Luftwaffe fighter pilot about the bombing of Berlin in 1944. We were in Munich at Der Königshof on February 10, 1973, discussing the first American bomber mission to Berlin, during which I had piloted a B-17 and the German, Kurt Barth, had opposed me in an Me-109 fighter. After "hangar flying" for a couple of hours, we were ready to part when Barth said he had flown fighters in the Berlin area until the end of the war and had never been shot down.

"In fact I flew escort for a Ju-52 floatplane the night of April 30, when the war was really over as far as we were concerned," Barth said.

April 30! "Don't you mean the twenty-ninth?" I asked.

He shook his head. "I flew escort for this Ju-52 on both the twenty-ninth and thirtieth," he insisted. "On the twenty-ninth we didn't pick up anyone, but on the thirtieth we—"

"You picked up someone on the thirtieth?"

Barth shrugged. "I was busy in the cockpit, so I don't really know. When the flight engineer gave me the signal I took off."

Now my curiosity was aroused. But Barth either couldn't or wouldn't say anything else about this mysterious mission, so I knew I would have to hunt elsewhere for further information. Fortunately I already had an appointment in Madrid to see Otto Skorzeny, Hitler's commando chief, who had promised to tell me about his visits with Eva Braun. I decided he would be an ideal person to query about the April 30 flight into Berlin, but I knew I would have to be very careful how I approached the subject. Skorzeny, during the years after the end of the Third Reich, had been accused many times of operating a clandestine organization that protected ex-Nazis in various parts of the world and made certain that they had adequate personal financing.

In Madrid on February 20 I went to the fourth floor of an office building on Montera Street and met with Skorzeny. The giant with the dueling scar on his cheek was jovial and very informative about the subject of my interview, Hitler's mistress. As delicately as I could, I led the conversation around to the last days of Hitler's life and then, playing on Skorzeny's vanity, said, "A man as clever as you should have been able to extricate Hitler from that bunker."

He looked at me for several long seconds, and I knew how the German officers who had tried to assassinate Hitler on July 20, 1944, must have felt when Skorzeny caught up to them a few days later. Finally Skorzeny said, "Do you think Hitler is dead?"

"Certainly," I lied.

He seemed relieved. "Yes, I could have gotten him out of Berlin easily. I had a plan."

As though anxious to tell someone about this plan, Skorzeny explained to me that after dark on the night of April 30 it would have been possible for Hitler to leave the bunker by a subterranean passage under the Reich Chancellery, climb to street level on the Hermann Göring Strasse, cut across the Tiergarten to the Zoo Station area near the Adolf Hitler Platz, and follow the railway lines to the Reichssportfeld. He could then have crossed the Scharndorfestrasse, traversed the Piechelsdorf Bridge, and walked to the Havel.

I nodded. "Once he reached the Havel he was trapped. Where could he go then?" Would he mention the Ju-52, I wondered?

Skorzeny grinned. "He could have been picked up by a seaplane that would have landed on the Havel."

I was shocked. Here was Hitler's commando chief actually telling me that the April 30 flight described by both Abert in Bari and Barth in Munich could have been made to pick up Hitler!

"Sounds plausible but not practical," I said. "I don't think Hitler could have followed the route you described, because the Soviet troops were everywhere."

"Zander, Johannmier, and Lorenz followed it the night before," Skorzeny insisted. "And others broke out from the bunker after the thirtieth. I *know* it could be done."

"How do you know? You were on the Oder?"

He laughed. "Was I?"

I didn't pursue the matter any further but changed my line of questioning. "It's a nice fairy-tale theory, but we all know Hitler took poison and then shot himself. Günsche, Kempka, Linge, and others saw his body, burned it, and buried it."

"If it wasn't a double," Skorzeny said.

I had heard the story about Hitler's doubles many times. Baur once mentioned that a man in Breslau who resembled Hitler a great deal may have been used at various times by the Führer's SS Bodyguard Regiment.

"Had Hitler decided to take part in a breakout," Skorzeny said, "a double could have been used to camouflage or facilitate his escape."

I also knew that Pauline Kohler, the maid at the Berghof, had insisted for years that Hitler had three doubles and only the Gestapo knew their names.

"One of the doubles is always at Berchtesgaden, another at Munich, and the third in Berlin," she vowed.

Now Skorzeny was insinuating that perhaps Hitler's double and not Hitler himself had been buried in the Reich Chancellery garden on April 30, 1945!

"Do you think it was a double?" I asked him.

Skorzeny laughed. "The Russian report states that the Führer is dead. They should know."

After my visit to Skorzeny, in 1973, I talked with many other Germans who were associated with Hitler in one way or another. None ever gave me an irrefutable answer about Hitler's death. When I visited Albert Speer at his mountain home in the Allgäu near Lake Constance in 1976, he, like most others, accepted that Hitler was dead. But he also stated that he felt certain Bormann was dead, despite the fact that no corpse was ever found and identified as Bormann's. However remarks and letters from former Hitler associates, such as Hanna Reitsch, Adolf Galland, and Leni Riefenstahl, gave me enough new information that I could determine what might have happened on April 30, 1945.

There are several indications that prior to this climactic day Hitler had carefully projected a false image of his mental and physical condition and had misled even Eva Braun about his plans. Undoubtedly Morell's drugs had affected Hitler's health, but he was not as weak or decrepit as he appeared. Several times during the final days in the bunker, he had shown flashes of his old energy and enthusiasm, especially when there was good news from the front in the daily report. During this period he determined who he could take into his confidence regarding his secret plan to escape from the bunker. It hadn't taken him long to discover that as the Third Reich fizzled out, many of his closest associates were deserting him. Bormann, Eva Braun, Gebbels, and the secretaries were loyal, but only' Bormann could aid him with his final plan.

At first Hitler thought he could be airlifted secretly from the bunker area by autogyro, and he had full confidence in Hanna Reitsch. He knew that she would not betray him. When he ordered Greim to Berlin, he asked Reitsch to fly him to the capital in an autogyro so it would be available for his escape. When he learned the last autogyro had been damaged by enemy action, Hitler had to abandon the idea. It was then that he decided to order Dönitz to send a Ju-52 floatplane to Berlin. He could have transmitted this order in one of at least two ways. Reitsch, who flew out of Berlin in the small Arado 96 on April 28, was ordered by Hitler to carry to Dönitz the information about Himmler's betrayal. Did he also send word with Reitsch for Dönitz to assign a Ju-52 to fly to Berlin on April 30 to pick him up? In addition, the wires between Berlin and Dönitz's headquarters in the north were still open: Goebbels transmitted the report about Hitler's "death" by telegram. Hitler could have notified Dönitz over the same wires to send the floatplane. It is known that someone in the bunker requested the Ju-52 to fly into Berlin and land on the Havel River on the night of April 29. Was this a test by Hitler to make certain the plane could get in and out successfully? It did; and despite the fact that a mix-up in communications caused the Ju-52 crew to miss the couriers Johannmeier, Lorenz, and Zander, who were carrying Hitler's last will and testament, Hitler was confident the crew (or another crew) could fly a similar mission the next night.

Fegelein's death has always mystified historians who have searched for a logical reason why Hitler ordered the execution of Eva Braun's brother-in-law. Fegelein played no important

role during the Third Reich, nor did he have any part in
Himmler's efforts to make a separate peace and betray Hitler.
He was a hard drinker and a womanizer who simply learned
too much about the Führer, according to an actress now living
near Potsdam, in East Germany. Kristina Reiman, a bit player
who appeared in several Karl Ritter films, was a casual companion of Fegelein's. I met her while visiting Potsdam in July
1975, doing research on the Hitler-Braun love affair. Referring
to Fegelein during our conversation about Eva and Gretl
Braun, Reiman stated she last saw him on April 27, 1945, in
Berlin.

"He was very worried. We had several drinks together, and
he kept repeating that there were two Hitlers in Berlin," she
said. "I thought he was drunk. Just before he left me, however,
he said that if the Führer ever discovered that he, Fegelein,
knew his secret, Hitler would kill him. He didn't tell me what
the secret was."

It may be that Fegelein, through his friends in the Führer's
SS Bodyguard Regiment—who would undoubtedly have handled the details of the plot—learned that Hitler intended to kill
his double, pretend it was himself, and then escape by
floatplane from Berlin. For learning this secret, he died.

If on some pretext Hitler had the double waiting for him out
of sight in the study, entered the room with Eva Braun after
saying their final farewells, and closed the door, the rest would
be easy. Eva would take the poison. Hitler would shoot the
double, force the poison capsule between the dead man's teeth
and crush it, and then slip out of the study by way of the door
leading from the study to his living room. From there he would
pass through the small conference room to the stairs leading to
the Reich Chancellery garden. By this time the stairway would
be clear, because Linge, Günsche, Kempka, Axmann, Gen.
Hans Krebs, army chief of staff, and the others would be
waiting outside the study door. Hitler had instructed Linge to
wait "at least ten minutes before entering the room." Hitler
could have been well on his way to the Havel river, protected
and guided by his SS Bodyguard Regiment, before the confused and frightened bunker dwellers opened the door to the
study. All the eyewitnesses have admitted several times that

they had only one thought in mind—get the corpses to the Reich Chancellery garden and burn them. The corpses were quickly wrapped in woollen military blankets and carried out of the study and up the stairs. No one thought to examine them closely. Why should they? Their Führer was dead. There was nothing they could do now but follow orders and then try to escape.

During the early hours of darkness on the evening of April 30, Hans Abert could have landed his Ju-52 on the Havel river, picked up Hitler and anyone else who was waiting, and then taken off before the Russians knew what was happening. The river was relatively free of surveillance by the Russians, since they did not anticipate the appearance of a floatplane. Back at the bunker, Bormann, who was undoubtedly in on any plan Hitler made, would be causing as much confusion as possible in order to cover Hitler's escape.

Fantasy?

In February, 1966—two years before the "official" Russian report on Hitler's death—four Americans were arrested in Brazil on smuggling charges. The four, Ralph Emerson Dial, of Oklahoma City; Sam Sexton, of Fort Smith, Arkansas; Joseph Addision Truehill, of Dallas; and Joseph McCutcheon, also of Fort Smith, had flown to Tres Marias from Miami in Truehill's B-26 carrying legal cargo. It was not the first trip to Brazil for the Americans, since for several months they had been purchasing ore samples and flying them back to the United States for analysis. This time, however, the four were arrested on landing and charged with smuggling. Even Professor Elisario Tavora, a former head of the Brazilian Atomic Energy Committee's department of mineralogy, called the arrest of the Americans "stupid and pernicious." However, the judge, Djalama de Cunna Melo, made several anti-U.S. statements, including the charge that "the accused are in the service of a powerful imperialist." The arrest and conviction of the four Americans shocked Washington. Despite the supposedly good relations between Brazil and the United States, the Brazilian government refused to commute their jail terms. Washington officials knew the charges were false but could not determine the real reason for the arrest. When all else had failed, the Americans made a daring escape from Brazil by airplane. Once they were in the United States, Washington refused to extradite them, as demanded by Brazil.

Why had they been arrested? Despite investigations, the answer remained a mystery until June 15, 1978. On that date I was in Berchtesgaden, the Bavarian mountain city near where Hitler's beloved Berghof stood and where the Eagle's Nest still perches high on Kehlstein peak. I had taken the bus and elevator ascent to the Eagle's Nest and was having a drink there when a German tourist sat down beside me. As was natural in such a setting, we began talking about Hitler and the Third Reich. I learned that the German had been in the Abwehr, the foreign and counterintelligence department of the high command of the armed forces. When he told me he lived in Leipzig now, I immediately suspected he was working for East German intelligence: The average East German is not permitted to leave the "Democratic Republic" to travel in West Germany. However I had no secrets to keep from him, so I enjoyed our conversation. Eventually our discussion got around to the missing Bormann and whether he was alive or not. The German, who never told me his name, laughed when I said I thought Bormann was dead.

"There are many Germans living in South America today," he said. "Don't you know that?"

"Yes, but not high-ranking ex-Nazis such as Bormann."

His face flushed. "You Americans underestimated the Nazis. I say Bormann is alive and in South America, and even higher-ranking leaders than him."

Higher-ranking than Bormann? I was startled. Speer was in Heidelberg. Goebbels and Göring were dead. I felt he was exaggerating and told him so.

"That I don't believe. Who—"

He interrupted and mentioned my acquaintances Dial, Sexton, Truehill, and McCutcheon, the four Americans arrested in Brazil on trumped-up charges. I couldn't believe my ears. He related the story of their arrest and conviction, with which I was familiar. I didn't interrupt. I wanted to hear his version.

"Do you know why they were detained?" he asked.

"No."

"Because they saw an old man near the landing strip at Tres Marias whom the Brazilian officials feared they recognized!" He shook his finger in my face. "You Americans don't know everything."

He walked away.

Hitler in Brazil? Fantasy?

In 1976 Enrique Jacabo Mürk, former aide to Adolf Eichmann and a Luftwaffe pilot, was arrested in Argentina. Walter Kutschmann, a former SS officer responsible for the execution of 1500 Jews in Poland, was later arrested in the same country. Bormann allegedly lives on a secluded estate just north of the General Paz Speedway in Argentina. Dr. Josef Mengele, the notorious "Angel of Death" who conducted hideous medical experiments on prisoners in concentration camps, lives in Paraguay. So why is it not possible that Hitler, who would now be an old man, lives in Brazil, protected by certain government officials? His dreams of a Fourth Reich would have been destroyed shortly after the end of World War II, when his treatment of the Jews became known worldwide. Yet he could live in peace and quiet, as he had always vowed he would do once his work was finished. The Allies certainly finished it for him in 1945. And if the story I was told in the Eagle's Nest in 1978 is true, he still has considerable influence, or the Americans would not have been arrested because he thought they recognized him. They didn't, of course; like the general public, they wouldn't have given a thought to the possibility that Hitler might be alive, and living in Brazil.

Fantasy?

On the 20th of April—Hitler's birthdate—in 1978 there was a meeting of Nazis from four nations at the Hotel Tyll in Itatiaia, Brazil. Throughout the morning a man with a German shepherd dog patrolled the front of the hotel, making certain that reporters, photographers, and all other outsiders stayed at a distance. When they refused to leave the area, other Nazis of Third Reich age appeared with whips and guns. One photographer was lashed by the whip, others were beaten. None of the Nazis were arrested, none were even warned by Brazilian police. The posture of the Brazilian government is puzzling. The justice ministry has ruled that meetings of Third Reich Nazis are not illegal, and an aide to Brazilian President Ernesto Geisel dismissed the Hotel Tyll meeting as "nothing more than a get-together of nostalgic old men."

Was one of the nostalgic old men Adolf Hitler?

More than three decades after the end of the Third Reich it is a secret. Hitler's final secret.

p. 1   *"I didn't come":* Interview Author with Audi Hetter at Berchtesgaden, West Germany June 16, 1978. Frau Hetter was ten years old when her father was gardener at Pension Moritz in 1922.

p. 1   *"He was aware of the strong anti-Semitic":* A dialogue between Dietrich Eckart and Adolf Hitler titled *Der Bolsheivismus von Moses bis Hitler* (Bolshevisim from Moses to Hitler), printed by Hohenreichen Verlag, Munich, 1923. In this published pamphlet Eckart gave Hitler credit for revealing that the Jews undertook a mass migration from Egypt because they had made a revolutionary, murderous assault on the Egyptian ruling class and had failed. This was Eckart's interpretation, of course. Eckart was also convinced that Moses was the first Bolshevist leader.

p. 2   *In his earlier years:* Snyder, p. 78.

p. 2   *Built in 1916:* Geiss, p. 70.

p. 3   *Romance, including romantic:* Geiss p. 32.

p. 6   *Sitting in Schweyer's office:* Heiden, 154. Schweyer had sent for Hitler out of respect and fear. He knew that some German officers were looking for a man who had the rightist political views they had, a man they could support in a revolt against the weak leaders of postwar Germany. Schweyer thought Hitler might be that man; he was curious and wanted to talk with him.

p. 6   *"If you continue":* Heiden, p. 155.

p. 7   *"You can tell":* Heiden, p. 376. Hitler was convinced that everything was possible; that all problems could be solved, big problems the most easily; that lies were often the way to achieve one's ends.

p. 7   *"Nothing would work":* Musmanno Papers. Justice Michael A.

Musmanno was naval aide to Gen. Mark W. Clark during World War II. Following the war General Clark appointed him president of the United States-Soviet Board of Forcible Repatriation. Later, Musmanno was a judge at the Nürnberg war crimes trials. Between 1945 and 1948 Musmanno interviewed over 200 persons who had been associated with Hitler in an effort to determine whether Hitler was dead. Musmanno's papers are now at Duquesne University Library, Pittsburgh, Pennsylvania.

p. 8   *It was a personal secret:* Interview with Rudolf Geiger, Ramsau, West Germany, June 1978. Geiger, born in 1888, was in charge of landscaping the grounds around Haus Wachenfeld after its first remodeling. Hitler often entered into long discussions with him, and he revealed his views about the putsch to Geiger in 1930.

p. 9   *"The national revolution has begun":* Snyder, p. 20.

p. 10   *"Don't worry":* Heiden, p. 187.

p. 10   *"Get me a stein": Ibid.,* p. 188.

p. 13   *"Very few people":* Hoffmann, p. 60.

p. 14   *"Having to change": Hitler's Secret Conversations,* p. 256.

p. 14   *"I had no income":* Tax declaration notice from Munich Finance Office to Hitler, May 1, 1925, with Hitler's reply noted in the margin May 19, 1925. Alderman Library, University of Virginia, Charlottesville, Virginia.

p. 15   *"Without my political activity":* Preliminary income tax declaration October 31, 1925. Alderman Library, University of Virginia, Charlottesville, Virginia. Hitler paid his private secretary 900 marks and his chauffeur 540 marks.

p. 16   *"This taxpayer travels":* Assessment decision, January 27, 1927. Alderman Library, University of Virginia, Charlottesville, Virginia.

p. 19   *"Placed under tight wraps":* Interview Author with Harvey M. Berg in Beaver Falls, Pennsylvania, May 21, 1978. Berg is now a businessman in Buffalo, New York.

p. 20   *On January 19, 1923:* Collier, p. 86.

p. 21   *Finally, at noon on Monday: Ibid.,* p. 88.

p. 21   *"Given God back to Italy": Ibid.,* p. 88.

p. 21   *"The high contracting parties":* New York Times, June 8, 1929.

p. 21   *"The Treaty reaffirms":* The Lateran Treaty, 1929.

p. 23   *"This meant nine dollars":* Letter of April 2, 1976, from Harvey Berg.

p. 23   *"In return for these loans":* Interview Author with Harvey Berg in Beaver Falls, Pennsylvania, May 21, 1978.

p. 23 *"When [Pacelli]"*: Papen, p. 279.

p. 24 *"The Vatican had an intimate knowledge"*: Papen, p. 279.

p. 25 *For a reason never explained:* Infield, p. 24. (1)

p. 25 *"I got to wondering"*: Robert Ludlum, *Bookviews,* July 1978, p. 12.

p. 25 *Berg's theory:* In a June 2, 1978, letter responding to his request to the U.S. National Archives Reference Branch for their experts to make a search for the Berg Report, the author was informed by letter that the U.S. National Archives was "unable to make a search because of insufficient information."

p. 26 *When, in 1928, Hitler bought Haus Wachenfeld:* Geiss, p. 68.

p. 26 *Hitler brought his stepsister:* Ibid., p. 3.

p. 27 *Needing 21 million votes:* Toland, p. 249.

p. 28 *In the September election: Ibid.,* p. 254.

p. 32 *"Take my offer"*: Interview June 17, 1978, Author with 72-year-old Heinz Jager in Winkl, West Germany, where he lives in retirement.

p. 32 *"For the first and only time": Ibid.*

p. 34 *"I never saw a man change": Ibid.*

p. 35 *"The garage was directly"*: Interview Author with Albert Speer at his mountain home on the Allgäu near Lake Constance, in West Germany, June 29, 1976.

p. 36 *"The salon is like something"*: Stahlenberg, p. 32. Elisabeth von Stahlenberg now lives in Texas and is married to an American businessman. Few people who know her today are aware of her former association with Third Reich officials.

p. 37 *"This particular room"*kohler, p. 57.

p. 37 *"When the dinner": Ibid.,* p. 58.

p. 38 *"The French books"*: Interview Author with a former SS officer who now lives in Berchtesgaden, West Germany and asks not to be identified. June 16, 1978.

p. 40 *"We had been briefed"*: Interview Author with Artur Kasche June 17, 1978, at Maria Gern, West Germany. Kasche was associated after the war, with Radio Free Europe and is now retired. He said that broadcasts from all over the world could be picked up at the Berghof, either directly or by a relay procedure. Hitler delighted in listening to speeches by President Franklin D. Roosevelt and ridiculing his statements for the benefit of his associates.

p. 42 *Eva Braun, for example:* Berlin Document Center. Much of the once-secret information about Hitler's mountain enclave came from the files of the Berlin Document Center, a U. S. State Department installation that contains NSDAP official and personal information. Material was obtained during the author's visit to the Berlin Document Center in July 1975.

p. 42 *The rooms were not cold:* The part of the underground tunnel system still accessible today is cold and damp. (It can be entered through the Hotel Zum Türken.) However only a short section can be transversed. The remainder of the tunnel system is considered too dangerous and is blocked off. Visit by Author, 1978.

p. 42 *"A national hotel would be erected":* Geiss, p. 132.

p. 43 *"If I did not know":* Ibid., p. 137.

p. 44 *When completed the new Platterhof:* Today the Platterhof is used as a recreation center for U. S. military personnel and is called the General Walker Hotel.

p. 45 *"A minister's uniform":* Geiss, p. 98.

p. 47 *"You will never learn":* Irving (2), p. 129.

p. 47 *"Once when I entered Hitler's room":* Kohler, p. 91.

p. 48 *A typical Führer-requested·menu:* Eva Braun album, U.S. National Archives.

p. 48 *At Wolfsschanze, Hitler's field headquarters:* Junge, p. 4. Traudl Junge, Hitler's private secretary, was with Hitler until the end of the Third Reich in 1945. She survived the Berlin bunker holocaust and lives in Munich today.

p. 49 *"I left Hitler's work room":* Ibid., p. 7.

p. 50 *"The Führer Headquarters was a cross":* Jodl at Nürnberg Military Court, June 3, 1946. Picker, p. 34.

p. 51 *"I sometimes had the impression":* Interview Author with Walther Horer, Munich, June 19, 1978.

p. 51 *"Once he wrote a very short letter":* U. S. Army Intelligence report based on an interview with Christa Schröder, Hitler's secretary, at Berchtesgaden on May 22, 1945. University of Pennsylvania Library, Philadelphia, Pennsylvania.

p. 51 *"Hitler dictated his major speeches":* Ibid.

p. 52 *"There is no one":* Ibid.

p. 53 *"Röhm's Revengers":* Kraus, p. 11. *Liberty* magazine, August 28, 1937.

p. 55 *"Blood is the cement of civilization":* Waite, p. 23.

p. 55 *"I couldn't believe the conversation":* Interview Author with Otto Skorzeny, Hitler's commando chief, in Madrid, Spain, February 20, 1973.

p. 56 *"When the German Army":* Junge, p. 29.

p. 56 *"My head will not roll":* Goebbels, p. 100.

p. 57 *"How would I look":* Musmanno Papers.

p. 58 *"But Führer, a wolf":* Interview Author with Otto Harz in Madrid, Spain, in February 21, 1973. Harz left Germany in 1938, when he was threatened by the SA because he publicly protested the treatment of the Jews. He became an importer.

p. 59 "It wasn't a flight": Dietrich, p. 25.

p. 61 Triumph of the Will *lasted 110 minutes:* Barsam, p. 26.

p. 63 *Hitler met Riefenstahl: Neue Rhein-Zeitung,* Düsseldorf, Germany, March 12, 1960.

p. 63 *"Riefenstahl was a very vital":* Hanfstängl, p. 203.

p. 64 *"According to a report":* Radziwill, p. 21. *Liberty* magazine, July 16, 1938.

p. 64 *When Goebbels heard that Riefenstahl:* Infield, p. 76. (2)

p. 64 *"I want to exploit the film": The New York Times,* April 16, 1933, Section 4, p. 2.

p. 65 *"I met with Hitler at lunch time":* Infield, p. 62. (2)

p. 65 *"I told Hitler that filming": Ibid.,* p. 62.

p. 66 *"I asked my husband":* Stahlenberg, p. 78.

p. 67 *"I told him no":* Interview with British Broadcasting Corporation, London, England, June 22, 1972.

p. 67 *"He looked at me": Ibid.*

p. 68 *"Leni Riefenstahl loved the Führer":* Interview with Frau Anni Winter, Hitler's housekeeper, in Munich, September 3, 1948. Musmanno Papers.

p. 68 *"You have a Monroe Doctrine":* Kaltenborn, p. 286.

p. 69 *"Jewish sports leaders":* Malitz, p. 21.

p. 69 *"I cannot alter a question":* Mandell, p. 104.

p. 70 *"When the film was first screened":* Hugo Müller was a member of the Reich Film Chamber from 1937 until 1944, when he was transferred into the army. He was in charge of a private screening of *Olympiad* for Hitler at the Berghof in early 1938. Müller interviewed by Author in Bad Reichenhall, West Germany, June 1978.

p. 71 *"It had to succeed here": Film Culture,* Spring 1973, p. 123.

p. 74 *"Incessant agitation against the Third Rch": The New York Times,* January 24, 1939, p. 17.

p. 76 *"If Hitler walked through the door": Time,* August 18, 1975, p. 33.

p. 77 *As security for the loan:* Maser, p. 200.

p. 78 *"When I worked for Frau Bechstein":* Interview by Author with Ilse Meirer in June 1978 at Ramsau, West Germany. Frau Meirer now operates a souvenir shop in Berchtesgaden.

p. 79 *"Sometimes girls are brought here":* Kohler, p. 72.

p. 79   *"Hitler made her undress":* Waite, p. 238.

p. 79   *"It was really funny":* Liberty magazine, December 20, 1941, p. 15.

p. 80   *"I should like to show you":* Ibid. p. 17.

p. 81   *"I let him do whatever he wanted":* Waite, p. 225.

p. 82   *"In her artless way":* Musmanno Papers.

p. 84   *Count Galeazzo Ciano:* Gibson, p. 85.

p. 84   *In the name of Fascism and Nazism:* Time, October 1, 1945, p. 29.

p. 85   *"I'm afraid of him":* Liberty magazine, November 29, 1941, p. 10.

p. 86   *"Well, after all, I shall be":* Ibid. p. 11.

p. 86   *"A day or so later":* Ibid., p. 52.

p. 88   *Winifred had visited Dr. Kurt Krüger:* Krüger, p. 314.

p. 89   *"Whether relations between":* Musmanno Papers. Dr. Karl Brandt interview.

p. 92   *These feats were accomplished:* Geiss, p. 104.

p. 94   *"In inviting me on the evening of October 17":* Official report of André François-Poncet to Georges Bonnet, French minister for foreign affairs. October 20, 1938.

p. 96   *"It is a tribute to Bormann":* Interview Author with Albert Speer at his home in Heidelberg, February 14, 1973.

p. 96   *The laborers who built the Eagle's Nest:* Geiss, p. 178.

p. 98   *"The Führer often came to the tunnel":* Interview Author with Anton Bose at Metzenleiter, West Germany, June 16, 1978. Bose is now a security agent for a trucking company.

p. 99   *"That elevator was the finest one":* Interview Author with Albert Hellmuth at Baden-Baden, July 1976. At that time Hellmuth was repairing electrical equipment at the casino at Baden-Baden.

p. 100 *Other previously unpublished facts about the Eagle's Nest:* Interview Author with Skorzeny in Madrid, February 20, 1973; and later correspondence with Skorzeny until his death in 1975.

p. 101 *The flight engineer:* Interview Author with Harry Owens in London, June 1978. On August 16, 1978, Owens and a companion were killed in a light-plane accident in Scotland.

p. 104 *"When I walked into Adolf Hitler's room":* Thompson; p. 3.

p. 104 *"When I dared to interrupt":* Ibid., p. 17.

p. 105 *"The front door of Matsuoka's train coach":* Schmidt, p. 221.

p. 105 "I can give no firm promise": Ibid., p. 222.

p. 107 "An invitation to visit Germany": Letter, from Truman Smith to Charles A. Lindbergh, on file at Yale University Library, New Haven, Connecticut.

p. 108 *"There can be no defense"*: Mosley, p. 290.

p. 109 *Actually the Luftwaffe had less than half:* German Military History Research Bureau, Specialty Group 6: Air Force and Aerial Warfare History. U. S. National Archives.

p. 110 *"Without a doubt the German air fleet"*: Mosley, p. 297.

p. 110 *"I am well aware":* Documents on German Foreign Policy. Germany and Czechslovakia, 1937–38. Document 487, p. 787. U.S. National Archives.

p. 111 *"I would gladly spare the Prime Minister"*: Ibid., p. 796.

p. 112 *"I have brought peace in our time"*: Snyder, p. 236.

p. 112 *"Ach, don't take it so seriously"*: Irving, p. 151. (2)

p. 112 *"Everything had to be worked out to the minute"*: Schmidt, p. 242.

p. 113 *"The German Foreign Minister has withdrawn"*: Ibid., p. 243.

p. 113 *"I withdraw my request"*: Ibid., p. 244.

p. 114 *"I sent for Chamberlain"*: Donaldson, p. 214.

p. 115 *"Ley had a powerful black Mercedes-Benz"*: Interview June 1978. Author with Hans Sopple in Munich, where Sopple owns a small clothing store.

p. 116 *"She would have made a good Queen"*: Schmidt, p. 75.

p. 116 *"The Duke's decision to see for himself":* The New York Times, October 23, 1937.

p. 118 *What terms might France expect?:* Liberty magazine, July 26, 1941. p. 23.

p. 120 *"Siegfried with a monocle"*: Snyder, p. 29.

p. 122 *"Blomberg has married a whore!"*: Irving, p. 5. (2)

p. 122 *"It turns out Fraulein Gruhn was the daughter"*: Stahlenberg, p. 140.

p. 123 *"The commander-in chief of the army"*: Ibid., p. 140.

p. 123 *"I was eventually called in"*: Irving, p. 9. (2)

p. 125 *"How many of the navy wives"*: Ibid., p. 213.

p. 127 *"I'll give you some good advice"*: Musmanno Papers. Interview with Erich Kempka in Munich on August 19, 1948.

p. 129 *"You can't imagine how overjoyed"*: Bormann, p. 39.

p. 130 *"You will have to see to it"*: Ibid., p. 42.

p. 130 *M., Manja Behrens:* Stevenson, p. 43.

p. 130 *"The room in which so many actresses"*: Tabori, p. 91.

p. 131 *"I saw Goebbels arrive"*: Kohler, p. 134.

p. 131 *"Sometimes he played the piano"*: Bleuel, p. 73.

p. 132 *"A narrow-minded humorless blonde female"*: Ibid., p. 205.

p. 133 *"She was a woman of rather faded prettiness"*: Kohler, p. 140.

p. 133 *"He treats me outrageously"*: Bleuel, p. 3.

p. 136 *"Should the courts, in applying Paragraph 55"*: Ibid., p. 147.

p. 137   *Morell was born in Traisa:* Hitler's Medical Report, OI Consolidated Interrogation Report (CIR) No. 4, U.S. National Archives, Annex I.

p. 139   *"Consultation at the Reich Chancellery":* Irving, p. 202. (2)

p. 140   *"You are my last hope":* Ibid., p. 202.

p. 140   *"Was suffering acutely from gastrointestinal disturbances":* Hitler's Medical Report, p. 2.

p. 142   *"Around 3:00 A.M. he had a heart attack:* Shirer, p. 447.

p. 144   *The German defector learned about the antigas pills:* This German police officer, who worked with the OSS during the war, wishes to remain unnamed. He lives in Munich today, having returned to his native city in 1946. I interviewed him twice: once in 1973 and once again in 1978. Subsequent investigation of his story verified the key facts he related to me. Recently released medical reports pertaining to Hitler's health in the 1940s further support his testimony.

p. 145   *"One day we were having pork":* Musmanno Papers. Interview with Frau Braun, Eva Braun's mother, at Rupoldingen, near Traunstein, September 4, 1948.

p. 146   *"After the effect of the injections wore off":* Ibid.

p. 146   *"The Führer took an unbelievable number of drugs":* Junge Memoirs, p. 107.

p. 147   *Twice a week she was to use a night pack:* Tabori, p. 73.

p. 147   *"I don't believe Morell":* Ibid. p. 73.

p. 147   *When Hoffmann became ill:* Hoffmann, p. 218.

p. 147   *Albert Speer had been troubled:* Speer, p. 425.

p. 148   *"The outstanding commander of the early part of the war":* Maser, p. 226.

p. 148   *Early in 1941 he developed edema:* Ibid., p. 279.

p. 150   *"What do you think about the Führer's health?":* Infield, p. 214. (1)

p. 152   *In front of an amazed Giesing:* Toland, p. 933.

p. 154   *"Morell, leave my room at once":* Junge, p. 143.

p. 157   *"All the stories about Eva's meeting":* Musmanno Papers. Interview with Frau Braun.

p. 158   *"I would like to have you come":* Hoffmann, p. 161.

p. 159   *"I think he is interested in the young girl":* Ibid., p. 161.

p. 160   *"She did it for the love of me":* Ibid., p. 162.

p. 160   *As Fritz Braun related the incident to his curious friends:* Musmanno Papers. Interview with Frau Braun.

p. 160   *As he told Hoffmann:* Hoffmann, p. 162.

p. 161   *"He received many women":* Musmanno Papers. Interview with Anni Winter in Munich, March 30, 1948.

p. 161 *Eva's plan worked out very well:* Musmanno Papers. Interview with Frau Braun. The entire episode about the meeting of Hitler and the Brauns is based on this interview.

p. 164 *"I have just sent him a letter":* National Archives, Record Group 242. Eva Braun's diary was found by Americans in 1945 in the possession of the mother of an officer of Hitler's personal bodyguard. It remained "undiscovered" there for nearly a quarter-century.

p. 167 *"I will never marry her":* Musmanno Papers. Interview with Julius Schaub at Garmisch, March 22, 1948.

p. 168 *"I want it delivered to the Chancellery":* Infield, p. 157. (1)

p. 170 *"He is only using me for very definite purposes":* U.S. National Archives. Eva Braun Diary, entry March 11, 1935.

p. 170 *"It must never happen again":* Tabori, p. 89.

p. 170 *"As if he wanted to memorize every movement":* Ibid., p. 70.

p. 171 *"You have been away from your wife too long":* Interview Author with Skorzeny.

p. 172 *"You are the only one who would say that":* Musmanno Papers. Interview with Traudl Junge in Munich, February 7, 1948.

p. 172 *"This time you will stay with me":* Musmanno Papers. Interview with Julius Schaub.

p. 177 *"No one had thought":* Junge, p. 30.

p. 178 *"They will sit there without moving":* Ibid., p. 31.

p. 181 *"It was an extremely dull, ugly room":* Musmanno Papers. Interview with Traudl Junge.

p. 182 *"In the years 1938-1939";* National Archives, U. S. Army Report No. 31. Dr. Hugo Johannes Blaschke, February 3, 1946.

p. 184 *"It was fascinating":* Junge *Memoirs,* p. 32.

p. 185 *"When I first met you":* Musmanno Papers. Interview with Frau Braun.

p. 187 *"I can't see films during the war":* Junge, p. 33.

p. 191 *"I never have a vacation":* Junge, p. 35.

p. 193 *"You can't revert back to the Stone Age":* Bleuel, p. 77.

p. 194 *"My favorite form of activity":* Klotz, p. 610.

p. 194 *"I have in my possession":* Ibid.

p. 195 *"The Supreme Command of the SA":* Bleuel, p. 97.

p. 196 *"I have nothing against Röhm":* Bormann letter of May 10, 1932, on file at the Institut für Zeitgeschichte, Munich FA36.

p. 196 *"If Adolf wants me dead":* Infield, p. 89. (1)

p. 197 *"Such accusations have no truth in them":* Interview Author with Albert Speer at Heidelberg.

p. 197 *"He was much too interested":* Interview Author with Skorzeny.

p. 197 *"Suppose you tell me how you have fared":* Krüger, p. 238.

p. 199 *"I was called to the Berghof":* Interview Author with Dr. Jacob Dressler at a farm a few miles from Berchtesgaden, June 1978.

p. 199 *"Hess's real name should have been 'Yes' ":* Kohler. p. 144.

p. 200 *"That is the real reason":* Interview Author with Skorzeny.

p. 200 *"In order to keep the SS and police free":* Institut für Zeitgeschichte, MA 333 BL 7977.

p. 200 *By the end of the war:* U.S. National Archives. U.S. Army Interrogation Report No. 4, November 29, 1945.

p. 201 *"The Führer is completely indifferent":* Junge, p. 110.

p. 203 *"It is hereby certified that Captain Göring":* Liberty Magazine, April 6, 1940, p. 8.

p. 206 *"Probably none of us is entirely normal":* Hitler's Secret Conversations, p. 127.

p. 207 *"It has come to the attention":* U.S. National Archives. Letter from J. Edgar Hoover to George S. Messersmith, State Department, May 23, 1939.

p. 211 *"Princess Hohenlohe's visit":* Hoover Institution. Letter to Lord Rothermere from Prince Wilhelm III, June 20, 1934.

p. 212 *"I have been informed how sincerely":* Whitehead, p. 233.

p. 213 *"You have been good enough":* Hoover Institution. Letter to Lord Rothermere from Adolf Hitler, December 7, 1933.

p. 213 *"I believe in timing things well":* Hoover Institution. Letter to Adolf Hitler from Lord Rothermere, December 6, 1935.

p. 217 *"My mission to create a better feeling":* Hoover Institution. Letter to Princess Hohenlohe from Lord Rothermere, January 19, 1938.

p. 218 *"There is no doubt in my mind":* Current Biography, 1940, p. 396.

p. 218 *"I have to acknowledge":* U.S. National Archives, Record Group 59. Letter from G.S. Messersmith to J. Edgar Hoover, March 7, 1939.

p. 219 *"The Baron's prestige among German":* U.S. National Archives. Letter from Bert Fish to the Secretary of State, July 31, 1939.

p. 219 *"Princess Stephanie Hohenlohe arrived in New York":* U.S. National Archives. Letter from Adolf A. Berle, Jr. to J. Edgar Hoover, July 8, 1940.

p. 220 *"I am extremely sorry that this matter":* U.S. National Archives. Letter from James Clement Dunn to Herschel V. Johnson, July 8, 1940.

p. 222 *"Honestly, this is getting to be the kind":* Whitehead, p. 236.

p. 225 *"Tolson: Please explain to her":* Federal Bureau of Investigation Archives. Memo from J. Edgar Hoover.

p. 226 *"As I have learned":* Federal Bureau of Investigation Archives. Letter from A. Nebe to J. Edgar Hoover, July 7, 1939.

p. 227 *"From a medical viewpoint":* Mitscherlich, p. 37.

p. 227 *"I agree to the proposal":* Ibid.

p. 231 *"Dante was never in Hell, either":* Interview Author with Skorzeny.

p. 231 *"I have ordered every officer":* Heinz Linge. *Revue,* December, 1955.

p. 233 *"SS Colonel Nebe called":* Czechoslovakia State Archives. Telegram from Braune to Eichmann, October 13, 1939.

p. 234 *"Reichsleiter Bouhler and Dr. Brandt are charged":* National Archives, Record Group 238. Document No. 630-PS, September 1, 1939.

p. 236 *"I also want to talk to you":* U.S. National Archives, Record Group 238. Document 1919-PS, October 4, 1943.

p. 237 *"Given you which dealt with":* National Archives, Record Group 238. Document No. 710-PS. July 31, 1941.

p. 237 *"The taking over of vehicles":* U.S. National Archives, Record Group 238. Document No. 501-PS, May 16, 1942.

p. 240 *"The Germans are coming":* Herzstein, p. 288.

p. 240 *"I've just been reading a fine article":* Hitler's Secret Conversations, p. 257.

p. 245 *"How many of the Me-262s":* Irving, p. 629. (1)

p. 249 *"Bombers fly over it all the time":* Musmanno Papers. Interview with Traudl Junge.

p. 250 *"Hitler's mountain retreat, the Berghof":* Letter to Author from Adolf Galland, January 31, 1978.

p. 253 *"Who else would come back?":* Musmanno Papers. Interview with Traudl Junge.

p. 255 *"You can take two suitcases":* Irving, p. 801. (1)

p. 258 *"The Führer's had a":* Irving, p. 805. (1)

p. 259 *"I knew you would come":* Junge, p. 134.

p. 259 *"When you see the Führer":* O'Donnell, p. 122.

p. 260 *"What do you think, Speer?":* Interview Author with Albert Speer, 1976.

p. 260 *"We slipped around the bunker":* Junge, p. 139.

p. 262 *"Do you know why I have summoned you?":* U.S. National Archives. Interrogation of Hanna Reitsch, October 8, 1945, by the Air Interrogation Unit of Headquarters, U. S. Forces in Austria. Microfilm No. 506-607A.

p. 262 *"She was so small and delicate"*: Junge, P. 146.

p. 263 *"Hitler is dead"*: U.S. National Archives. Interrogation of Hanna Reitsch.

p. 265 *"In a short while my family"*: Junge, p. 150.

p. 266 *"One evening when Hanna and Eva"*: Ibid.

p. 267 *"Our children would rather die"*: Ibid.

p. 268 *"If I am killed in battle now"*: Musmanno Papers. Interview with Julius Schaub.

p. 268 *"Tonight you will cry"*: Musmanno Papers. Interview with Traudl Junge.

p. 268 *"Although during my years of struggle"*: The William R. Philip Collection, Hoover Institution.

p. 269 *"Benito Mussolini is dead"*: Reuters, April 28, 1945.

p. 270 *"Would my dog Blondi respond?"*: Musmanno Papers. Interview with Julius Schaub..

p. 270 *"I want you to have this coat"*: Junge, p. 158.

p. 271 *"Tell everyone in Munich farewell"*: Ibid.

p. 272 *"HITLER DEAD IN CHANCELLERY"*: The New York Times, May 2, 1945.

p. 275 *"On the body, considerably damaged by fire"*: Bezymenski, p. 49.

p. 279 *"Not as far as I am concerned"*: Interview Author with Hans Abert at Bari, Italy, on March 21, 1970.

p. 280 *"In fact I flew escort"*: Interview Author with Karl Barth at Munich, February 10, 1973.

p. 281 *"Do you think Hitler is dead?"*: nterview Author with Skorzeny.

p. 282 *"Had Hitler decided to take part in a breakout"*: O'Donnell, p. 366.

p. 282 *"One of the doubles is always at Berchtesgaden"*: Kohler, p. 99.

p. 284 *"At least ten minutes"*: O'Donnell, p. 232.

p. 285 *"The accused are in the service"*: San Antonio Express, May 29, 1966.

p. 286 *"There are many Germans"*: Interview Author with a German from Leipzig at Berchtesgaden (Eagle's Nest), June 15, 1978.

p. 287 *On the 20th of April*: The Washington Post, July 31, 1978.

Selected Bibliography

BARSAM, RICHARD M. *Filmguide to Triumph of the Will.* Bloomington: Indiana University Press, 1978.

BEZYMENSKI, LEV. *The Death of Adolf Hitler.* Hamburg: Christian Wegner Verlag, 1968.

BLEUEL, HANS PETER. *Sex and Society in Nazi Germany.* New York: J. B. Lippincott, 1973.

BORMANN, MARTIN. *The Bormann Letters.* London: Weidenfeld and Nicolson, 1954.

CIANO, GALEAZZO. *The Ciano Diaries.* New York: Garden City Publishing Company, 1947.

COLLIER, RICHARD. *Duce!* New York: The Viking Press, 1971.

CRANKSHAW, EDWARD. *The Gestapo.* London: Putnam & Co., Ltd., 1956

DIETRICH, OTTO. *With Hitler on the Road to Power.* (Republished) Reedy: Liberty Bell Publication, 1978

DONALDSON, FRANCES. *Edward VIII.* New York: J. B. Lippincott, 1974

DRIMMER, FREDERICK. *Very Special People.* New York: Bantam Books, 1976

ECKART, DIETRICH. *Der Bolshevismus von Moses bis Hitler.* Munich: Hohenreichen Verlag, 1923

EISENHOWER, DWIGHT D. *Crusade in Europe.* New York: Doubleday & Co., 1949.

FIEDLER, LESLIE. *Freaks.* New York: Simon & Schuster, 1978

GEISS, JOSEF. *Obersalzberg.* Berchtesgaden: Plenk KG, Druckerei und Verlag, 1977

GOEBBELS, JOSEPH. *The Early Goebbels Diaries 1925-1926.* New York: Oliver Watson, 1962

HEIDEN, KONRAD. *Der Fuehrer.* Boston: Houghton Mifflin Company, 1944

HANFSTANGL, ERNST. *Unheard Witness.* Philadelphia: J. B. Lippincott, 1957

HERZSTEIN, ROBERT EDWIN. *The War That Hitler Won.* New York: G. P. Putnam's Sons, 1978.

HITLER, ADOLF. *Hitler's Secret Conversations,* 1941-1944 New York: Farrar, Straus & Young, Inc., 1953.

—*Mein Kampf,* Boston: Houghton Mifflin Co., 1943

HOFFMANN, HEINRICH. *Hitler was my Friend.* London: Burke Publishing Company, Ltd., 1955

HULL, DAVID STEWART. *Film in the Third Reich.* Los Angeles: University of California Press, 1969

INFIELD, GLENN B. (1) *Eva and Adolf.* New York: Grosset & Dunlap, Inc., 1974

—*Leni Riefenstahl: The Fallen Film Goddess.* (2) New York: Thomas Y. Crowell Co., 1976

IRVING, DAVID. (1) *Hitler's War.* New York; The Viking Press, 1977 (2) *The War Path.* London: Michael Joseph, Ltd., 1978

JUNGE, TRAUDL. *Unpublished Memoirs.*

KLOTZ, HELMUT. *Der Fall Röhm.* Berlin: 1932.

KOHLER, PAULINE. *The Woman Who Lived in Hitler's House.* New York: Sheridan House, Inc., 1940

KRÜGER, KURT, M.D. *Inside Hitler.* New York: Avalon Press, 1941

LANGER, WALTER C. *The Mind of Adolf Hitler.* New York: Basic Books, 1972

MALITZ, BRUNO. *Die Leibesubungen in der Nationalsozialistischen Idee.* Munich: F. Eher, 1933

MANDELL, RICHARD D. *The Nazi Olympics.* New York: Ballantine, 1972

MANVELL, ROGER and FRÄNKEL, HEINRICH. *Himmler.* New York: Paperback Library, 1968

MASER, WERNER. *Hitler: Legend, Myth and Reality.* New York: Harper & Row, 1973

MITSCHERLICH, ALEXANDER. *Doctors of Infamy.* New York: Henry Shuman, 1949

MOSLEY, LEONARD. *Lindbergh.* New York: Doubleday & Company, 1976

MUSMANNO, MICHAEL A. *Ten Days to Die.* New York: Doubleday & Company, 1950

GEISS, JOSEF. *Obersalzberg.* Berchtesgaden: Verlag A. Plenk KG, 1976

O'DONNELL, JAMES P. *The Bunker.* Boston: Hougton Mifflin, 1978

PAPEN, FRANZ VON. *Memoirs.* London: Andre Deutsch, Ltd., 1952

PICKER, HENRY and HOFFMANN, HEINRICH. *Hitler Close Up.* New York: Macmillan Publishing Co., 1973

POOL, JAMES and SUZANNE. *Who Financed Hitler?* New York: The Dial Press, 1978

SCHMIDT, PAUL. *Hitler's Interpreter.* London: William Heinemann, Ltd., 1951

SHIRER, WILLIAM L. *The Rise and Fall of the Third Reich.* New York: Simon and Schuster, 1960

SNYDER, LOUIS. *Encyclopedia of the Third Reich.* New York: McGraw-Hill, 1976

SPEER, ALBERT. *Inside the Third Reich.* New York: Macmillan Publishing Co., 1970

STAHLENBERG, ELISABETH VON. *Nazi Lady.* London: Blond and Briggs, Ltd., 1978

STEVENSON, WILLIAM. *The Bormann Brotherhood.* New York: Harcourt Brace Jovanovich, 1973

TABORI, PAUL. *The Private Life of Adolf Hitler.* London: Aldus Publications, Ltd., 1947

THOMPSON, DOROTHY. *I Saw Hitler.* New York: Farrar & Rinehart, 1932

TOLAND, JOHN. *Adolf Hitler.* Garden City: Doubleday & Company, 1976

WAITE, ROBERT G. L. *Adolf Hitler: The Psychopathic God.* New York: Basic Books, 1977

WHITEHEAD, DON. *The FBI Story.* New York: Random House, 1956

Index

Abert, Hans, 285, 300*n*
Abetz, Otto, 212
Adlerhorst headquarters, 172,
    244, 246
Adolf Hitler Free Corps, 251
African campaign (1942), 149
Air Club (Berlin), 108
Albrecht, Lt. Com. Alwin-
    Broder, 125-26, 249
Albrecht, Frau Grete, 125
Allied Control Commission, 272
Alpine redoubt *(Alpenfestung),*
    100, 249
American Jewish Congress, 71
Amort firm (Josef and Stefan), 2
Amt 500 (communications
    center), 254
Anschluss, 233
Ardennes offensive, 172, 244-47
Auschwitz (concentration camp),
    227, 235
Axmann, Artur, 273, 274, 284

Baarova, Lida, 131, 132, 135
Bacteriological Research
    Institute, 140
Bad Nauheim headquarters, 249
Baillet-Latour, Count Henri, 69-
    70
Barcarole (motion picture), 131
Barth, Kurt, 280, 300*n*

Baumbach, Gen. Werner, 246
Baur, Hans, 58, 59, 252, 255, 270,
    274, 279, 282
Bayreuth Festival, 118, 132
Bechstein, Carl, 5, 18, 77
Bechstein, Frau Helene, 5, 18, 77,
    78, 293*n*
Beer Hall Putsch (1923), 3, 7-12,
    17, 54, 203
Behrens, M., Manja, 130, 295*n*
Below, Frau von, 183
Beneš, Eduard, 215
Berchtesgaden, 1-12, 14, 15, 19,
    26-46, 216, 251, 252, 286, 292*n;*
    see also Berghof
Berg, Harvey M., 19-25, 290*n*,
    291*n*
Berghof, 2-12, 30-46, 86, 87, 110,
    112, 161, 167, 172, 214, 216,
    232, 236, 243-44, 245, 247, 282,
    286, 291*n*, 298*n;* bodyguards,
    36, 38, 39, 45-46, 54-55;
    communications system, 39-
    40; development of, 30-32, 45-
    46; furniture and living
    arrangements, 35-40, 174-82;
    Hitler's habits and behavior at,
    47-59; *"Hoheitsgebiet,"* 45-46;
    invitations to, 46, 183-86;
    pornography, 38; property
    surrounding, 32-35; RAF

Berghof *(cont.)*
  bombings, 249; tunnel system,
  40, 50; typical daily activities,
  174–92; *see also* Eagle's Nest
Berle, Adolf A., Jr., 298*n*
Bernadotte, Count Folke, 254
Bettschnüffelei (bed-sniffing), 193
Bismarck, Princess Ann Mari
  von, 85
Bismarck, Prince Otto von, 85
Blaschke, Dr. Hugo Johannes,
  182, 190–91, 276, 277, 297*n*
Blomberg, Field Marshal Werner
  von, 67, 120–23, 125, 126, 295*n*
Blondi (dog), 50–51, 190, 232,
  243, 270, 300*n*
Blue Light, The (motion picture),
  60, 63
Board of Forcible Repatriation,
  290*n*
Bonnet, Georges, 94–95, 216,
  294*n*
Borman, Albert, 252–53
Bormann, Frau Gerda, 128–29,
  130
Bormann, Martin, 5, 30–32, 43–
  45, 71, 182, 184, 191–92, 195–
  96, 246, 252, 272, 274, 279–80,
  282, 283, 285, 286, 287, 294*n,*
  297*n;* Berghof quarters, 42; in
  the bunker (April, 1945), 257,
  259, 264; Eagle's Nest and, 91,
  94, 96–97, 98, 102, 103; love
  affairs, 129–30; power of, 128,
  254–55
Bose, Anton, 98, 99, 294*n*
Bouhler, Philip, 233–34
Bradley, Gen. Omar, 246
Brahms, Johannes, 4
Brandt, Frau Anni, 183
Brandt, Col. Heinz, 151
Brandt, Dr. Karl, 89, 144, 152,
  183, 199, 234, 269, 294*n*, 299*n*

Brauchitsch, Gen. Walther von,
  124
Braun, Eva, 4, 5, 51, 56, 90, 91,
  102, 103, 143, 147, 149–50,
  155–73, 184, 243–44, 246–47,
  251, 273, 280, 282, 287, 291–
  92*n*, 297*n;* attempted suicides
  of, 159–60, 165; background
  of, 155–56; at the Berghof, 40,
  42, 174, 178, 183, 185, 186–87,
  190, 191–92; death of, 271,
  284; first meeting with Hitler,
  145–58; job in Hoffmann's
  studio, 156–59, 160; last days
  (in the bunker), 255, 256, 257,
  259, 260, 264, 267–71;
  marriage of, 268–69; Nürnberg
  rally (1935), 165–67; obsession
  with clothes, 168, 188; visit to
  Italy, 142–43
Braun, Frau Franziska, 143, 144,
  155, 157, 160, 161–64, 172–73,
  183, 274, 296*n*, 297*n*
Braun, Fritz, 155, 158, 160, 161–
  64, 183, 274
Braun, Gretl, *see* Fegelein, Frau
  Gretl
Brazilian Atomic Energy
  Committee, 285
Brenner Pass Conference, 112–14
Brinkmann, Dr. E., 278
Britain, Battle of, 206, 221, 228
British Broadcasting Corporation
  (BBC), 41, 103, 293*n*
Brown House, 79, 146, 184, 189
Bruckmann, Frau Elsa, 18, 78
Bruckmann, Hugo, 18
Buch, Walter, 128
Bulge, Battle of the, 244
Bürgerbrau Keller, 8–9, 10, 11

Café Heck, 157
Cardiazol (drug), 148–49

Castrations, 119
Chamberlain, Neville, 109, 110–12, 191, 215, 216, 217
Christian, Gen. Eckhardt, 255
Christian, Frau Gerda, 57, 255, 258, 270, 273, 274
Churchill, Winston, 77
Ciano, Count Galeazzo, 84, 294n
Clark, Gen. Mark W., 290n
Communism, 17, 23, 28
Concordat of 1933, 23–24
Coolidge, Calvin, 223
Cooper, James Fenimore, 240
Coramine (drug), 148–49
Counter Intelligence Corps (U.S. Army), 19
Cromwell, Oliver, 56
Czechoslovakia, Nazi occupation of, 110–12, 224

Dachau (concentration camp), 34, 227, 234
Daily Mail (of London), 209, 210, 213–14
Daluege, Kurt, 227, 228, 229
Darlan, Adm. Jean François, 117–18
Day of Freedom (motion picture), 67
Deutsch, Frank, 81
Development of Criminality in the German Reich from the Outbreak of War until 1943, The (Reich Bureau of Statistics), 119
Dial, Ralph Emerson, 285–87
Dietrich, Otto, 56, 59, 183, 251, 293n
Dietrich, Gen. Sepp, 196, 244
Dr. Koster's Anti-gas Pills, 141, 142, 145, 152, 296n
"Doctors' revolution" of 1944, 152–53

Dönitz, Adm. Karl, 254, 260, 261, 263–64, 272–73, 283
Dressler, Dr. Jacob, 199, 226, 298n
Dulles, Allen W., 143, 144
Dunn, James Clement, 220, 298n
Dwarfs, extermination of, 235

Eagle's Nest, 34, 49, 91–103, 104, 132, 236, 247, 248, 249, 254, 286, 287, 294n; construction of, 91–92, 94, 96–97, 99; cost of, 94; Hitler's feelings about, 97–98; location of, 100; purpose of, 91, 100; rooms and layout, 92–94; staff, 98
Eckart, Dietrich, 1–3, 5, 6, 77, 247, 289n
Eckart, Frau Dulcinea, 2
Eckert, Heinrich, 77
Eher Verlag (publisher), 19
Eichmann, Adolf, 233, 235–36, 287, 299n
Eicken, Dr. Karl von, 139–40, 152, 242, 243
Eighth Air Force (U.S.), 249
Einsatzgruppe B, 224
Einsatzgruppe D, 233
Einstein, Albert, 230
Eisenhower, Gen. Dwight D., 246, 273
Enabling Act (1933), 24
Esser, Hermann, 134–36
Esser, Frau Therese, 136
Europa (liner), 71
Euthanasia program, 233–34, 235
Exner, Frau Marlene von, 48

Fanck, Arnold, 61
Farah Diba, Empress, 222
Federal Bureau of Investigation (FBI), 207, 219, 220, 221, 222, 223, 228, 229, 299n

Fegelein, Frau Gretl, 102, 169, 183, 186, 244, 251, 284
Fegelein, Gen. Hermann, 102, 243, 244, 246, 257, 264, 283-84
Feldherrn Hall, 8
Fick, Roderich, 34
Fifth Panzer Army, 246
Film of the Nation award, 239
Final Solution *(Endlösung)*, 224, 235-36
First Army (U.S.), 244, 246
Fischbach (artist), 165
Fish, Bert, 219, 298n
Flügge. Baron von. 219
Fock. Carin. *see* Göring. Frau Carin
Formis, Heinz, 54
François-Poncet, André, 94-96, 104, 294n
Frank, Hans, 136
Frank, Richard, 77
Franz Salvador, Archduke, 209
Frederick the Great, 56, 200
Frederick William I, King, 56
Frederika, Queen, 222
Freemasons, 23
Freikorps, 194
French Resistance, 40, 103
Frentz, Walther, 178
Fritsch, Gen. Werner Freiherr von, 123-24, 194, 196-97
Führer's Decree Relating to the Maintenance of Purity in the SS and Police (1941), 200
Fürstner, Capt. Wolfgang, 69

Galland, Gen. Adolf, 249-50, 282, 299
Gallegos (artist), 165
Ganghofer, Ludwig, 4
Gasparri, Cardinal Pietro, 20, 21
Geiger, Rudolf, 290n

Geisel, Ernesto, 288
German Labor Front, 85, 132
German National Film Prize (1935), 67
German National People's Party, 27
German News Service (DNB), 114
German Olympic Committee, 69
Gestapo (State Secret Police), 54, 124, 224, 225-26, 233, 235, 282; *see also* SS
Giesing, Dr. Erwin, 144, 152, 153, 201, 278
Gimczynski, Count, 208
Goebbels, Joseph, 28-30, 36, 51, 52, 56, 60, 63, 66, 69, 86, 87, 98, 128, 136, 190, 191, 212, 239, 240-41, 242, 251, 272-73, 283, 286, 292n, 293n, 295n; death of, 132; jealousy of Riefenstahl, 64-68; last days (in the bunker), 258, 264-68, 271; love affairs, 130-32, 135; marriage of, 87
Goebbels, Frau Magda, 86-87, 130, 132, 253-54, 262, 264, 265, 266-67
Goebbels family, 56-57, 265-66
Goelz, Erwin, 71
Göring, Frau Carin, 203
Göring, Hermann, 10, 12, 13, 52, 53, 80, 124, 134, 182, 190, 191, 212, 215-16, 236-37, 245, 246, 250, 251, 254, 258, 261, 262, 264, 273, 278-79, 286, 298n; addiction to drugs, 86, 200, 203-5, 206; air attack on Allies (1945), 247; Berghof quarters, 42; Blomberg scandal and, 121-22; entertainment of foreign visitors, 106, 107, 108,

109, 115; marriage of, 85–86; power struggle with Himmler, 215; toy trains of, 106
Gottesleben, Das (Ganghofer), 4
Grace, Princess, 222
Graf, Lia, 235
Great Dictator, The (motion picture), 10
Greim, Gen. Robert Ritter von, 261–63, 264, 283
Grossman, Hermann, 267–68
Gruber, Max von, 193
Gruhn, Erna, 120–22
Guderian, Gen. Heinz, 251
Günsche, Otto, 179–80, 201–2, 257, 264, 270, 274, 282, 284
Günther (cook), 49
Gürtner, Dr. Franz, 84
Gustavus V, King, 254
Gypsies, 227, 232–33

Hácha, Emil, 142, 215
Halder, Gen. Franz, 7, 47
Halifax, Lord, 215, 216
Hamburg South American Line, 137
Hamilton, Duke of, 199
Hanfstängl, Ernst, 12, 293*n*
Hanfstängl, Frau Helene, 12
Hanke, Karl, 132
Hapsburg family, 210, 211
Harz, Otto, 58, 293*n*
Hasselbach, Dr. Hanskarl von, 153, 183
Haus Wachenfeld, 2–3, 5, 14, 19, 26, 175, 177, 290*n*, 291*n;* renamed, 28–30
Hause Wahnfried, 88
Heilbronn salt mines, 250
Heimkehr (motion picture), 238–40
Heines, Edmund, 194, 196

Hellmuth, Albert, 99, 294*n*
Henlein, Konrad, 215
Hermann Göring Division, 150
Hess, Rudolf, 11, 12, 30, 52, 81, 84, 196; flight to Scotland, 199–200
Hesse, Fritz, 114
Hesse, Hermann, 230
Hessen, Grand Duke von, 156
Hetter, Audi, 289*n*
Heusemann, Käte, 276, 277
Heusinger, Gen. Adolf, 151
Hewel, Walter, 150, 181, 185–86, 257, 258
Heydrich, Reinhard, 126, 132, 224, 227–28, 229, 235–36, 237
Himmler, Heinrich, 38, 52, 56, 80–81, 84, 102, 123, 126, 132–33, 191, 224, 226–27, 235–36, 243, 251, 254, 263–64, 284; betrayal of Hitler, 264; mistress of, 132; power struggle with Göring, 214
Himmler, Frau Marga, 132–33
Hindenburg, Paul von, 28, 120
Hindenburg (dirigible), 70
Hitler, Adolf: airplane travel, 58–59; attempted assassination of, 151, 171, 201, 243; in Berlin (World War II), 242–71; banned from speaking (1925), 18; Brenner Pass Conference, 112–14; bunker events (April, 1945), 256–71; death of, 100, 271, 272–73; drug dependency, 145–46, 147, 148–49, 150, 152, 153–54, 197, 200–201, 253, 282–83; entertainment of visitors, 105–18; fantasy of bombing New York, 246; fascination with cowboys and Indians, 230–41; fascination

Hitler, Adolf *(cont.)*
with nudity, 170–71; favorite
actress of, 60–75; final secret,
272–88; flatulence of, 139, 141;
forelock and mustache, 57;
funds and finances (1920s), 13–
25, 77, 78; imprisonment, 5–6,
12, 17, 20, 77; insomnia, 52–55,
139; last will and testament,
269, 274, 283; marriage of,
268–69; meals and eating
habits, 48–49, 56, 76, 139, 184–
85, 188–89, 190; medical
treatments, 139–54; named
chancellor, 28, 120, 205;
obsession with blood, 55–56;
personal habits and behavior,
47–59; physical deterioration,
150; recordings of, 51–52; sex,
women, and romance, 76–90,
98; tantrums, 104, 113; throat
operation, 139, 242, 243; visit
to Switzerland, 14; World War
I, 208, 211
Hitler, Paula, 57–58
Hitler's Medical Report, 277–78
"Hitler's run" (section of the
Obersalzberg), 182–83
Hitler Youth, 123, 124, 194, 273
Hodges, Gen. Courtney, 246
Hoepner, Gen. Erich, 151
Hofer, Franz, 248–49
Hoffmann, Carola, 78
Hoffmann, Heinrich, 13, 14, 24–
35, 82, 138–39, 140, 147, 159–
60, 183, 290*n*, 296*n*
Hohenzollern family, 210, 211
Hollywood Anti-Nazi League, 71
Holocaust, 235–38; *see also* Jews
Holy Mountain, The (motion
picture), 61

Homosexuality, 119, 123–24,
193–200; Fritsch scandal, 123–
24, 194, 196–97
Hoover, J. Edgar, 207, 218, 219,
233, 298*n,* 299*n;* duped by
Hitler, 223–29
Horer, Walther, 51, 292*n*
Horthy, Madame, 118
Horthy, Adm. Miklós von, 118,
150
Hugenberg, Alfred, 27
Hugo, Victor, 95

I.G.-Farben (cartel), 126
Inskip, Sir Thomas, 108
Inter-Allied Commission, 138
Internal Revenue Service, 222
International Military Tribunal,
225
International Olympic
Committee, 69
International Police Radio
Technical Committee, 226
Interpol (International Criminal
Police Commission), 224–25,
228–29
Italian Film Price (1936), 67

Jager, Heinz, 32–34, 291*n*
Jana, La (motion picture), 36
Jeurjo (Eckart), 1
Jewish Labor Committee, 71
Jews, 17, 23, 38, 68, 69, 74, 81,
225, 235–38, 249, 252, 287,
289*n,* 293*n;* Concordat (1933)
and, 24–25; *see also* Final
Solution; Holocaust
Jodl, Gen. Alfred, 40, 51, 246,
253, 256, 292*n*
Johannmeier, Willi, 279, 281, 283
Johnson, Herschel V., 298*n*

Johnson, Lyndon B., 222
Junge, Traudl, 49, 57, 146, 149–
  50, 174–82, 184, 191, 201–2,
  236, 247, 249, 255, 258, 261,
  262, 265, 267, 268, 269, 270,
  271, 273, 274, 292n, 296n, 297n,
  299n, 300n

Kadow, Walther, 30–32
Kahr, Gustav Ritter von, 6, 10,
  11
Kaltenborn, H. V., 68, 293n
Kantzow, Thomas, 203
Karajan, Herbert von, 118
Karinhall, 106, 115, 215–16
Karl May Museum, 241
Kasche, Artur, 40, 291n
Keitel, Field Marshal Wilhelm,
  113, 150, 246, 253–54, 256, 258
Keitner, Erik, 79
Kempka, Erich, 52, 127, 236, 242,
  273, 274, 276, 282, 284, 295n
Kempka, Frau Maja, 127
Kennedy, John F., 222
Kennedy, Joseph P., 109
Kersten, Dr. Felix, 149
Kesselring, Field Marshal Albert,
  279
Kielce ghetto, 233
Kinberg, Olaf, 203–4
Klessheim Castle, 150
Kluge, Field Marshal Günther
  Hans von, 151
Kochendorf salt mines, 250
Kohler, Pauline, 36–38, 47, 79,
  131, 133, 199, 282, 291n, 292n,
  293n, 295n, 300n
Konradsberg Lunatic Asylum,
  205
Krebs, Gen. Hans, 284
Krüger, Else, 274

Krüger, Dr. Kurt, 89, 197–99,
  294n
Kutschmann, Walter, 287

Lammers, Hans, 251
Landsberg Prison, 3, 12, 17, 18,
  28, 78, 156, 194, 199, 209
Langbro Psychopathic Hospital,
  205
Lappus, Sigrid von, 84
Last of the Mohicans, The
  (Cooper), 240
Lateran Treaty (1929), 21–22, 25,
  290n
Laval, Pierre, 117
Lenbach, Franz von, 4
Lewald, Dr. Theodor, 69
Ley, Frau Inge, 85
Ley, Dr. Robert, 114–16, 132, 251
Lilienthal Aeronautical
  Congress, 109
Lindbergh, Charles A., 58, 106–
  10, 112, 115, 294n
Linde, Carl von, 5
Lindhagen, Carl, 203
Linge, Heinz, 184, 236, 274, 282,
  284, 299n
Linz Museum, 202–3
Liptauer, Suzi, 85
Locarno Pact, 214
Loehlein, Dr. Walter, 278
Lorenz, Heinz, 183, 263, 279, 281,
  283
Lossow, Gen. Otto von, 8, 10, 11
Lubianka Prison, 274
Lublin ghetto, 233
Ludendorff, Gen. Erich, 9, 10–11,
  12, 194
Ludlum, Robert, 25, 291n
Luftwaffe, 106, 107, 109, 134,
  227, 240, 245, 246, 247, 253,

Luftwaffe *(cont.)*
  261, 262, 269, 278-79, 280, 287,
  295*n*
Luitpold, Prince-Regent, 4
Lundberg, Dr. Karl A. R., 203

MacDonald, Jeanette, 239
Mackensen, Field Marshal
  August von, 70
Magistrati, Countess Maria, 84
Malitz, Bruno, 69
Mansfeld, Count Coloredo, 209
Manzialy, Konstanze, 255, 270
Marx, Dr., 165
Marxism, 17
Mason-Perkins collection, 250
Masur, Norbert, 254
Matsuoka, Yosuke, 105-6, 115,
  294*n*
Maurice, Emil, 82
May, Karl, 230-31, 232, 234, 236,
  237, 240-41
Mayer, Mauritia, 4, 5
Maytime (motion picture), 239
Medical Diagnostic Institute
  (Berlin), 278
Mein Kampf (Hitler), 7, 12, 13,
  14, 17, 19, 38, 76, 78, 180, 194;
  number of copies sold, 15, 18,
  19
Meirer, Ilse, 78, 293*n*
Meistersinger, Die (opera), 118
Melo, Djalama de Cunna, 285
Mengele, Dr. Josef, 287
Mengershausen, Henry, 274, 275
Messersmith, George S., 217,
  218, 298*n*
Midgard (artist), 165
Milch, Field Marshal Erhard,
  108, 245
Mitford, Unity, 90, 91, 143
Mittelstrasse, Frau Margaret, 175

Montgomery, Field Marshal Sir
  Bernard Law, 149
Morell, Dr. Theodor, 42, 48, 55,
  137-54, 170, 172, 183, 192, 197,
  201, 202, 203, 252-53, 269,
  277-78, 282, 296*n;* background
  of, 137-38; criticism of, 142,
  145; medical treatment of
  Hitler, 139-54; party
  membership, 138; physical
  appearance, 140; visit to
  Switzerland, 143-44
Morgan, J. P., 235
Müller, Adolf, 13
Müller, Hugo, 70, 293*n*
Müller, Karl Alexander von, 232
Müller, Renate, 79-81
Munich Finance Office, 14, 15-
  16, 17, 19
Munich Pact, 112, 216, 220
Mürk, Enrique Jacabo, 287
Musmanno, Michael A., 273,
  274, 278, 289-90*n*, 293*n*, 294*n*,
  295*n*, 296*n*, 297*n*, 299*n*, 300*n*
Mussolini, Benito, 13, 20-21, 38,
  70, 84, 105, 132, 300*n;* Brenner
  Pass Conference, 112-14;
  death of, 269; rescue of (1943),
  55, 171
Mussolini, Edda, 84
Mutaflor, 141

National Archives, 276, 291*n*,
  295*n*, 297*n*, 298*n*, 300*n*
National Commission on Law
  Enforcement and Social
  Justice, 223
National Police Academy, 223
Nazi Party, 7, 8, 13, 14, 18, 20, 23,
  52, 54, 69, 76, 78, 83, 88, 103,
  120, 121, 132, 190, 193, 210,

213, 220; Brazil meeting (1978), 287–88; death of Horst Wessel, 27–28; election of 1930 and 1932, 28; first party rally, 6; Hitler's resignation from, 208–9; membership, 6; refounded (1925), 17; street brawls, 28; swastika emblem, 240–41

Nebe, Arthur, 224, 226, 227, 228, 229, 233, 299

Negus (dog), 165, 178

Neufforge collection, 250

New York Times, The, 21, 116, 272, 290*n*, 293*n*, 295*n*

Nissle, Dr. A., 140, 278

North German Lloyd Line, 137

NSDAP (National Socialist German Workers' Party), *see* Nazi Party

Nürnberg laws, 55, 233

Nürnberg rally (1935), 165–67

Obersalzberg, 1–12, 14, 15, 19, 26–47, 77, 87, 219, 230, 232, 247, 249, 252, 254, 255, 258; failure of Allies to bomb, 250; history and background, 3–4, 5; "Hitler's run," 182–83; location of, 3; popularity of, 4, 5; *see also* Berghof; Eagle's Nest

Olbricht, Gen. Friedrich, 151

Olga, Princess, 118

Olympia (motion picture), 70–75

Olympics of 1936, 68–75, 108

Olympic Village, 69

Operation Barbarossa, 149

Operation Seraglio, 255, 257

Order of the German Red Cross, 212–13

Ordinance for the Safeguarding

of German National Military Potential, 119

Osten, Lina Mathilde von der, 126

Oster. Col. Hans. 151

Owens. Flt.. Sgt. Harry. 101–2. 294*n*

Owens, Jesse, 70

Pacelli, Eugenio, *see* Pius XII, Pope

Papen, Franz von, 23, 28, 291*n*

Paul, Prince Regent, 118

Pension Moritz (the Platterhof), 4–5, 6, 7, 11, 14, 19, 25, 30, 42–43, 44–45, 182, 289*n*, 292*n*

Penthesilea (motion picture), 75

Perugia collection, 250

Petacci, Clara, 269

Pétain, Marshal Philippe, 117

Phipps, Sir Eric, 191

Pius XI, Pope, 20, 21

Pius XII, Pope, 22, 23–24, 25

Plate, Dr., 159

Platterhof, *see* Pension Moritz

Poland, invasion of (1939), 75, 99, 148

Popp (artist), 165

Pornography, 38, 82–83, 132–33

Potthast, Hedwig, 132

Prussian State Opera, 118

Puttkamer, Adm. Karl-Jesco von, 177–78, 252–53

Quandt, Günther, 86

Quick (magazine), 222

Raeder, Adm. Erich, 125, 126

Rapprochement policy, 110

Rastenburg headquarters, 50, 174, 242

Rattenhuber, Johann, 264

Raubal, Angela, 26, 81, 83, 165, 167
Raubal, Geli, 26, 79, 81–84, 152, 158, 159, 165; death of, 83–84, 128, 159
Reich Security Service, 126
Reiman, Kristina, 284
Reiter, Mimi, 81
Reitsch, Hanna, 261–63, 264, 266, 279, 282, 283, 299*n*, 300*n*
Rhineland, German occupation of, 114, 214
Ribbentrop, Joachim von, 96, 105, 112, 113, 117, 149, 181, 212, 216, 221, 258
Richter, Frau Ludmilla Kuranda, 207–8
Richter, Dr. Rudolf, 207–8
Ride Through the Desert, The (May), 240
Riefenstahl, Leni, 60–75, 134, 282, 293*n;* background of, 61; filming of the Olympics, 68–75; first meeting with Hitler, 63; Goebbels jealousy of, 67–68; U.S. visit (1938), 71
Ringling Brothers Barnum and Bailey Circus, 235
Ritter, Karl, 284
Röhm, Ernst, 54, 84, 194–95, 196, 197, 199, 209, 237, 297*n*
Röhm's Revengers, 53–54, 55, 292*n*
Roman Catholic Church, 20–25
Rommel, Field Marshal Erwin, 40, 149, 150, 151
Roosevelt, Franklin D., 77, 222, 291*n*
Rosenberg, Alfred, 8
Rosl (artist), 165
Rothermere, Lord, 209–10, 211, 212, 213–14, 216–17, 220, 298*n*

Rothschild collection, 250
Royal Air Force (RAF), 101, 245, 249, 251
Rüffer, Charlotte, 124
Ruhr, French occupation of (1923), 18
Runciman, Lord, 214–15, 217
Rundstedt, Field Marshal Gerd von, 148
Rupprecht, Crown Prince, 11
Ruprecht, Dr. Leopold, 203

SA *(Sturmabteilung),* 6, 8, 9, 10, 11, 13, 18, 22, 23, 32, 54, 60, 66, 67, 69, 70, 138, 158, 195, 209, 293*n*
Saint-Germain-en-Laye, Treaty of (1919), 215
Salzburg Music Festival, 215
Scarlatti Inheritance, The (Ludlum), 25
Schaub, Julius, 132, 167, 253, 257, 297*n*, 300*n*
Schloss Leopoldskron, 216
Schmidt, Otto, 123, 124
Schmidt, Paul, 112–14
Schmundt, Rudolf, 58, 150, 152, 177–78
Schneider, Herta, 56, 172–73, 183
Schofield, Maj. Lemuel B., 221, 222
Schörner, Field Marshal Ferdinand, 272, 279
Schreck, Julius, 139, 140
Schröder, Christa, 51, 52, 174, 175, 177, 178, 180, 252–53, 255, 292*n*
Schröder, Kurt von, 28
Schultz, Dr. Bruno, 228
Schumann, Clara, 4
Schwarz, Franz, 84
Schweitzer, Albert, 230

Schweyer, Dr. Franz, 6–7, 11, 12, 289*n*
Security Intelligence Corps (SIC), 19, 22
Seidl, Fritz, 240
Seiler, Gen., 219
Seisser, Col. Hans von, 8, 10, 11
Seitz, Anni, 134
Seitz, Dr., 5
Seventh Army (U.S.), 75
Sex and sexual escapades. 119–36: Albrecht escapade, 125–26: Blomberg affair, 120–23: Fritsch scandal, 123–24; homosexuality, 119, 123–24, 193–200; laws, 119–20, 135; love affairs, 127–36
Sexton, Sam, 285–87
Seydlitz, Gertrud von, 78
Siegesmund, Hermann, 194–95
Sixteenth Bavarian Reserve Infantry Regiment, 208
Sixth Panzer Army, 244
Skorzeny, Otto, 55–56, 100, 171, 197, 199–200, 231, 280–82, 292*n*, 294*n*, 297*n*, 298*n*, 299*n*, 300*n*
Smith, Truman, 107, 294*n*
Soggnaes, Dr. Reidar, 276–77
Sonnemann, Emmy, 85–86
Sopple, Hans, 115, 295*n*
Soviet Union, invasion of (1941), 105, 149
Spandau Prison, 200
Speer, Albert, 35, 66, 96, 132, 142, 147–48, 171, 197, 251, 258–60, 264, 282, 286, 291*n*, 294*n*, 296*n*, 297*n*, 299*n*
Spirit of St. Louis (airplane). 106–7
SS *(Schutzstaffel),* 38, 66, 67, 78, 79, 92, 98, 99, 102, 110, 112, 169, 170, 182, 191, 200, 224, 226–27, 234–35, 236, 237, 251, 256, 258, 262, 274, 282, 284, 287, 291*n; see also* Gestapo
Stadelheim Prison, 5–6, 196
Stahlenberg, Elisabeth von, 36, 66, 122, 123, 291*n*, 293*n*, 295*n*
Stalin, Joseph, 77, 242, 247, 251
Stasi (dog), 165, 178
Stauffenberg. Lt. Col. Claus Schenk. Graf von. 151
Stehlin. Capt.. 94
Steiner, Gen. Felix, 257
Stern (publication), 222
Strasser, Otto, 79, 82
Streicher, Julius, 12, 76; pornographic collection of, 132–33
Stuelpnagel, Gen. Karl Heinrich von, 151
Stumpfegger, Dr. Ludwig, 269–70
Sudetenland, 111, 215
Szcpessy, Baroness, 219

Tavora, Elisario, 285
Terina (singer), 5
Theater an der Wien, 208
Thiele. Hugo. 156
Thompson. Dorothy. 104–5
Thyssen. August. 18
Thyssen, Fritz, 18
Tiefland (motion picture), 75
Todt, Fritz, 91, 96
Trenker, Luis, 61
Tresckow, Gen. Henning von, 151
Trevor-Roper, Hugh, 273, 274–75, 276, 278
Trianon, Treaty of (1920), 209
Tristan and Isolde (opera), 132

Triumph of the Will (motion picture), 60, 61, 65–67, 68–69, 74, 293*n*
Troost, Isabel, 186
Troost, Paul, 186
Truehill, Joseph Addison, 285–87
Tucker, Justice, 217–18
Twelfth Army Group, 246

Ucicky, Gustav, 239
Udet, Ernst, 109, 134, 202
UFA (motion picture company), 79
Ufa-Palast-am-Zoo Theater, 60
U.S. Department of State, 207, 219, 221, 224, 298*n*
U.S. Immigration and Naturalization Service, 221
Universal Motor Company, 229
University of Giessen, 137
University of Grenoble, 137
University of Heidelberg, 137
University of Pennsylvania, 182

Vatican, 20–25
Veendam (steamship), 219
Verlaine, Paul, 40
Versailles Treaty, 114
Vichy France, 117–18
Victor Emmanuel II, King, 20
Völkischer Beobachter, 1, 8, 17, 18, 209
V-1 and V-2 rockets, 244–45, 246
Vorkuta Prison, 274
Voss, Richard, 3–4

Wagner, Friedelind, 89
Wagner, Richard, 76, 88, 118
Wagner, Siegfried, 88

Wagner, Walter, 268–69
Wagner, Winifred, 76, 78, 87–90
Waldenburg-Schillingsfürst, Prince Frederick Franz Augustin Hohenlohe von, 208, 209
Waldenburg-Schillingsfürst, Princess Stephanie Hohenlohe von. "Steffi." 207–22. 298*n;* arrest and internment. 222: background of, 207–8; lawsuit, 217–18; marriage and divorce, 208; in U.S., 219–22
Waltenberger, George, 5
Warsaw ghetto, 233
Washington *Diplomat,* 222
Washington Post, The, 300*n*
Weber, Dr. Karln, 278
Wehrmacht, 50, 197
Weimar Republic, 8, 24, 193–94, 210
Wermelskirch, Fritz, 123, 124
Werwolf headquarters, 57
Wessel, Horst, 27–28
Westinghouse Corporation, 238
Wiedemann, Fritz, 207, 210–11, 216, 218, 219, 220
Wilhelm II, Emperor, 225
Wilhelm III, Prince, 108, 210, 211–12, 298*n*
Windsor, Duke and Duchess, 114–16
Winter, Anni, 68, 84, 161, 293*n*, 296*n*
Winter, Herr, 2, 5, 26
Witzleben, Field Marshal Erwin von, 151
Wöehmann Line, 137
Wolf, Johanna, 58, 252–53, 255
Wolfsschanze headquarters, 50, 57, 151–52, 242, 292*n*

Wolfsschlucht headquarters, 57
World Jewish Conference, 254
World War I, 6, 9, 109, 138, 194, 208, 224; reparations payments, 8, 27
World War II, 19, 103, 143, 228, 287, 290*n*
Wurmbrand, Count Ferdinand, 209

Young Plan, 27

Zander, Wilhelm, 279, 281, 283
Zeppelin Field, 66
Zhukov, Marshal Georgi, 273
Zielke, Willy, 70
Ziessler, Adolf, 80
Zossen headquarters, 254
Zwei Menschen (Voss), 3–4, 5